D1554129

The Trauma and the Triumph

The Trauma and the Triumph

Gender and Partition in Eastern India

Edited by

Jasodhara Bagchi
and
Subhoranjan Dasgupta

THE TRAUMA AND THE TRIUMPH,
Gender and Partition in Eastern India,
edited by JASODHARA BAGCHI and SUBHORANJAN DASGUPTA
was first published in February 2003 by STREE,
an imprint of Bhatkal and Sen,
16 Southern Avenue, Kolkata 700 026.

First reprint, paperback, January 2006

© 2006 Jasodhara Bagchi and Subhoranjan Dasgupta

ISBN 81-85604-64-9

Typesetting and design by Compuset International,
85 Park St, Kolkata 700 016 and
printed by Webimpressions (India) Pvt Ltd,
34/2 Beadon St, Kolkata 700 006.

Published by Mandira Sen for STREE,
an imprint of Bhatkal and Sen,
16 Southern Avenue, Kolkata 700 026

To Ashoka Gupta, and women like her,
who stood by their sisters in distress
and showed the courage of their convictions

Acknowledgements

WE ARE GRATEFUL to the School of Women's Studies (SWS) Jadavpur University, and its two successive directors, Dr Anuradha Chanda and Dr Malini Bhattacharya, for encouraging and housing this project. We also thank Sarbani Goswami, Abhijit Sen and other members of SWS who were always ready to render any assistance that we needed. The project began with funding from Oxfam India and has continued with financial assistance from Hivos India. The research that went into the making of this book and ones to follow owe not a little to the imaginative and hard work put in by Mouli Mishra, Debjani Dutta and Aparajita Dhar in Kolkata and Subhasree Ghosh in New Delhi. Dr Gargi Chakravartty not only contributed interviews and gave access to the writings of her mother, Sabitri Roy, but was also ready to share her ideas with us. Our translators—Sudeshna Chakravarti, Subhasree Ghosh, Barnita Bagchi, Kumkum Chakravarti, Sipra Bhattacharya, Chandreyee Niyogi, and Kalyani Chowdhury— have helped us by communicating the authenticity of the original texts. Pradeep Biswas, Surangama Dasgupta and Lokeshwari helped us with the computer.

No words are enough to thank those—Manju Chattopadhyay, Hasna Saha and Hena Chowdhury in particular—who gave their time and shared their invaluable experiences with us in the interviews. The compilation of this book was facilitated considerably by the special issue that *Seminar* brought out (February 2002) titled *Porous Borders, Divided Selves*. *Seminar* has also generously permitted us to reproduce the following pieces that also appear in this volume, albeit with some changes: 'The

Problem', which the Introduction draws upon; 'Freedom in an
Idiom of Loss'; 'History's Creative Counterpart'; 'Hoina'; the
extract from *Meghe Dhaka Tara*; 'Poems on Partition'; 'A Partition Diary'; 'East Is East, West Is West'; 'Uprooted and Divided'; 'The Nowhere People'; and the interviews with Nalini
Mitra, Sukumari Chaudhuri and Bithi Chakravarti.

We are thankful to Rathindranath Roy for permitting us to
reproduce the chapter 'And Still They Come' from *My Reminiscences* by Renuka Roy, which appears as the fifth essay and to
Selina Hossain for letting us translate the pages from *Kanta Tare
Prajapati* that appear in the third essay in this volume. We are
grateful to the following who let us reproduce the material that
appears in Part 3, Creative Texts: to Amitananda Das for permission to translate and publish two poems of Jibanananda Das
from *Ruposhi Bangla*; to Taslima Nasreen for permission to
translate and publish two poems, 'Broken Bengal' and 'Denial';
to Ritaban Ghatak of the Ritwik Memorial Trust for permission
to translate and publish an extract from *Megha Dhaka Tara*; to
Kakali Chakravarti for permission to translate and publish her
father's short story 'Hoina', to Kumar Roy, editor *Bohurupee*, for
permission to translate and publish an extract from *Natun
Yehudi*.

Many others helped in several ways and we are grateful to
them. Our last word of thanks goes to Ashoka Gupta.

Contents

List of Contributors

JASODHARA BAGCHI is chairperson, West Bengal Commission of Women and former director, School of Women's Studies, Jadavpur University.

URVASHI BUTALIA is co-publisher, Kali for Women, and an activist.

SUBHORANJAN DASGUPTA is Professor of Human Sciences at the Institute of Development Studies, Kolkata.

MEGHNA GUHA THAKURTA is a specialist in gender studies and teaches in the Department of International Relations, University of Dhaka.

ASHOKA GUPTA has tried to follow Gandhian principles in her lifelong work as an activist and a social worker.

RENUKA ROY was a life-long Gandhian, a member of the Constituent Assembly and Provisional Parliament which framed the Constitution of India. She became minister for Relief and Rehabilitation, Government of West Bengal, 1952-1957.

MEENAKSHI SEN is a writer and member-secretary, Tripura Commission for Women.

RACHEL WEBER is assistant professor, Urban Planning and Policy Program, Cornell University.

Introduction

THE PARTITION OF India in 1947 provoked massive transfers of population both in the eastern and western parts of the sub-continent. Like the exodus of the Jews during the days of the Third Reich, this movement of millions in the subcontinent is also another example of 'Coerced Migration'—to use the category of Charles Tilly (1990)—which 'entails obligatory departure, forced severing of most or all ties at the origin.' But all 'coerced migrations' have their own region-specific distinctions and, in this sense, the exodus in Punjab differed and continues to differ from the displacement in Bengal.

Urvashi Butalia, author of *The Other Side of Silence* (1998)— a remarkable text on the *human* history of the Partition in Punjab—recognized this distinction when she wrote in the August 1994 issue of *Seminar*: 'A serious gap is the omission of experiences in Bengal and East Pakistan (Bangladesh). But these require detailed attention of their own: better not to pay lip service by including an interview or two.' Like Urvashi Butalia, Ritu Menon and Kamla Bhasin, co-authors of another remarkable text, *Borders and Boundaries* (1998), on the gender-accent of the Partition Narrative, confined themselves to the West because the Partition of Bengal in the East, they correctly concluded, deserved a separate treatment. In this book our focus is on the human dimension of the second Partition of Bengal (1947) with a clear emphasis on the gender-perspective.[1] Our aim is to fill the 'serious gap'.

The Partition of Bengal, despite some obvious political and existential convergences, differs from the Partition of Punjab in at least four important aspects. These are:

(i)   While the Partition of Punjab was a one-time event with mayhem and forced migration restricted primarily to three years (1947-1950), the Partition of Bengal has turned out to be a continuing process. Displacement and migration from East to West, that is, from former East Pakistan and Bangladesh to West Bengal, is still an inescapable part of our reality, as the most recent exodus following post-election violence in Bangladesh in October 2001 illustrates.

(ii) The extent and depth of sheer violence and cruelty leading to a massive two-way exodus in Punjab was not repeated in the East. The *kafilas*, long columns of people on the move, from East Bengal to West Bengal, were not matched by kafilas from West to East.[2] Moreover, even after recalling the carnages in Kolkata and Noakhali in 1946, Dhaka-Narayanganj in 1962, Bhola and Jessore in 2001, it needs to be said that the 'one fell swoop' in Punjab was much more bloody and destructive. In contrast, the Partition of Bengal has produced a process of slow and agonizing terror and trauma accelerated by intermittent outbursts of violence.

(iii) While history and politics have been constant and definitive in the context of Punjab, the Partition of Bengal has been refracted through conflicting prisms during the last six decades. For example, the two-nation theory which proved to be sacrosanct in Punjab was challenged for the first time in East Pakistan by the historic Language movement which erupted in 1952. A policy of determined resistance against the rulers of West Pakistan followed that ultimately led to the creation of Bangladesh in 1971. As Taslima Nasreen phrased it eloquently in her poem 'Denial', '1971 challenged and rejected 1947'.

However, the emergence of 'secular' and 'democratic' Bangladesh did not signal the end of history. Forces opposed to it continued to be active and the 'irony' of history was repeated when the fundamentalist Jamat-i-Islami, an inveterate enemy of the Liberation War, began to share power with the Bangladesh National Party after their combined electoral victory in October 2001.

(iv) Compared to the nature of border and boundary in the West where political, strategic and military considerations have converted the entire region into two rigid divisions, the dividing line in the East is porous and flexible. So much so, constant cross-border movement and migration impelled by human and economic considerations have given to this region, where the two countries meet, a composite character which questions the strictly demarcated preconditions of nationalism and the nation-state.

There, is, however, one compelling similarity between the experiences in Punjab and Bengal. In both these divided states, women (minors included) were targeted as the prime object of persecution. Along with the loss of home, native land and dear ones, the women, in particular, were subjected to defilement (rape) before death, or defilement and abandonment, or defilement and compulsion that followed to raise a new home with a new man belonging to the oppressor-community. Creative texts which are being analysed focus on this distinctive tragedy of the woman who at times chose to commit suicide in order to thwart the corporeal holocaust. This deathwish and act of immolation construct the tragic dialectic of the 'Women in Partition' trapped between the extremes of a life desecrated and a redemptive death. We find that women who were sexually molested while leaving their homes and found shelter in All Bengal Women's Union, are still not ready to be interviewed about their experience. Through indirect means we even came to know how some of them were taken advantage of by males of the same community and not of the other. In point of fact, not only in Punjab and Bengal, but also in all other countries where two or more communities incited by religion, race, colour or language fall upon one another, women are identified as the main object of ruthless conquest. Confronted by the same reality in Bosnia-Herzegovina, the reality of mass rape of women, Stasa Zajovic (1994) concluded, 'the female womb becomes occupied territory'. We had a confirmation of this nearer home in Gujarat.

Living under patriliny women are the original 'displaced

persons', leaving the usually safe haven of the natal home to the humiliation-riddled anxiety of the marital one. In the strict gender division of spaces women are given charge of the quotidian reproduction of life. The Partition, read in history as an event in the public arena, wrenches the fabric of the quotidian life apart, depriving her of home and hearth. The 'micro' aspect of this tearing apart gets immediately lost in the public story of re-setting the boundaries. Moreover, the distasteful aspect of a vivisection in which nations are defined in terms of religious communities is the way it renders women's bodies and sexuality vulnerable. Women, even in ordinary peaceful times, are seen as icons of the honour of the community. The easiest way to assail a community, therefore, is to define the sexual purity of its women. As Pradip Datta's work on Bengal (1999) has brought out, the fear of 'abduction' or 'rape' by the 'other' community had been played up in the communal divide of the Hindus and Muslims and had prepared the ground for the 'two-nation' theory. It is only to be expected that this fear psychosis had free play in the Bengal Partition. Here, too, we have a re-play of Ritu Menon and Kamla Bhasin's observation that 'All of them treat women's bodies as territory to be conquered, claimed or marked by the assailants'. This is the area which has produced its own veil of silence, the most difficult one to penetrate, though there is a general belief that rape was less marked a presence in the Bengal Partition. The fear of rape was enough to marginalize women and to prevent them from being accepted by their own community. For the bhadralok middle class refugees, this particular brand of gender-ideology entered the domain of 'commonsense'. Nilanjana Chatterjee's interviews (1992) with various kinds of male refugees resulted in this significant pointer:

> The 'chastity' of married and unmarried Hindu women seemed to symbolize most potently, the honour, exclusivity and continuity of the community—and to represent its site of transgression. Violence against Hindu women featured widely in the minority's complaints of ill-treatment in Pakistan and as a topic of concern in West Bengal—the sexual possession of Hindu women by Muslim men being made to

stand for Muslim domination, 'miscegenation', the loss and humiliation of the male Hindu self (p 77).

Satish Chandra Banerjee, the President of the West Bengal Provincial Congress Committee, explained to his party cadres, that as an East Bengali himself (though living in Calcutta!) he could vouch that the Hindus were leaving East Pakistan because they 'prized their self-respect and the honour of their women above everything else' (ibid: 78). If we follow Dorothy Smith's formulation of the 'everyday world as a problematic' and not as 'phenomenon', we see the need to critique the patterns of domination that got reflected even in the ways in which Partition was read only as an exercise in making two nations out of one colonized landmass. Up to now the major feminist inroad into this hegemonic discourse of Partition has been to bring out the ways in which the intensely 'private sphere' of women's sexuality was deployed in this major redrawing of the 'public' borders and boundaries. But there are still other areas in civil society in which gender ideology may operate as a critique of the dominant ruling categories.

In a situation of such mass-scale displacement, the categories that inevitably get silenced are the ways in which women retrieve the daily requirements of social reproduction. Since this is the aspect that gets least spoken about, what gets elided is the agency of women who start up the family routine in changed circumstances, re-build the rhythms of daily subsistence, if not the actual search, at least the organization of shelter. The caring, nurturing role of women hounds them in these moments of public rupture. Nita's famous cry that resounds on the hills at the end of Ritwik Ghatak's *Meghe Dhaka Tara*, 'I wanted to live', is the most living indictment of this aspect of the Bengal Partition. Nita, the breadwinner, was denied its gendered privileges and became the victim at the sacrificial altar of the displaced family. Her tragedy was an integral part of her diurnal survival and struggle.

In a remarkable study of the role of the women in recreating the space in the process of resettling in the outskirts of Calcutta, Rachel Weber makes a nuanced discrimination between the traditional and privileged women making the passage from the home to the world and the passage in the case of the displaced 'refugee' women:

> The type of analysis which separates spaces so rigidly and then speaks of a 'coming out' does not reflect the complex relations between women, power and space. Women do not simply cross these borders when they cross the thresholds of their houses. It is not as simple as the scene in Satyajit Ray's interpretation of Tagore's *Ghare Baire* (The Home and the World) when Bimala walks through the splendidly-lit corridor into the public world of men and nationalist politics. Refugee women did not really move into public life, but rather the domestic world expanded to include their participation in political, community and economic affairs (see Essay 4, 'Re[creating] the Home'; this volume).

While Weber is right in reading a re-defined power relation in what she calls the complex relations between women, power and space, it is a little misleading to think of the microcosm of the refugee 'colony' as the entire macrocosm.

The same women, uprooted and raising new shelters, refused to succumb to the dictates of fate. Both in Punjab and Bengal they displayed exemplary resilience, fortitude, patience and strength to emerge victors against the combined nightmare of assault, exodus, displacement, grinding poverty and broken psyche. They kept their new shelter in camps and refugee settlements intact and also ventured out to acquire skills and earn. In West Bengal, in particular, the historic assertion of the refugee-woman as the tireless breadwinner changed the digits of feminine aspiration of the Bengali bhadramahila and altered the social landscape irrevocably. In the words of Butalia who traced the same emphatic advance in Punjab, 'Just as a whole generation of women were destroyed by Partition, so also Partition provided an opportunity for many to move into the public sphere in a hitherto unprecedented way.' Two interviews, with Bithi Chakravarti and Sukumari Chaudhuri, and the translation of the last section of Ritwik Ghatak's screenplay *Meghe Dhaka Tara* in this book attest to this grim struggle, tragic and triumphant in the same breath.

This progress from trauma to triumph in West Bengal was,

to a large extent, guided and inspired by the undivided Communist Party. The standard acknowledgement of this Communist involvement with the post-Partition problem of the Bengali 'refugees' is in terms articulated by Nilanjana Chatterjee (1992):

> The refugees were gradually identified with the Left, particularly the Communists, although the latter were at first actually suspicious of the refugees as being potentially reactionary and anti-Muslim. Soon, however, the grievances of the refugee have-nots became a major issue in leftist opposition politics and a factor behind the radicalization of politics in the state.

Her observation is endorsed by Sukumari Chaudhuri, who was a militant leader in the workers' struggle in the Bengal Lamp factory. According to her testimony,

> 'Our salary was very low. In 1955, the agitation for payment of bonus sharpened. Marching shoulder to shoulder with our male counterparts, we refugee women participated wholeheartedly in the agitation. It was a great morale booster for our male colleagues. The agitation was spearheaded by the undivided Communist Party of India (CPI) which was active and helpful in our colonies also' (Interview, this volume).

Indeed, this pronounced leftist impulse is one of the major aspects of the story of women's involvement in the post-Partition narrative of renewal and refurbishing of life that has given the Partition in the East a very different flavour and deserves a much more nuanced scrutiny than is currently acceptable: viewing the Partition only in terms of individual suffering and the sexual exploitation of women.

What is better recorded is the involvement of very strong Gandhian activist-women like Suhasini Das or Ashalata Sen who had honoured the commitment of Gandhiji towards communal harmony and had stayed back in East Pakistan to continue to spread education and self-help among women. But the involvement of the Communists with the victims of Partition arose out of years of work in the towns and villages of undi-

vided Bengal. The cultural movement of the Indian People's
Theatre Association (IPTA) was a direct response to the hunger
and death of the people of Bengal in the 1943 famine, a per-
verse enterprise of the British government towards 'war effort'!
The Communist women had responded with the formation of
the Mahila Atma Raksha Samiti, a women's collective with innumerable branches, for self-defence, except that the boundaries of 'self' extended far beyond stray individuals. The Bengal
of the 1940s was a time of great political excitement: apart from
the struggle against famine, there was the heroic peasant
struggle against the unjust demands of the zamindars and the
large jotedars or tenant farmers. The killings in Calcutta, followed by Noakhali, which gradually made Partition acceptable,
were seen as the great betrayal of the Communist organization
among peasants and workers. Thus, Manikuntala Sen, the remarkable chronicler of women's activities in this movement
(1987; 2000), talks about the Partition as having arrived after
breaking the unity of people and workers that had been built
up, so painstakingly. The women-activists of the Communist
movement had mobilized women in the Tebhaga movement
under the banner of the Mahila Atma Raksha Samiti, and they
were able to muster this support system in the struggle to establish a life of dignity for the refugee women of Bengal.
Manikuntala Sen's rhetoric is unmistakable: 'Independence
came through partitioning the country, along with it, in divided
West Bengal there came rows of human beings who had lost
everything, rending the sky through their slogan "Who are we?
The Refugee!" '

The political turmoil of the 1940s caused many leftist
women activists to go back to East Pakistan to resume their unfinished work. After Partition, this intricate meshing of the political life of the women meant a drastic restructuring of the
private-public dichotomy. Gender ideology is found within this
niche of state formation. The post-Partition state in Bengal (if one
can talk about it in these terms) was an attempt to fit the new
into the old. An exclusive focus on women's sexuality in the
making of two nation-states out of one polity puts an unneces-
sary limitation on the theme of 'embodiment'. Such large-scale
displacement of women suggests that we need to think anew
about workplaces where women are a new presence, and on po-

litical mobilization where women figure in greater numbers. The impact cannot be minimized especially when we see the results of shameful state-sponsored communal violence against the minorities, as took place recently in Gujarat.

Without being complacent in any way, we would like to emphasize that by extending the gendered notion of 'embodiment' from an exclusive reliance on sexual exploitation of women to include the negotiation, often physical, in everyday struggles of survival, the challenge of the workplace and that of politically establishing one's discovery of civil existence in a changed setting, we who are studying the Partition in the Eastern India, are contributing to de-essentializing the gender ideology. There is enough evidence in the writings and testimony of women that the new challenges shielded them from the unhealthy heritage of cultural nationalism. From a mere passive receptacle of the community's honour, gender ideology helped to challenge the post-Partition state in newer ways.

The epic novels of Sabitri Roy (1952; 1964; 1972, 1984) stand as a proof of this multiple challenge. Since Roy was involved with the Left movement in Bengal, she had not hesitated to use her pen as an active weapon in the movement. In her writings the personal aspect of gender ideology enters into an extremely significant symbiosis with the political and enriches the horizon of our understanding of the gendering of post-Partition lives. Though she succeeds in shedding the obsession with female chastity that marked Hindu nationalism, she is very conscious of the ways in which women's sexuality acts as a manipulating device even in progressive politics. In her novel *Swaralipi* (1952) she openly attacked the way the Party leader expects sexual service from a promising woman-comrade who is on the way to attaining leadership status. By refusing him and the adventurism of the current party line she ends up a martyr. This is the kind of challenge that women catapulted into the public sphere had to endure. Sabitri Roy had to pay the price by having her book banned by the Communist Party. Her suffering comes out in a personal communication where she expresses her deep disappointment that this book, on which she had spent so much of her craft, will simply be used to make *thongas* or paper bags to pack groceries!

Roy's novels and stories express the suffering that the creative women in the political movement had to undergo after the deracination of Partition. Her work is again being pulled out of oblivion and brought before public readership mostly through activist researchers. Tanika Sarkar has written about the conflict that a woman-artist has to go through in balancing the demands of the individual and the collective, as in the writings of Sabitri Roy, and observes:

> All artists have to go through such contradictions and conflicts, but the kind of haemorrhage that a woman artist has to go through in this cold war is unparalleled. Because the household is not just a chain of servitude for the artist, it is also her very own. Yet she has to destroy her own creativity by being enslaved by it. The few blossoms that escape this untimely death are not excused by the patriarchal family, the literary circles and even the progressive Left organizations. (Introduction. Sabitri Roy, *Nirbachita Rachana Sankalan*, translated by JB)

Obviously, the Grand Narrative of the history of Partition which concentrates on the politics and on the main perpetrators, on deals and negotiations, on the exchange of territories and reckless redrawing of borders ignores this crucial human and creative aspect. If we want to recapture this essential human history, this epic saga of suffering and struggle, we have to excavate the memory of protagonists with the help of interviews which constitute an important segment of oral history and by examining diaries and memoirs. These hidden histories, once revealed, will compose their own Partition Narrative where the veil of silence that has shrouded people's experiences, especially that of women, will be lifted.

This resurgence of memory, hymnic and elegiac at the same time—to use the adjectives of Walter Benjamin (1973)—needs to be juxtaposed with the creative literature on the Partition because the latter too embodies the triumph and the trauma of actual men and women (not political leaders) in authentic statements where transcription of reality and literary imagination form one indivisible structure of experience. Both memoirs and fiction together articulate the totality of experience by combining the creative and confessional modes of expression.

One could profitably employ Pierre Macheray's famous binary model of the 'Explicit/Implicit' or the 'Spoken/Unspoken' to define the relationship between concealed memoirs gradually coming to light and creative literature already read or films already seen (1978). In Macheray's words, the Implicit-Unspoken (memoirs) represents the 'silence which gives (explicit) literature life'. While memory acts as the tormented margin bordering the centrality of creative texts, both together script the reality of Partition which is still very much a part of our present condition, burdened as it is by Partition of our minds. When this deep-seated internal rupture provokes us to link its external eruptions—Kolkata, Noakhali, Nellie, Bhagalpur, Babri, Ahmedabad, Jessore, Bhola and Gujarat—spanning six decades in one single chain, we realize the unrelenting immediacy of Partition in 1947 even today.

A NOTE ON THE CONTENTS

This volume, the first in our planned series, will be followed by three more which will concentrate on interviews and reminiscences, documentation and creative texts. Accordingly, in the first we have attempted to project briefly what is to follow and constructed the theoretical bases of our research. This book is divided into four Parts.

PART I   ANALYSIS AND LITERARY EVIDENCE

This focuses on the gender-narrative of Partition—an area hitherto ignored, even suppressed—and highlights the political failure of Partition viewed from the perspective of Tebhaga: 1 'Freedom in an Idiom of Loss' by Jasodhara Bagchi; 2 'History's Creative Counterpart' by Subhoranjan Dasgupta. This is followed by a translation of a memorable chapter from Selina Hossain's novel *Kantatare Projapati:* 3 'Butterfly on Barbed Wire', depicting the historic struggle of Ila Mitra, and also providing the crucial gender dimension to the Tebhaga revolt. Her own statement is appended with the translation: 'How Humanity [Is]Attacked under Liakat-Nurul Amin Regime'. Rachel Weber, 4 'Re[creating] the Home' and Renuka Roy, 5 'And Still They Come' have also been included. While Weber's essay is a remarkable exploration

of the refugee women's struggle in the private and public domains (one of the earliest on this theme), Renuka Roy (former
Minister of Relief and Rehabilitation in the West Bengal government) writes candidly and compassionately of those turbulent
years. It helps us to correct a few entrenched notions and throws
new light on centre-state relations vis-à-vis the refugee problem.
Meghna Guha Thakurta's research, 6 'Uprooted and Divided',
brings us back to the focal point of the disrupted family, its hopes
and fears, against the broader canvas of ongoing Partition in the
East. Urvashi Butalia's field study, 7 'The Nowhere People', em-
phasizes the agony of the hapless people, women in particular, who struggle in the enclaves on both sides of the
Bangladesh-West Bengal border. They are the nowhere victims
living in the no man's land of *chitmahal*. Meenakshi Sen exam-
ines the gender-question in her essay 'Tripura: The Aftermath',
where Partition and exodus influenced the life patterns of both
indigenous tribal women and Bengalis, Hindus and Muslims,
who crossed over or had to leave.

PART II   INTERVIEWS AND REMINISCENCES

The interviews in this Part recall the first outbreak of riots in
Dhaka and deteriorating communal relations (Nalini Mitra), the
trauma and the triumph of women-refugees in West Bengal
(Sukumari Chaudhuri and Bithi Chakravarti). Another interview
(Nibedita Nag) recalls the forgotten phase of history which witnessed the heroic resistance put up by leftist women cadres in
the late 1940s and early 1950s in East Pakistan. Indeed, Nag and
other activists opposed the prevailing current of exodus from east
to west and decided to fight it out in the fields, factories and
prisons of East Pakistan. This was a resolute protest of another
kind against the divisive logic of Partition. While the reminiscences of Ashoka Gupta and Suhasini Das focus on two historic
events—the carnage in Noakhali and Gandhi's mission, and the
division of Sylhet—the recollection of Sonarang, a village in East
Bengal lost forever for the refugees, is a moving example of
nostalgia enveloped in grief. This Part closes with a short interview with the very aged widows of Brindavan whose broken,
disjointed accounts after five decades expose the tragic essence
of the rupture.

PART III CREATIVE TEXTS

These texts not only dispute the claim that the persistent agony of Partition in the East has been ignored by creative writers but also depict the complex web of feelings this experience provoked. From compensatory nostalgia to limitless despair, from gnawing distrust (women were singled out as victims) to resolute defiance, from diurnal trauma in railway platform to epic struggles in refugee colonies—all these motifs have been recreated in the poems, short story, play-extract and screenplay. Appropriately, this Part closes with the last phase of Ritwik Ghatak's masterpiece *Meghe Dhaka Tara*.

PART IV DOCUMENTARY EVIDENCE

This Part records the impact of the Partition in a nutshell. While 23 'East Is East, West Is West', provides irrefutable facts and figures to underline the gross discriminatory treatment meted out to refugees in the East, the two letters of the aggrieved MLAs of East Bengal, belonging to the minority community, predict why Partition and exodus have turned out to be a continuing process in Bengal.

We have tried to make the Bibliography as comprehensive as possible. However, some omissions are inevitable when the area of research is so vast, spread over several decades and is still an emergent one.

NOTES

1. The viceroy Lord Curzon made the first Partition of Bengal, 1905, to curb the nationalist movement by creating two provinces, where the eastern part was joined to Assam while the western part was joined to Bihar and Orissa. It was revoked in 1911 and the capital was moved to Delhi.

2. Kafilas are long columns of people on the move, often stretching for miles. The longest kafila, comprising 4,00,000 refugees, travelled from western Punjab (Pakistan) eastwards to India.

REFERENCES

Benjamin, Walter. 1973. *Illuminations*. Glasgow: Fontana
Butalia, Urvashi. 1998. *The Other Side of Silence: Voices from the Partition of India*. Delhi: Viking.
Chatterjee, Nilanjana. 1992. Midnight's Unwanted Children. PhD diss. Brown University.
Datta, Pradip. 1999. *Carving Blocs: Communal Ideology in Early Twentieth-Century Bengal*. Delhi: Oxford University Press.
Macheray, Pierre. 1978. *A Theory of Literary Production*. London: Routledge and Kegan Paul.
Menon, Ritu with Kamla Bhasin. 1998. *Borders and Boundaries: Women in India's Partition*. Delhi: Kali for Women.
Nasreen, Taslima. 1994. *Ay Kasto Jhenpe/Jiban Debo Mepe*. Dhaka: Gyankosh.
Roy, Sabitri. 1964; 1965. *Meghna Padma*, vols 1, 2. Kolkata: Mitralay
——. 1972. *Badwip*. Kolkata: Nabapatra.
——. 1984. *Paka Dhaner Gan*. Kolkata: Suprakashani; as *Harvest Song*, trans into English by Chandrima Bhattacharya and Adrita Mukherjee. Kolkata: Stree, in press.
——. 1952. rpt 1992. *Swaralipi*. Kolkata: Ratna Prakashan.
——. 1999. *Sabitri Rayer Nirbachito Rachana Sankalan*. Kolkata, Dey's Publishing and School of Women's Studies, Jadavpur University.
Sen, Manikuntala. 1982. *Shediner Katha*. Kolkata: Nabapatra.
——. 2001. *In Search of Freedom: An Unfinished Journey*. Kolkata: Stree.
Tilly, Charles. 1990. *Immigration Reconsidered: History, Sociology and Politics*, edited by Virginia Yans-Mclaughlin. New York: Oxford University Press.
Zajovic, Stasa. 1994. Women and Ethnic Cleansing. *Women Against Fundamentalism* 1, 5. London.

PART I

Analysis and Literary Evidence

1

Freedom in an Idiom of Loss

Jasodhara Bagchi

THE FIRST TWENTY years of independence in Bengal were clouded over by Partition. The women's chronicle in this man-made uprooting by and large remains untold and here I only hint at some of the signposts in an attempt to open the deep scar on the mind and body of Sonar Bangla, the youthful golden Bengal, the honey-tongued mother whose *sons* weep if there is a flicker of sadness on her face. Partition was an ever-unfolding story of the abduction of this young mother from which there was no recovery, state planned or otherwise.

I must, at the beginning, confess that the Partition of Bengal has continued to haunt me in an ever-continuing dialogue with myself. At one level, I feel myself to be one of the real beneficiaries of the Nehruvian thrust into a reasonably self-respecting sense of modernity. Those of us who studied abroad in the late 1950s and 1960s will surely recall the sense of being prized as mini-ambassadors of a new India, committed to democracy, humanitarianism and political justice.

The pull at home, however, was one of being uprooted, loss of dignity and honour. Families huddled together on Sealdah Station platform and the streets of Calcutta. The sense of being uprooted had overtaken the psyche of Bengal. A little pressure here or there and the sense of pain gushed out. As I had once commented on a paper by Gyan Pandey that in a way the Partition never ended for us (Dutta et al 1996) Just as the Sikh riots in 1984 and the earlier riots in Bhagalpur made some activist scholars look back on women's agency in the state-sponsored uprooting and the so-called recovery programme of abducted women, the events of the 1970s and our involvement in the War of Liberation in Bangladesh also made us live through the pain of Partition.

> May the earth of Bengal and the water of Bengal,
> The air of Bengal and her fruits,
> Be blessed, blessed again, and thrice blessed, my lord.
> May Bengali dreams and Bengali words,
> And the love that wells up in a Bengali home,
> Be blessed, blessed again, and thrice blessed, my lord.

('Banglar Mati, Banglar Jal'
translated by Chandreyee Niyogi)

This was a declaration by Rabindranath Tagore of the indivisibility of Bengal: its soil, water, earth, fruit and the first partition of Bengal attempted by Lord Curzon in 1905. The resistance produced the swadeshi anti-colonial movement in which Bengal/India was effectively represented as a feminine form: She was both the avenging and the affectionate reassuring mother.

In the words of Rabindranath again:

> A scimitar shines in your right hand,
> And your left hand quells our fears,
> Your eyes are tender and smiling,
> But your third eye scorches and sears.
> O mother, we cannot turn our eyes from you.
> Your temple of gold has opened its doors to
>   ever enduring view.

('Aji Bangladesher Hriday Hote'
translated by Chandreyee Niyogi)

The ghost of the later holocaust of the second partition of Bengal lay, as the Bengali proverb goes, in the mustard seed of this representation itself. This extreme Hinduized form of the three-eyed mother goddess made cultural nationalism a strongly divisive force in the long run. In the darkening horizon of the ever-growing rift between Hindus and Muslims, Qazi Nazrul Islam sounded a clear note of warning.

> Are they Hindus? Are they Muslims? Dare one ask again?
> O Captain tell them men are drowning, each of our
>   mother born.
> A mountain steep, a desert deep and a seething ocean ahead;
> Take heed my crew, for we must cross at night.

('Durgam Giri Kantaro Moru',
translated by Chandreyi Niyogi)

The warning went in vain. The Great Calcutta Killing of 1946 and the Noakhali riots ended on 15 August 1947, but the land was divided.

In Bengal though women were not exchanged in lieu of property and chattel, the chastity belt of women's heroism to save the family honour was a signifier of the most important defence against total social disaster. The nationalist obsession with preserving the honour of the community by valorizing sati and jauhar was directed, by a strange twist of logic, less against the white ruler than against the Yavana compatriots. Tod's *Annals of Rajasthan* provided a model of chaste women who were seen as custodians of India's national glory. As Atulprasad Sen a younger contemporary of Rabindranath, declared in the heady days of anti-colonial resistance:

> Those who keep their honour by embracing the pyre,
> Give up their lives happily for their sons and children's sires,
> We are their children all.
> Sing, sing again with a hundred lutes and flutes,
> .'India will reclaim the grandest place in the conference
>   of nations.'

('Balo, Balo, Balo Sabe',
translated by Chandreyee Niyogi)

What started off as an image of anti-colonial resistance helped to turn the women of the subcontinent into potential victims of communal conflicts. The abduction of women occurs as an in-

evitable refrain in all accounts of the Bengal Partition. Young
scholars who have worked among refugees (J. Chatterjee 1995,
Weber 1996) have testified to the emphasis on the sexuality of
the womenfolk to be carefully protected almost in lieu of the
property over which they had forfeited their claims by turning
foreigners in their own land and soil. This anxiety was shared
by both communities as this was the historical juncture when two
nations were born out of one nationalist struggle. This harping
on abducted women as a central core of nation building is a
pointer to the nation-community nexus. I notice in current dis-
cussions on women's rights and citizenship a tendency to pit the
community as a greater ally of women as against the nation-state
posed as site of harsh surveillance.

The nation is, in the current postmodernist onslaught on all
things that smack of 'modernity', a metanarrative in which the
entire hegemonic establishment is implicated. Assessing the
event from a feminist perspective one cannot help noticing the
deep collusion between the community at one end of the spec-
trum and the nation on the other. The majoritarian religious
ideology turning into natural commonsense is thus not just the
threat posed by the nation-state. It is also the threat of the community and the family that make such naturalization possible.

Moral regulation or, rather, a hypocritical obsession with
women's sexual purity, marks the patriarchal foundation of the
hegemonic class in India. A woman's body is a pawn even in
the game of nation building. Rather skilfully, Jyotirmoyee Devi
narrates the story of the birth of two nation-states on the Indian
subcontinent through the holocaust of pre-Partition and Partition violence, as the story of a Hindu Bengali girl, Sutara Datta.
Jyotirmoyee Devi's *Epar Ganga Opar Ganga* (1968) *(The River
Churning;* 1995) is a rare example of a Partition novel in Bengali
written by a woman. It focuses on violence and, possibly, the
rape of a Hindu girl in East Bengal and her subsequent
marginalization by her own community in post-Partition 'secular' India. With restraint, yet daring rare in a septuagenarian of
her generation, Jyotirmoyee presents the physical trauma of the
young adolescent girl. Her sexuality is the great violation, 'un-
spoken' in the novel; yet it remains the stake in a sinister game
in which the community teams up with nationhood in order to
keep alive the class-caste entente of the ruling classes in India.

Epar Ganga Opar Ganga was originally published in 1967 as *Itihashe Stree-Parva* (The Woman Chapter in History) in the reputed Bengali periodical *Prabashi,* in its annual autumn issue. The *Stree-Parva* of the *Mahabharata* was no conventional chapter on women: for Jyotirmoyee it contained the potential of crosscutting 'myth' with 'history', the great 'open secret' that is kept carefully hidden from the public eye by a manipulative patriarchy. In the novel she tries to uncover the core of the subjugation of women by a specifically male violence on which the social order is dependent, an order that is shot through with hypocrisy and cowardice. Our history is full of such male aggression, socially condoned by patriarchal values that make women pay for crimes of which they are the chief victims. Jyotirmoyee Devi detected such injustice at the heart of the vivisection of the subcontinent into two and, later, three states. The tragedy of this holocaust, carefully elided in our history, is brought home by Jyotirmoyee through the life of a Bengali middle class girl. The stories of girls like her deserve to be told by people with special sensibilities and special pains using indirect strategies. The author locates such a strategy in the *Stree-Parva* of the *Mahabharata*: 'I do not know of historical writings in any other culture except the *Mahabharata* which has a chapter called Stree-Parva.' But as she points out, the chapter hardly deserves the name; 'In actual fact, even Vedavyasa could not bear to write the real Stree-Parva . . . Cowards do not write history. There are no great poets among women, and even if there were, they could not have written about the violation of their own dignity.

> Hence there is no recorded history of the real Stree-Parva . . . The Stree-Parva of humiliation by men? The Stree-Parva of all time? The chapter that remains in the control of husband, son, father and one's own community—there is no history of that silent humiliation, that final pain . . . The Stree-Parva has not yet ended; the last word is not yet spoken.
>
> (my translation).

The defilement of communal honour through the violation of female sexuality is a thesis that resonates through the entire process of our nation building, to which our popular mass media bear ample testimony. At one level, the anger in Jyotirmoyee Devi's Preface may read like yet another familiar tune. But the construction of her narratives shows that the anger is directed as much against the violation of a woman's body as an expression of the triumph and intimidation of one community over another, as it is against the way it is then used as an exclusionary boundary with which the woman's own community preserves its caste-class purity.

Epar Bangla Opar Bangla was intended to lift the veil on a Stree-Parva in history—the blood-stained, chequered history of 'secular' modern India. It is no accident that Sutara grows to be a teacher of history in the capital city of India, and that the novel opens in one of her 'modern' Indian history classes. We hear Sutara speaking to her students:

> 'Does history remain confined to the written page? The victors blacken the vanquished on the pages of history and which history has ever talked about the weak and the suffering? . . . and . . . ?
>
> (all translations are by me)

Sutara pauses, and in the pause her story becomes history. In a flashback we are transported to a night in 1946, when a sudden blaze of communal frenzy destroys the peace of a neighbourhood in a village in East Bengal, where Hindus and Muslims had lived in peace and amity. Within a few hours, there is complete havoc in the Hindu household. Even before they have registered what is happening, the father disappears, the mother jumps into the pond to save her honour, the married sister disappears and the young adolescent girl, Sutara, loses consciousness as a result of assault and molestation.

She is the only surviving member of her family to be nursed back to health by their Muslim neighbour. Through a haze of fear and physical pain she tries to piece together the nature of the outrage, since people are too embarrassed to answer her questions. Those who were involved with riots and Partition will instantly catch on that the trials of Sutara are not likely to end with the assault on her body but, instead, are about to begin.

Tamijuddin, Sutara's father's friend whose family nurtured

her, faces a threat from his own community. He reports to his family, 'I tried to tell them, why are you meddling with the women [of the Hindu community], we have women in our homes too. Do you know what they said? "When were women not dragged and pulled out? Read their *Puranas*—didn't Ravan abduct Sita? And what about Draupadi?" I said, that was not right, everyone knows. They said, "Let us not talk about right or wrong—it happens in every country. We know."'

When finally, Sutara's brother who is living in Calcutta gets to hear about her survival, his response is lukewarm. It is Tamij Sahib's wife who, as a woman, understands the dynamics of this social situation. 'Why not let her remain here? She can go back later. And, will they accept her if she goes back . . . ?'

Their fears are fully justified. After she is escorted back into the riot-torn Calcutta of 1946-47 by Tamijuddin and his eldest son (taking, one should note, considerable personal risk), Sutara has to move in as a guest of her brother's father-in-law in whose home the family had taken temporary refuge. Having been touched by a Muslim is never openly mentioned as the reason for the discrimination against her, but from the beginning she is treated as an untouchable, outside the fold of caste and community. Her exclusion is most rigidly enforced as far as entry to the kitchen and drinking water are concerned. On one occasion she overhears the mistress of the house saying,

'Six months in a Muslim household—What caste purity could such a girl be left with! All right, you have brought her here, but at least let her remain in a corner like *hadis* and *bagdis*! Instead, you have let her enter into all the household activities. Who knows what she has eaten and done in the past few months! What are we left with!'

She is sent off to a hostel run by Christian missionaries where she meets girls in similar ambiguous situations:

Once again she was engulfed by fear. Everything was unfamiliar, the teachers were European. Most of the girls were orphans, their parents lost in the famine of '42 [sic], others were victims of Partition. These young girls had forgotten which tradition they belonged to.

In a much acclaimed book by Partha Chatterjee, *The Nation and Its Fragments* (1992), 'community' and 'women' are presented as two fragments of the nation. At the moment of the birth of two nation-states in the place of one colonial state, the bodies of numberless women are brought under the control of their respective communities to complete the grand act of vivisection. The 'limit to the realm of disciplinary power' that is supposed to 'mark the idea of a community' is a gruesome chimera to the hordes of women who, like Sutara, witnessed (from the margins of the community) the incomprehensible birth of two nation-states.

Contrary to what the rhetoric might suggest, the author's anger is not the righteous anger of the patriarch protesting against *our* women being violated by *them*; it is, rather, directed against the dual control exercised by patriarchy. Thus riot victims like Sutara are hit twice by patriarchy: first by the male of one community who establishes his own 'identity' by exercising his territoriality over her body: second by her 'own' community which invokes compulsions of ritual purity to exclude her from the ritually pure domains of hearth and marriage, and drinking water. Her anger is focused on this reduplicated aggression: the first as physical assault on a woman's body and sexuality; the second, a prolonged and unbearable panoptic gaze by the community over her body and mind.

It is against this ideology of the 'purity' of the community that the protagonist of Jyotirmoyee Devi's novel has transgressed. No histrionics or heroism attends the act, for she has been robbed of her agency. Had it not been for 'education' Sutara would have been washed away like so much flotsam. (Small wonder that in the formative years of gender ideology, women's education was seen as a threat to female sexuality—Hindu girls in Bengal were threatened with widowhood in the early years of female education.)

The marginalization by the community persists; Sutara is particularly unwanted at weddings and is considered an obstruction to the marriage prospects of future generations. As a single girl she is free to take a job in Delhi where she meets victims of the Punjab partition. Somewhere she begins to comprehend the game—it is bodies like hers that have to be expunged in order that the community may nestle and breed in the bosom of the nation-state.

Bengali fiction, short stories in particular, abounds in stories of Partition and of Hindu-Muslim riots. In *Jaiba* (The Biological) by Narendranath Mitra, a Hindu woman raped just before Partition is not allowed to abort because her scientifically-minded husband makes a guinea pig of the baby to study the impact of environment during conception on the formation of the child's personality. The bourgeois freedom that the woman is supposed to enjoy in the newly liberated India turns into a nightmare for her—raped, restored and then made an object of a scientific experiment.

II

There was no official programme of recovery of the abducted women in the Bengal Partition. In a recent interview Phulrenu Guha said that she did not agree with Mridula Sarabhai, though she was a close friend of hers, that women should be exchanged.[1] She said that if a woman had made a new home for herself she should not be uprooted yet again. However, the absence of this state-run surveillance did not make the monstrous displacement of Partition any less of a physical and psychological holocaust. The massive influx and exodus of people belonging to the same linguistic group signalled a displacement at a scale that was unimaginable. This is the kind of displacement that happens during war and the systematic carnage that follows ethnic violence. As Ashoka Gupta, the well-known social worker and Gandhian activist, said in a panel discussion organized by the School of Women's Studies, they were appalled that this terrible displacement, loss of lives and property happened due to cool, calculated agreement between leaders at the top who remained virtually unscathed by this unprecedented violence.

The early years of Independence were scarred by this upheaval. From about 1949 Calcutta started swarming with refugees who first occupied the railway platforms of Sealdah then formed refugee colonies that dotted the outskirts of the city. The indignity of their existence was summed up in the word

'refugee' designated as 'marginal men' by Prafulla Chakraborty
who was a militant leader of the refugees. It is Jyotirmoyee
Devi who once again sums up this liminal existence.

WE ARE THE VALUELESS PRICE

So you no longer seem to recognize us,
We who have, over long thirty years, been trekking
through village after village.
Leaving the land of our birth,
Across the country, past rivers, canals, swamps and seas,
Past hill and wide stretches of land till—till what?
Our journey's end?
Will it ever, or will it be one long ceaseless trek
for all time to come?
. . . .
Our womenfolk? Our wives and our daughters?
They have been abducted en route.
And our parents and our children are either dead
Or half-dead through fatigue and lack of food.
Still we come,
We who are the valueless counters you used
As pawns for winning dominion over your country.
The disgraceful symbol of your freedom
won with a beggar's bowl and folded hands.
. . . .
You have given us a new name: 'Refugees'.
. . . .
Driven out from our land, despised and disgraced in
      our new habitat,
We are the valueless price paid for your acquisition
      of dominions Delhi and Dacca.
Our minds have ceased to hope, our anguish finds no tongue,
The open road offers us no asylum.
. . . .
We are the slaves of your Ministers who hold sway over
      your land for five year terms.

They pretend to give us rehabilitation, or should it
    better be called exile at Dandakaranya.

. . . .

For Harijans, Islamis, Tribals, Scheduled Castes
There is no limit to words of sympathy that drop from
    your lips
Or to tears you pretend to shed.
Are they men or Gods that so much sympathy is reserved
    for them
and none is spared for us? Which country do they belong to?
And which do we?

(Translated by Saibal Kumar Gupta; first published in *Alekhya*,
Baishakh-Asad 1385, April June 1978)

A play that ran to full houses in Calcutta and was subsequently
made into a film called *The New Jews* by Salil Sen (reproduced
in this volume) point to the supportless, dangling condition of
the thousands of Bengalis rendered homeless. Women's protest
against this wanton uprooting is recorded in a memorable shot
in Nemai Ghosh's film *Chhinnomool*, showing a group of Hindu
peasants leaving East Bengal. An old woman of the community
does not see the point of leaving the ancestral home (*bastu*).

The 'refugee' population transformed Calcutta from a city
of arm-chair babus devoted to genteel culture into a militant,
angry, leftist city where middle class women uprooted from
the shelter of their village homes came out to work. As Rachel
Weber discovered through her interviews, not all women were
happy about this freedom thrust upon them. This individual
freedom was also articulated in an idiom of loss. Ritwik
Ghatak, *the* filmmaker of the Bengal Partition, has epitomized
the new refugee women in the resettled colonies on the outskirts of Calcutta in the epic figure of Nita, the heroine of
Meghe Dhaka Tara (The Star Veiled by Clouds).

This is the tragedy and triumph of the displaced women of
Bengal. Myth and reality enter into a convenient symbiosis in
these rare chronicles of women's suffering.

NOTE

1.   Phulrenu Guha (1911-), a member of the Rajya Sabha and minis-
     ter for social welfare in the union cabinet in 1969; in 1971 she
     chaired the Committee on the Status of Women that produced
     the landmark report (1975).
       Mridula Sarabhai (1911-78) was a Gandhian who fought for
     the rights of the working class, women and minorities. She led
     the attempt to return abducted women to India. See Menon and
     Bhasin 1996.

REFERENCES

Bagchi, Jasodhara. 1990. Representing Nationalism: Ideology of Moth-
     'erhood in Colonial Bengal, Review of Women's Studies, *Economic
     and Political Weekly (EPW)* 20-27 October.
——. ed. 1995. *Indian Women: Myth and Reality*. Kolkata: Orient
     Longman.
——. 1996a. Secularism as Identity, and Comments on Gyanendra
     Pandey. In *The Nation, the State and Indian Identity*, edited by
     Madhusree Dutta, Flavia Agnes and Neera Adarkar. Kolkata:
     Samya.
——. 1996b. Ethnicity and Women's Empowerment: The Colonial
     Legacy. In *Embodied Violence*, edited by Kumari Jayawardena and
     Malathi de Alwis. Delhi: Kali for Women.
Bandyopadhyay, Manabendra, ed. 1995. *Bhed-Bibhed* I, II (in Bengali),
     an all-India compilation of stories about riots, partition and anti-
     communalism. Kolkata: Dey's Publishing.
Bandyopadhyay, Sandip. 1997. Partition and the Forgotten People,
     Frontier, 2-8 August.
——. 1997. The Riddles of Partition. Memories of Bengali Hindus. In
     Reflections on Partition in the East, edited by Ranbir Samaddar.
     Delhi: Vikas.
Butalia, Urvashi. 1993. Community, State and Gender. On Women's
     Agency During Partition, Review of Women's Studies, *EPW*, WS
     12-24, 24 April.
Chatterjee, Jaya. 1995. *Bengal Divided: Hindu Communalism and Parti-
     tion, 1932-47*. Cambridge: Cambridge University Press.
Chatterjee, Partha. 1986. *Nationalist Thought and the Colonial World: A
     Derivative Discourse*. Delhi: Oxford University Press.
——. 1997. The Second Partition of Bengal. In *Reflections on Partition in
     the East*, edited by Ranabir Samaddar. Delhi: Vikas.

Chowdhury, Indira. 1993. The Return of the Sati: A Note on Heroism and Domesticity in Colonial Bengal, *RFR/DRF* 22,3/4: 41-44.

Das, Suranjan. 1995. *Communal Riots in Bengal, 1905-1947*. Delhi: Oxford University Press.

Devi, Jyotirmoyee. 1968. *Epar Bangla,Opar Bangla*. Calcutta, Dey's Publishing; English translation, 1995. *The River Churning*. Delhi: Kali for Women.

Jayawardena, K., and Malathi de Alwis, eds. 1996. *Embodied Violence: Communalising Women's Sexuality in South Asia*. Delhi: Kali for Women.

Menon, Ritu, and Kamala Bhasin. 1993. Recovery, Rupture, Resistance, Indian State and the Abduction of Women during Partition', Review of Women's Studies *EPW*, WS 2-11.

——. 1996. Abducted Women, the State and Questions of Honour. In *Embodied Violence, Communalising Women's Sexuality in South Asia*, edited by K. Jayawardena and Malathi de Alwis, Delhi: Kali for Women.

Ranabir Samaddar, ed. 1997. *Reflections on Partition in the East*. Delhi: Vikas.

Sangari, Kumkum, and Sudesh Vaid, eds. 1989. *Recasting Women: Essays in Colonial History*. Delhi: Kali for Women.

Sangari, Kumkum. 1993. Consent, Agency and Rhetorics of Incitement, *EPW* 28(8): 867-883.

Sarkar, Tanika. 1985. Communal Riots in Bengal. In *Communal and Pan-Islamic Trends in Colonial India*, edited by Mushirul Hasan. Delhi: Oxford University Press.

Sarkar, Tanika, and Urvashi Butalia. 1995. *Women and the Hindu Right*. Delhi: Kali for Women.

2

History's Creative Counterpart—Partition in Akhtaruzzaman Elias' *Khowabnama*

Subhoranjan Dasgupta

INTRODUCTION

SHOULD WE DISREGARD the great examples of creative literature, especially fiction, as 'non-history' or applaud them as imaginative transcriptions of history, where the writers uncover the reality surrounding them as well as the reality of the past by threading together actuality with memory, events with legends, and the struggle of the exploited with its mythic correlative? I propose that such fiction is not non-history per se but a historical narrative of another genre where, in the words of Brian Fay (1998), the meaningful reality is given its 'poetic-rhetoric' representation. We can even call this narrative suggesting the possible and imagined 'metahistory'. The most remarkable part of contemporary fiction produced by the Latin American novelists, the German Gunter Grass, the Czech Milan Kundera and—much nearer to us—Akhtaruzzaman Elias belongs to this genre. Replete with the inner reality of legends, memory and myths and at the same time close to diurnal actuality, this narrative, to quote Hayden White (1973; 1998), serves 'as an illumination of a world that we inhabit'. In this essay, I have examined the fiction of Akhtaruzzaman Elias, his epic-like *Khowabnama* (Dream-Elegy) in particular, to show how fiction acts as history's creative counterpart by focusing on the cognitive as well as the aesthetic modes.

ELIAS' WORLD OF FICTION

Neither Lucien Goldmann (1977), who traced the course of human history of post-war France in the novels of Alain Robbe-Grillet in the sixties, nor Hayden White who deliberately expanded the borders of historical discourse by underlining the 'Rhetorical Attitude' and the 'Linguistic Turn' was the first to propose literature, primarily fiction, as history's creative counterpart. The term 'counterpart', in this specific context, means neither duplication of history nor opposition to it, but, essentially, an extension and even completion of it. One could even try to sound modest and claim that fiction is viewed here as history's creative complement.

Both Lucien Goldmann and Hayden White as well as many other theorists of our age who have posited metanarratives of different kinds to enrich the so-called 'objective' narrative of history were preceded by Friedrich Engels (Marx and Engels 1975). In that oft-quoted letter written to Laura Lafargue on 13 December 1883, Engels proposed Balzac as an excellent historian. He wrote,

> By the by I have been reading scarcely anything but Balzac while laid up and enjoyed the grand fellow thoroughly. There is the history of France from 1815 to 1848, far more than in all the Vaulabelles, Capefigues, Louis Blancs et tuttiquanti. And what boldness! What a revolutionary dialectic in his poetic justice.

Marx and Engels clearly stated why they favoured Balzac. While Marx found him 'remarkable for his profound grasp of reality', Engels—in the words of Georg Lukacs—honoured him for having 'inexorably exposed the vices and weakness of royalist feudal France and [having] described its death-agony with magnificent poetic vigour' (Lukacs 1972). The question is do we have a Balzac in our midst who in his fiction has also exhibited a similar 'profound grasp of reality' and 'exposed the vices and weaknesses of the contemporary regimes'. If we look around and seek honestly, our eyes will come to focus on one author who has attained an iconic status in both

Bangladesh and West Bengal after writing only two novels
and a handful of short stories. I am speaking here of
Akhtaruzzaman Elias who refused to be prolific in the age of
slick and smart quickies and who has been hailed by critics as
the most scintillating creative writer in the modern history of
Bengali Literature after Manik Bandyopadhyay.

Mahasweta Devi in a candid interview confessed that she
would have considered herself thrice blessed if she had one
tenth of the creative ability of Elias. Badruddin Umar and
Soukat Ali—to name only two more renowned admirers—re-
garded his two novels *Chilekothar Sepai* (Soldier of the Attic)
and *Khowabnama* (Dream Elegy) as exceptional texts. Why?
Precisely because Elias in these two novels and in his short
stories emerged and established himself as the Ideal Chronicler who not only depicted the many layers of reality in
imaginative terms but also as a sociologist explored the twists
and turns, pressures and processes which made such a reality
possible. Elias, himself, was convinced of this dual role, of this
double yet related allegiance to the poetic and epistemological
dimensions of fiction as history and he told his wife before his
death in January 1997: 'This book, I tell you, will help students of history and sociologists in the future.' By 'this book'
he meant *Khowabnama*. I feel tempted to quote the words of
Elias' wife, Suraiya Elias, at this point. She told me, 'Oh!
When I recall the amount of scholarship that went behind
Khowabnama—the history of Partition, the history of Tebhaga,
the history of the Fakir-Sanyasi uprising—texts on agriculture,
especially cultivation of paddy and, above all, his ideological
and emotional engagement with the Partition of Bengal.'

Akhtaruzzaman Elias condemned the Partition of Bengal in
unequivocal terms. Not once but on several occasions he said,

> My father, like many other members of the educated Mus-
> lim middle class of that time, earnestly wanted that Muslim
> boys and girls should keep pace with their Hindu counter-
> parts, that they live with equal dignity. But, let us not for-
> get, these Muslim boys and girls belonged to a particular
> class, to the Muslim middle class. It also needs to be empha-
> sized that only the progress of this middle class was aspired
> for. But the movement they unleashed in order to fulfil this

aspiration simply cannot be approved of. The Partition of 1947 was so catastrophic, so deplorable, so heartrending and meaningless that we are realizing it more every day.

(interview, Lyric)

Elias was born in 1943, four years before the traumatic division. Hence no personal memory of that horror provoked him to voice his rejection of the attainment of a homeland for Bengali Muslims. Like others, he had to live in East Pakistan first and then in Bangladesh, but he could never accept the division of Bengal.

When we deconstruct Elias' denunciation of the division, what strikes us is his emphatically Marxist point of view. He denounced Partition for that very reason which made it so appealing, even irresistible, to the members of his own class. Moreover, he did not have to wait for the Pakistani persecution of twenty long years to ascertain that the promise of a Muslim homeland was meant to be broken. In his context, no experiential afterthought was required to conclude that Partition was a calculated class collusion, if not conspiracy, between the Muslim League and the Congress, between the upper middle class leaderships of both these power blocs reinforced as they were by the share-the-pie stratagem of the Birlas and Ispahanis. In other words, Nehru's Congress and Jinnah's League were impatient to grab power and in the helter-skelter of things they chose to forget the trials and travails of the suffering majority. Those who dared to act and think otherwise, for example, the fighters of Tebhaga, were ruthlessly persecuted by the powers-that-be of both Hindustan and Pakistan. Elias' condemnation therefore did not emanate from a shocked middle class reaction but from an aware class-determined Marxian vision which stressed:

(i) Muslim League's emphasis on Islam as the religion of social liberation was a calculated ploy meant to dupe the masses, not to redeem them. On the other hand, Tebhaga from the very start was an agrarian movement of exploited peasants drawing its sustenance from the Marxian category of class struggle and directed to a large extent by the Communist Party.

(ii) Partition was used to establish the authority of the
Muslim middle and upper middle classes who were no
less apathetic than the Hindus towards the exploited
who were Muslims. Hence Partition did not promise
the *Ranga Prabhat* (Red Dawn) of Abul Fazl or offer the
Nongor (Anchor) of Abu Rushd to the Muslim majority.

(iii) Finally, 25 years of colonial Pakistani rule did not
mould his basic evaluation of Partition. Rather, his
class-dictated Marxian weltanschauung influenced his
judgement His friend, Syed Abdul Maqsud, attested to
this view. 'The little that I knew him, I can tell that he
was profoundly influenced by Marxism in the late sixties. He was a Marxist and he remained Marxist till his
death.' Had Elias been alive, we could have asked,
'What alternative do you propose from your Marxian
standpoint?'

No doubt leftist intellectuals like Badruddin Umar (1990), Sirajul
Islam Chaudhury (1993) and Ahmed Rafique (1986) had similar
comments to make on Partition and Tebhaga. Badruddin Umar
did not fail to glorify Tebhaga as the principle of opposition to
Partition. Sirajul Islam Chaudhury echoed Elias or vice versa
when he wrote, 'The real issue was the clash between the Hindu
and Muslim middle class. The Hindu middle class hoped to
enjoy all the fruits; the Muslims claimed we want our share.'
Ahmed Rafique even categorized the entire cultural protest
which reached its apex in the historic Language movement as
hemmed on all sides by the hesitant middle class. To paraphrase
his critique, it encircled the main road in contented pride, it did
not reach the harvested fields or grimy factories. But none among
them, I feel, phrased such an unequivocal condemnation of Partition as Elias did. He did not label it as others have done as
'historically incorrect' (Rafiuddin Ahmed 1981), or as a 'false
promise' and so on, but as a calculated betrayal of the exploited,
irrespective of their religious identity, on both sides.

Khowabnama recreates this treachery and indicts it. The
gameplan of the Muslim League shedding copious tears over
the fate of Muslim peasants oppressed by Hindu zamindars is
exposed by the loner Choto Mia who refuses to accept that the

'social responsibility of the Muslim zamindar' will grow once Pakistan is created. Castigating the rule of the Muslim League in Bengal which 'had only Famine to offer as its achievement', Choto Mia debunks the tirades of Muslim League demagogues who spout Islamic socialism. His question is sharp and pointed. 'All the bigwigs of your League are rich people and zamindars. If you expel them how can you ensure the survival of the party?' The party had to flourish and therefore it borrowed the slogans of Tebhaga to waylay the Muslim peasants. This was not the case of the exploited usurping the language of the exploiter as described by Ranajit Guha (1953), but its exact opposite. The exploiter stole the promise of the militants and when the battle for Pakistan was finally won, conveniently forgot what he had promised.

Tamij, the hero of the novel, who even on the day of Partition looked forward to the imminent implementation of Tebhaga could hardly believe his ears when the Muslim League politician Abdul Kader dismissed the demand as pointless and denigrated the defiant peasants of Nachol as hotheaded lumpens. Abdul Kader also informed Tamij, not without a sense of smug satisfaction, that the new Bill in Assembly had omitted the clause of the bargadars. Hence Tebhaga was nothing more than a pipedream, and Partition was designed to facilitate the speedy ascent of a jotedar like Sharafat Mandal, who stepped into the shoes of the Hindu zamindar and persisted with the same tyranny. Sharafat emerges, like Tamij, as another crucial character of the novel illustrating the process of change in rural overlordship.

In all fairness, Elias also pinpointed the contribution of the Hindu bhadralok who viewed the ascendancy of the Muslim League based on the combination of the jotedar-ashraf with disgust and alarm. In fear of being swamped by the Muslims, who till the other day were mostly petty subordinates, Satish Mokhtar charted his Hindu scheme of deliverance, 'Our Shyamaprasad is right. We demand a divided Bengal even in an undivided India. No more with the barbarian Mohamedans.' This emphasis on hostility in the creative text finds its historical sanction in Partha Sarathi Gupta's statement (2000), 'The campaign for partitioning Bengal began with Hindu politicians who used the Noakhali riots to criticize the Muslim League government . . . Some of the

[Hindu Mahasabha] resolutions, dated mid-May 1947, also have hostile comments on the move to have a united Bengal, indicating some alarm that the Bose-Suharwardy-Abul Hashim plan might be taken seriously by the high command.'

In *Khowabnama* vanquished Tebhaga is posited against victorious Partition. Further, this defiant agrarian revolt and whatever it embodies invoke the scenario of true redemption. It actualizes the Principle of Hope and exposes the actuality of Partition as something vacuous and catastrophic. This is accomplished by Elias with enviable artistry because none else in the contemporary world of Bengali literature is able to transform a thwarted reality into irresistible dream with more power and poignancy. Tebhaga does not occupy the centre-stage of the novel, as Partition does. It wells up in the background from time to time like a symphonic movement played at a distance. It recedes, advances, intervenes and also disrupts the narrative of Partition with its corrective accent. Even when it is not physically present, its traces persist, like a signature that refuses to be erased. If Partition is what the world is, Tebhaga voices Michel Foucault's political intent (1991): 'To refuse what we are' and if the power of Partition 'is like a productive network which runs through the whole social body, it is much more than an agent and actor of repression', Tebhaga, to use Foucault's expression again 'promotes new forms of subjectivity through refusal'.

The first mention of Tebhaga, which coincided with the phase that led to Partition, occurs on page 20 of the novel. In one revealing sentence Elias condenses the essence of the movement, 'New and new waves are advancing from north and east. The bargadars are coming together to store the paddy in their homes.' What is more striking is the impact of this single statement on the exploited villagers like Kulsum and Tamij. Kulsum is in the same breath amazed and excited though Tamij turns grave in wonder. The second mention occurs after 23 pages when the hapless Tamij begs the rising jotedar Sharafat Mandal to allow him to work as a sharecropper. While deliberations are on between the two, the elder son of Sharafat, Abdul Aziz, a staunch Muslim League activist, ridicules the audacity of the poor peasants who have demanded two thirds of the produce they have cultivated with their own hands and who will permit only a meagre one third to be given to the landowner.

Aziz's condemnation of Tebhaga is categorical, 'Yes [they] can jolly well demand. You don't have to pay taxes to voice your demand. But, one word, the land does not walk on its own to the zamindar's house . . . to acquire one tiny piece of land an ounce of blood needs to be released in the form of sultry sweat from the body. Is the peasant aware of this sacrifice?' These words, and not the million promises made by Muslim League politicians (faithfully recorded in the novel) that the land will belong to the tiller in the Islamic paradise, exhibit the real attitude. They echo as a clashing counterpoint whenever politicians claim that Pakistan will ensure the eradication of zamindars, jotedars and mahajans. As a result, the promise of a politician like Ismael rings hollow when he says, 'Only the Hindus will gain if Muslims fight among themselves. Tebhaga will be automatically implemented in Pakistan.'

Ismael is not indulging in any reckless invention. He is merely following the Draft Manifesto of the Muslim League (published in March 1945) which harped on the abolition of the zamindari-mahajani system. In fact, the Muslim League did not hesitate to go beyond the resolution of the Communist Party and its fighting peasants by declaring that not only Tebhaga, but Choubhaga (all the produce) would belong to the tiller. Taj ul-Islam Hashmi (1994), who has narrated in fine detail the Muslim League's hijacking of the rebellious agrarian politics of Tebhaga in the crucial years 1945-47, observes, 'Ghiasuddin Pathan, a prominent Muslim League leader of the district [Mymensingh] is said to have told the Muslim sharecroppers who were with the Communists that they should not waste time and energy for Tebhaga . . . since Pakistan was in the offing and they would get all lands or Choubhaga after the mass expropriation of all Hindu landlords.'

This deceptive usurpation of the Tebhaga ideology and its deft placement in the matrix of the false utopia of Pakistan paid rich dividends. Elias however is determined to demolish this very Utopia in order to denounce Partition without the slightest misgiving. His objective is to posit his own idealized reality and this he achieves by granting Tebhaga an elevated, aesthetic immutability. The consummately crafted prose of Elias flutters in fervour when he narrates the brave acts of the Tebhaga war-

riors. Challenging the thesis of Abdul Aziz in the previous page
(p 43), Tamij recollects,

> 'The jotedars, presumably, had spoken to the police. But to
> how many fields can the police possibly go . . . Even the
> wives and daughters of peasants attacked with brooms,
> cooking spuds, kitchen knives. Had he not run through the
> paddy fields, leapt over sheaves of corn, one or two blows
> of spuds and brooms would have certainly hit him. Who
> knows if he had not suffered some hits? Who broadcasts
> willingly the news of being assaulted by women?'

The narrator Tamij, in this first phase of the novel, is a sul-
len opponent of the peasant's temerity. Yearning to be an obe-
dient sharecropper himself, he says, 'The paddy is the dear life
of the landowner. How can he possibly survive if this paddy is
the object of pulls and thrusts?' But the metamorphosis occurs
at an unrelenting pace. Fisherman Tamij turns into the sharecropper Tamij and after Partition when Tebhaga is actually
crumbling he opts to fight for it. Rejecting the instruction of his
political boss to go to Dhaka, he proceeds towards that unde-
fined region where the paddy belongs to the tiller. By deciding
his own course not only does he challenge Engels' prediction on
the progressive pauperization of the small peasant (1975): 'Our
small peasant, like every other survival of a past mode of production, is hopelessly doomed. He is a future proletarian,' but
also etches the real consciousness, the real praxis and the real
Utopia.

The most inspired prose in the novel recreates Tamij's quest
for emancipation:

> Though he is illiterate, for the first time in his life he is able
> to read the word 'Shantahar'. Going to Shantahar means,
> you go to Jaipur from there, to Akkelpur, to Hili . . . So
> many policemen are going, which means peasants are lift-
> ing the paddy into their barns, the cloth covering the arses
> of jotedars has fallen, the scoundrels are running, hiding in
> the arseholes of the police. And in the midst of all these the
> soil is being readied for aman . . . Once the soil is ready the
> sapling will be brought and seeds will be planted in joyous

abandon. Ah! It rained last night, the soil is as soft as but-
ter, the moment the plough touches it, the plough delves
deep down inside the earth, Tamij can even extract water
from there. In the fumes of the Shantahar train you again
inscribe the picture of paddy fields. Ah, what fields. The
stalk flourishes in a flash, it bends below under the weight
of the milk. Innumerable peasants have descended on the
fields to thresh the thick clusters of paddy. The jotedars
have come with the police. Trains filled with police are
spreading out in every station. They come down like chol-
era, like smallpox. Peasants attack them with their scythes
and sickles. The scoundrels gasping for breath cannot find
the path to escape.

(my translation)

This memorable account sums up the politics of
Akhtaruzzman Elias. He is not only against Partition but also
opposed to any measure in any part of the world that deprives
the worker and peasant of the fruit of their labour. Elias is
not prepared to view Tebhaga as an isolated eruption of
emancipatory zeal. His worldview prompts him to regard it as
one significant phase of the cyclic chain of rebellions which is
linked to others that have preceded it.

In *Khowabnama* this counter-narrative does not begin with
Tebhaga but from the historic Sanyasi-Fakir uprising against the
colonial rulers. The first half of the 1770s witnessed the spread
of this challenge in Rangpur, Coochbehar, Bagura, Purnea,
Mymensingh and Dinajpur, though it proved to be abortive.
The memory of the battles fought, especially the valour of the
two leaders, Majnu Shah and Bhabani Pathak, crystallize into a
series of exquisite lyrics whose mood sway from the warlike to
the elegiac.

'Majnu,' shouts Bhabani Sanyasi,
'Catch the Whites and hang them straight!'
Bhabani roars and the Giris flash swords
They send the whites to Yama's door.

(my translation)

Even after positing Tebhaga and the redemptive memory of

past revolts against divisive Partition, Elias decides to leave history or fiction as open-ended. The last few pages of *Khowabnama*, for instance, extract the essence out of history, popular memory, legend, folktale and fantasy to dwell on one overwhelming truth of Bengal's past and present, namely, hunger. At his cognitive best in this closing phase, Elias impels Tamij's daughter, Sakhina, to say that she is hungry for rice. This primordial urge is granted its 'linguistic turn' by the poetic prose of Elias and, as a result, the cognitive acquires its aesthetic and ethical connotations. When we read this section of the novel—once again the partial translation is a poor echo of the original—we realize how history and fiction can be both truthful and creative in the best sense and can avoid the pitfall of wishful, one-sided prediction.

The hunger of the Bengali people stretching over ten centuries is invoked through the hallucinatory voice of Sakhina, 'Ma, The kitchen burns, the kitchen burns. I will eat rice, Ma cooks rice, I will eat.' This accumulated hunger of the exploited is fused with the flow of revolts and the 'slokas' which depicted it. As she tries to quench the hunger of her daughter, Tamij's wife, Phuljan, succumbs to the pervasive, mythic recollection and ruminates, 'Phuljan has heard Munshi's slokas in the past. She has heard so many slokas praising Majnu and Bhabani Sanyasi in the Poradaha fair. Tamij used to tell him all these and she herself used to recite a few.' In this surreal atmosphere redolent with the defiant spirit of the past, Tamij himself shot to death while fighting for Tebhaga enters the body of the moon. He becomes an integral part of the legendary battle for rice celebrated in folk memory and under his pressure the moon turns ghostly and threatening. The novel ends with the kitchen burning under the wounded moon. Nothing more.

When Elias was not writing a novel, this same overwhelming reality of hunger ignored the 'poetic-rhetoric' and turned into biting prose. In his essay on Gunter Grass he observed, 'Since ages we have not eaten well. Bengali poetry which was written a thousand years ago began with the news of riceless pots. Those who have no food in their stomachs, their stomachs burn and rage. Yes, starvation and half-fed stomachs are the prime cause of our gastric ulcer' (1997). A race condemned to this hunger-struck gastric ulcer for centuries has the right to rebel, to dream of revolts, to layer its memory and legend with the strains of these uprisings and ultimately present the archetype of this history of hunger in Tamij's daughter Sakhina. Indeed, Sakhina crosses the limits of actuality and becomes a voice of the race whose remembrance and future, reality and fantasy, history and metahistory revolve around the one, compelling statement, 'Ma has put the rice to boil. Ma I shall eat.'

This very brief assessment of *Khowabnama* intends to show how the logic of Elias' creative narration, to borrow the words of Louis Mink (1998), shifts from 'explanation' to 'understanding' and scripts a poetics of fiction as well as history. The moment he accomplishes this dual task, he enters the realm of hermeneutics which is true to the kindred points of aesthetic as well as historical consciousness. But this truth, Hans Georg Gadamer (1976) reminds us, is transcribed with the help of language. And when Elias wields this all-important weapon of language, he allows, to quote Gadamer, 'everything human to be spoken to us'. Abjuring the photographic actuality attempted by chroniclers, he 'emplots' history with constructive imagination and enriches the surface of diurnal existence with a multi-layered perspective of memory, myth, legends. He begins *Khowabnama* with a myth vibrating with history and he ends by transforming a hungry girl into a figure of fantasy.

Till date he remains as the supreme example of magic realism in Bengali literature. Elias, himself, has explained the quest and components of this realism, 'I have never observed reality with any specific philosophy in mind. I want to explore reality from inside, I want to decipher its inner dreams, desires, resolutions, beliefs. This inner reality is all-important.' (Interview, *Lyric*). No wonder he professed a special love for the Latin American novelists, Jorges Luis Borges and Gunter Grass. Their creative formats sustained by legends, folktales, history and myths was his format too.

CONCLUSION

Every gifted writer has his talismanic passage which reveals to the fullest extent his magic power. In the case of Elias, this pas-

sage, perhaps, is to be found in Chapter 21 of his other masterpiece, *Chilekothar Sepai,* where he describes the death-defying
struggle of the people of East Bengal against Ayub Khan's regime in 1969. This text fuses the ideological and the aesthetic in
one unbreakable bond and merges the politics of the moment
with the tumult of history. Obliterating the borders between
memory, legend, past, present and the future aspired-for, the
particular text recreates a pageant of rebellions which floundered
but did not fail to inscribe the promise of hope. Almost all critics of Elias have singled out this passage as the key to Elias'
political aesthetic and creative assimilation of history. Here is an
imperfect translation of this unique passage:

> This flow of people ... Clothes of many and physiognomy
> appear unfamiliar to him. Who are they? Have the people
> of long, distant past also joined this march? There in the
> exact middle march the residents of Dhaka of Islam Khan's
> reign in their short dhoties! Even those of earlier times who
> used to go to Sonargaon in their boats filled with sacks of
> rice have come. The residents of Banglabazar and Tantibazar
> have emerged from the cold heart of the vanished canal?
> There stand the turbaned, dead soldiers of Ibrahim Khan's
> reign who battled with Shahjada Khasru. Osman trembles
> seeing the men who died of hunger in Sayestha Khan's days
> when the cost of rice was Taka 1 for eight maunds. They
> have not eaten for 400 years ... Flying their waves of black
> hair they advance. This procession cannot be so massive
> unless all the battered are here ... Battered by the Moghuls,
> by the Mags, by the company merchants. Breaking the dry
> layer of bricks of Racecourse Kalibari, the Maratha priest
> has come swinging his falchion, the fakirs of Majnu Shah
> have come; there throwing rings of finger-torn clenched fists
> the Muslim weavers come, their black bodies burn in the
> sun. The bone-all, starving naked bodies of weavers who
> weave jamdanis worth Taka 4,000 a piece are walking erect.
> The Imam, muezzins, musallis of Babubazar Mosque shot
> by the sahibs are walking, instead of muttering their ayat
> they are now roaring, 'We shall not let it go in vain.' The

sepoys of Lalbagh Fort mangled by the beasts let loose by
Nabab Abdul Ghani—Ruplal and Mohini Mohan—lackeys
of the redfaced sahibs come. The sepoys of Meerut arrive
after tearing down their nooses hanging from the palm trees
of Victoria Park, sepoys of Barreilly, Sandwip, Sirajganj,
Goaland. No, my friend, even that is not enough. The
youths of Jugantar and Anusilan in their dhoties and ban-
yans and devoted to their mother march, in their midst you
can identify separately those two youths who were killed in
Kaltabazar. Carrying the bloody waves of Dolai canal on his
head Somen Chanda jumps out of Narinder Bridge. There is
Barkat! His skull blown off . . . So many people, Dhaka's
past-present-future is overflowing with the tide of new water, morning-afternoon-evening-night stand forgotten and
dissolved, today it has no east-west-north-south, all the
separation marks of seventeenth, eighteenth, nineteenth and
twentieth centuries have been erased. Dhaka is intent to occupy limitless time and limitless space! Osman's heart
trembles! How far can he go with this tidal surge? How far?

(my translation)

Is there any point in dissecting this text? Fragments of history
and memory are woven here together to articulate the utopian
message of the author. They read as related particles of some,
single, immense story: the story of the class struggle as depicted
in *The Communist Manifesto*. Both *Chilekothar Sepai* and *Khowabnama*, then, excavate the political unconscious, so eloquently
theorized by Fredric Jameson (1989), and with their orchestrated
surfeit of memory and myth, legends and tales, dreams and fan-
tasies serve as history's creative counterpart. The boldness, the
dialectic, the grasp of reality which Marx and Engels read in
Balzac we read here again. There is, however, one difference.
Balzac had described the death agony of royalist feudal France
with poetic vigour but Elias, true to his times, projected the
bravery and agony of the struggle only. He did not impose the
facile wish-fulfillment of victory. He closed the circle, so to speak,
by articulating the rhetoric of redemption in a realm still bound
by the crushing limits of necessity.

REFERENCES

Ahmed, Rafiuddin, 1981. *The Bengali Muslims: A Quest for Identity 1871-1906*. Delhi: Oxford University Press.
Choudhury, Sirajul Islam, 1993. *Dwijati Tattver Satyamithya.* Dhaka: Bidyaprakash.
Elias, Akhtaruzzaman, 1986. *Chilekothar Sepai.* Dhaka: University Press Ltd.
——, 1992. Interview. *Lyric,* Akhtaruzzaman Elias Number. Dhaka.
——, 1996. *Khowabnama.* Kolkata: Naya Udyog.
——, 1997. *Sangskritir Bhanga Setu.* Kolkata: Naya Udyog.
Engels, Friedrich, 1975. The Peasant Question in France and Germany. 1894. In Karl Marx and Friedrich Engels, *Selected Works,* vol 2. Moscow: Progress Publishers.
Fay, Brian, 1998. The Linguistic Turn and Beyond in Contemporary Theory of History. In *History and Theory: Contemporary Readings,* edited by Brian Fay, Philip Pomper and R.T. Vann. Oxford: Blackwell.
Fazl, Abul, 1994. *Ranga Probhat,* vol 1, *Abul Fazl Rachanabali,* edited by Alauddin al Azad. Dhaka: Bangla Academy.
Foucault, Michel, 1991.*The Foucault Reader.* London: Penguin.
Gadamer, Hans G. 1976. *Philosophical Hermeneutics.* Berkeley: University of California Press.
Goldmann, Lucien, 1977. *Cultural Creation.* Oxford: Blackwell.
Guha, Ranajit, 1953. *Elementary Aspects of Peasant Insurgency in Colonial India.* Delhi: Oxford University Press.
Gupta, Partha Sarathi, 2000. 'Who Divided the Bengalis?' In *The Partition Retrospect,* edited by Amrik Singh. Delhi: Anamika Publishers with National Institute of Panjab Studies.
Hashmi, Taj-ul Islam, 1994. *Peasant Utopia: The Communalisation of Class Politics in East Bengal 1920-1947.* Dhaka: University Press Ltd.
Jameson, Fredric, 1998. *The Political Unconscious: Narrative as a Socially Symbolic Act.* London: Routledge.
Lukacs, Georg. 1972. Introduction, in *Studies in European Realism.* London: Merlin.
Maqsud, Syed Abdul, 1997. Akhtaruzzaman Eliaser Sange Anekta Path. *Ajker Kagoj,* 11 Jan. Dhaka.
Marx, Karl, and Friedrich Engels, 1976. *On Literature and Art.* Moscow: Progress Publishers.
Mink, Louis. 1998. History and Fiction as Modes of Comprehension. In *History and Theory: Contemporary Readings* edited by Brian Fay, Philip Pomper and R.T. Vann. Oxford: Blackwell.

Rafique, Ahmed, 1986. *Buddhijibir Sangskriti.* Dhaka: Muktadhara.

Rushd, Abu. 1997. *Nongor.* Dhaka: Bud Publications.

Umar, Badruddin, 1990. Musalmander Swadesh Pratyabartan. In *Bangladesh: Bangali, Atmaparichayer Sandhane,* edited by Mustafa Nurul Islam. Dhaka: Sagar Publications.

White, Hayden, 1973. *Metahistory: The Historical Imagination in Nineteenth-Century Europe.* Baltimore: Johns Hopkins.

——, 1998. The Historical Text as Literary Artifact. In *History and Theory: Contemporary Readings.* Oxford: Blackwell.

3

Kanta Tare Prajapati/Butterfly on Barbed Wire
Selina Hossain

HER BODY CRUMPLED up, not touched now even by the icy cold, ghostly silence in the cell, Ila lies motionless on the floor, the weals on her back burning. Blood still drips near her forehead, she doesn't try to reach out and touch it. Feet aching and heavy, a strange sound in her breast, she is unable to close her eyes. Harek's face floats before her eyes the moment she closes them. But who was this Harek? Not a word on his lips, as helpless as his beloved cow, his eyes focused far away . . . repeatedly crushed beneath their boots, stretching out again, till, at last, he goes away, rising above their grasp. The S.I.'s voice—exactly like an executioner's—drifts to her, 'If you don't confess all about the murders now, you'll be stripped!' She's naked now. Her clothes have been forcibly taken away. She's imprisoned in a tiny cell. Clothes are only an outer covering, what does it matter if they are taken away? Harek has given something so much larger—a black-coloured heart as big as this earth. Her head hums with pain. Ramen would stroke her forehead gently when she had a headache. If she suffered too much, her mother-in-law would mix Jabakusum hair oil with a little water, and massage it into her scalp, 'You have to take care of yourself, Bouma,' she'd say, 'you don't take care of your body!'

Body? There never was any time to take care of it. And the wounds of a thousand vulture-talons upon it now. There were countless palms all around the twelve villages. Hundreds of vultures would roost on the crowns of those palms, their wings outspread, soaking up the sunshine. She had never thought that their talons would be so poisonous, that they'd burn her to ashes from head to toe in an instant, tear her apart, lacerate a human life! Aaah! Ila moans with pain. Water? Her dry tongue longs for water. Who would give her some water? There was no Sukhiya here. No one had collected water from the pond, boiled it, strained it through a piece of fine cloth, then stored it in an urn for her! Could you get water the moment you wanted it? She licked her dry lips. There was nothing even remotely wet, anywhere here ... in Baisakh, the soil of Chandipur would be like this hard, parched, cracked in a thousand directions. Aaah! Again that moan in Ila's throat. O Ma ... her hand creeps up to her head, strokes her forehead. I have given up everything I have! If my life is fulfilled by giving that which they want, I am ready! But in exchange, let them give me back the people of this place, let the bloodstains be washed away!

Aaah! She rests her head on the floor. In the evening, the sepoys had hit her head with their rifle butts, and a strange sound hummed in her ears ... 'Buzz ... z .. z.' That childhood game, The Blind, Buzzing Fly! Some days ago, in Chandara's house, a huge wasp had drifted round her nose, making that same sound, ' Buzz–z-z.' She was, in fact, quite enjoying it! There was a certain regal air about the wasp's colourful torso. But Chandara hadn't liked it. She took a broom, and after much effort, she managed to beat the life out of it. It lay flat on Chandara's floor. Ila asked, 'Why did you kill it, Chandara?'

'It was troubling you, wasn't it?'

'But it was flying about in its own fancy!'

'If it troubles you, why should I bear it?'

Where was Chandara now? The sepoys had put a thousand wasps into her head. Blood flows from her nostrils after the beating—streams of blood! Her clothes are soaked with blood. Harek had found a sari for her from a Santhal, that sari is wet with blood now. What can she do to stop the flow? The S.I. sits before her, glaring at her with bloodshot eyes, ready to pounce on her.

'We've done nothing as yet ... confess! Otherwise it won't do you any good, let me tell you!'

Whom is he talking to? Who will listen to this animal's threats? Ila looks at her blood-stained sari. She looks at all the

people around her, they look the same: their bodies are similar, their dress is similar. Not one is different, they are all
alike. Her lips tremble, but do not part. When she had been a
teenager, out on the playfield, she'd press her lips tightly together, and run hard. As if she were flying like a bird towards
the finishing line!

Pounding the floor with his boots, the S.I says, 'Here, you
bitch, will you open your mouth or not?'

Bitch? Ah, a fitting tribute to this human life! No one had
ever addressed her in this way!

'Got it, the straight road won't do for her! Bitch, whelp of
a bitch! Here, take her and lock her up in a cell!'

How large is this cell? Space enough for just this much
space! Actually, even standing space would be enough for me!
I've seen the huts of the Santhals, without light or air; they live
out their lives in darkness. They don't get proper sleep; rainwa-
ter seeps into their huts in the monsoon; in summer, the heat is
stifling. What does their backbreaking labour fetch them? At
least you've given me enough space to lie down! The whimper
in her throat gets feebler now. She is gradually getting listless.
If she closes her eyes, she no longer sees Harek, but thousands
and thousands of arrows come flying over the crowns of the
palms in Chandipur.

The door opens with a click. A beam of torchlight flashes
over her body. She does not move, or make a sound. They
shouldn't see the slightest movement, hear the tiniest whisper
of sound. The next instant, some clothes are tossed to her.

'Here are your clothes, put them on!'

The torch is switched off. She fumbles into her clothes in
the darkness. The door is open, her knees knock together in the
acute cold. Yet, she likes the cold. The throbbing headache
seems to recede. The cold acts like a gentle, tender touch, like a
healing balm. She sits with her head against the wall. The conversation of the sepoys outside filters in. Listening to them, she
makes out, it is now midnight. It is pitch dark outside, nothing
can be seen. Yet Ila stares out into that darkness, thirst locked
in her chest. She's had no contact with the outside world since
yesterday.

'Here, you dame! Get up—so!'

A sepoy pulls her violently to her feet. She doesn't know

where she's supposed to go. She doesn't wish to know. Crossing a patch of darkness, they come to a house; it seems to her, to someone's home. Perhaps the S.I's house. Again that harsh voice growls, 'You can still confess. There'll be no place for you till you've made a confession.'

Ila gets irritated. She has no wish to hear the same thing over and over again. She keeps her face averted, unaware of the bruises beneath her eyes. There is a window within the line of her vision. Somewhere nearby, an owl hoots. Back home in Ramchandrapur-haat, if an owl hooted, her mother-in-law would hold a piece of iron in the flame of a lamp. She would say, 'The owl's hooting is inauspicious. If you burn a piece of iron, that evil is destroyed.' Ila thinks, 'There is no evil here. Let me fill my ears with the owl's hooting. At least, the fresh breeze from the outside world brings me this sound. A single word from those animals makes my wounds bleed again, makes me sick!' Again that voice, which makes her sick, is heard. 'It's clear she won't open her month. Come on, use the things which will make her speak! Then she'll know what she's sown and what she'll reap!'

'Actually sir, we've never seen such a wicked female in our lives!'

'I haven't, either! I'd like to see the mother who gave birth to her.'

'Mother, or witch! Who knows?'

A howl of laughter rises among the soldiers. Ila transfers her gaze from the darkness to the white wall in front of her. The owl's hooting has stopped now. That sound had been like a shelter for her. As soon as it stops, her shelter too crumbles, falls apart.

Two sepoys come, catch her arms and lay her flat on the floor. They place two sticks on either side: above and below her feet, and begin pressing down. They tie a cloth tightly round her mouth so that her screams won't be heard. Her body is lacerated with pain, violent pain. She stretches out her hand as if to cling on to something, finding nothing, she tears at her hair. She hears the voices of many people. 'This Pakistani injection will make her open her mouth.'

'See how it has puckered up, she can't help but open her mouth now!'

'Her pa must have fed her with cat's meat, that's why she is so strong!'

Ila thinks, why don't they put some Pakistani thing! After some time, they get tired, they let her go. Before she knows what's happening, one soldier yanks out a huge handful of her hair. Her eyes begin to water with terrible pain. She feels she's about to faint, she's suffocating. She thinks she'll soon go looking for Harek. Harek's father had told her, 'Rani Ma, I'll get Harek married now. I've selected a girl.' Ila had been pleased. 'That's good news! What fun we'll have!' But Harek had opposed the idea violently, 'I won't marry now, I'll work for the revolution all my life, Rani Ma, like you!' Ila had patted his back 'Pooh, foolish boy!' Harek had said sullenly, 'If I don't work for our cause, I'll go and live in the forest. I'll eat fruit and roots, catch birds. I won't come back to the village!'

The S.I's voice thunders, 'Take her to the cell.'

They open the cloth binding her mouth. Her head flops sideways. Her breathing is weak. She can't get up because of that Pakistani injection. The sepoys grab her arms and legs and carry her to the cell. Ila keeps her eyes closed. Not even the weakest of sounds would escape her lips.

After she is brought to her cell, the S.I. shouts, 'She'll have to blab. Get me four hot boiled eggs, one of you.'

Ila hears the departing footsteps of a sepoy. What hell awaits her now? How much more would they do? Some one is pacing outside, the sound of booted footsteps slams her chest. She can see lights red, blue, green and yellow lights—a thousand butterflies flitting inside her head—the colours dazzle her eyes. Next to the bamboo grove in Ramchandrapur–haat, hundred, and hundreds of Lajjabati flowers would bloom in a small patch. Sometime she would stand silently, looking at them. Harek would ask, 'Rani Ma, shall I pluck some for you?' But Ila would stop him, 'No, no, they'll close up if you pluck them. They look lovely now!' Nishikanto's daughter, Parag, was very fond of wearing flowers in her hair. Ila had never seen her without them. She had a beautiful figure, once you saw her, you couldn't take your eyes off her! Was she alive? Half-conscious, Ila mutters, 'You're looking beautiful, wearing those palash flowers, Parag. Keep well, be happy.' The palash grows bright before her eyes, she can't think of anything except palash. And then, with a terrible scream, her whole body begins to shake. Four or five sepoys hold her down forcibly and another one pushes a hot boiled egg into her vagina. Fire . . . the earth is entirely engulfed in fire! With one horrific scream, she loses consciousness.

She doesn't know how many endless nights have gone by. When at last, consciousness returns and she awakes to light in her cell, she's incapable of movement. A doel calls, very close to her window. Ila can see its black back, its white breast. Rubbing away her tears with her palm, she says, 'Please give me the strength to endure! Please say just one thing. That I shouldn't be defeated! Let a procession of sepoys pass over my body before I utter even a single word in front of them!' The doel flies away, and the next instant, the S.I. enters the room with some sepoys

'Oh, so you are conscious, I see. You have guts, I have to say!'

The S.I. kicks her stomach, the boot's kick turns her insides upside-down. The soldiers do not hold back. Each one has his kick.

'Here, push the screws into her heels!'

They had brought the screws, immediately one was pushed into her heel. Ila becomes aware that the floor is getting wet. Her hair is spread all about her head. Butterflies invade her consciousness, all red, blue, green and yellow. Half-conscious, she hears the arrogant boots, the harsh voice, 'We'll return at night. If your don't confess, the sepoys will rape you one by one.'

They go away. The outside world is shut out. A ray of late December sunlight has entered through the skylight and lies diagonally on the floor. Ila stretches out her hand to that sunbeam, it seems Mohan is crawling towards her, there's nobody else nearby. Mohan's face wears a divine smile. Ila feels no hunger, no thirst, nothing. She cannot stay within herself. She sees, Mohan has come very close to her breast, he's lying there, going to sleep in the curve of her bosom. Her throat hums with a lullaby. As she sings, she feels drowsy, but she can't sleep. She has no strength left, and so she cannot sleep. But bubbles keep rising up in her subconscious, then float away like foam.

They return. Her eyes are blinded by the beam of the flashlight. Again the threats, she'll be raped if she doesn't confess.

She's clutching Mohan closely, she doesn't hear anything they say. In the next moment, a scream rises to her threat. Mohan has fallen, has been flung away somewhere, she can't find him anywhere. Her body is naked and bared . . . her body is being bared. Even then, she doesn't say a word.

The S.I. screams, 'Talk, you bitch!'

She whimpers with pain, fire spreads all over her body. Three or four of them pin her down, and when one begins to rape her, her consciousness turns itself away from the barbarity, she is lost. She does not remember anymore.

Then a time comes when the deep night is over. The darkness fades away, light flowers, birds call outside, leaves stir in the breeze, flowers bloom; it is dark in her cell, faint light filters in through the cracks and corners in the doorway. Opening her eyes is painful, she glances up once, then closes them again, she bites her lips with her teeth . . . no, not defeat, ever. She'd give her last drop of blood to stop this beastly torture . . . Harek had died without making a sound, wouldn't she be able to do it then? She becomes aware that her clothes are soaking in blood, her body is growing limp because of that severe bleeding, she feels the world all around is getting cold. As if she'd come to some far corner of the earth, how was she to cross this icy frontier? Ila lies motionless, her head resting on her forehead. She takes no notice of the heavy flow of blood, let it flow . . . flow! She is brought in this condition from Nachol to Nawabganj. The sepoys at the gate of Nawabganj Jail greet her with merciless blows. Fawning curs who licked their masters' boots, unaware how puny their rights were, or what their station was!

The Court Inspector and a few sepoys carry her to the cell of Nawabganj jail. Now, fever has come as an adjunct to her heavy bleeding, her head feels as if it will be torn off. Fever scorches her body, Ramen's face floats before her eyes, shrivelled, devastated. Ila cannot recognize him. They leave her in the cell and go away. After that a doctor arrives. He places a thermometer in her armpit. Reading the temperature he shudders. 'This is terrible! It is 105°!'

After five days, she detects a note of concern and she looks straight at the man. So, some humans still remain on this earth! All these days, she'd lived with a band of ferocious wolves in a deep forest. She clings to the doctor's hand, 'Doctor, I am bleeding profusely!'

'I know. I could see at once what torture you've had to endure! I'll do my best for you. I'll get a female nurse to arrange for your treatment. My name is Ayub Ali.'

Ila doesn't let go of the doctor's hand. She says brokenly, 'I've heard a lot about your skill, though I've never met you!'

Laughing, he said, 'You've raised a storm in this entire area!'

Ila looks back with dull eyes. She is in such a precarious state, that it is painful even to laugh. The corners of her eyes glint. She is overwhelmed by the warmth and sincerity of the doctor.

Ayub Ali says confidently, 'I am hopeful that you won't face any ill treatment, here. The O.C. of this police station, Mr. Rahman, knows you. He's told me himself that while you were a student at Bethune, he was studying at Scottish Church College.'

She cannot recall Rahman. She doesn't even try. Shattered, in great pain, Ila faints once more. Dr. Ayub Ali brings some medicines and some scraps of a blanket. She has the medicine when she regains her senses. If nothing else, her headache eases.

The next day, a nurse from the government hospital at Nawabganj comes to examine her. She doesn't have to tell her anything, the nurse understands everything at a glance. Ila's fever doesn't come down, the bleeding does not stop. She loses consciousness from time to time. She remains under the treatment of Dr. Ayub Ali in that solitary cell. She doesn't know what the nurse's report contains, she sees that they give her a fresh sari in place of the bloodstained one. She feels just a shade better for that. Occasionally, the doctor comes and says a few words, gives some medicines, she is getting some easily-digestible food. The days here pass by in relative quiet. She finds it difficult to swallow even a spoonful of the mushy, over-cooked rice. As if all the mechanisms in her body had broken down and were rejecting even the slightest morsel of food. O.C. Rahman comes secretly, mostly at might. He wipes her forehead to cool it. Presses a few segments of an orange into her palm. Asks a brief question. 'How do you feel now?' Ila cannot say, 'I'm all right.' Nothing is all right anywhere around her. Her fever doesn't come down, her bleeding doesn't stop, the solitary cell weighs down upon her like a stone on her chest, the pain is unbearable; she loses consciousness.

O.C. Rahman assures her, 'You needn't worry. You have nothing to fear here. I will not allow anything to harm you.' Ila responds weakly, 'Fear of what? What do I have? I've lost everything! If only I could have saved Harek in exchange of giving all I had!'

'Let it be, you mustn't talk too much. Please rest. And please eat the sago at night.'

She spends seven days in this cell. Every night, Rahman visits her, gives her some medicine. One afternoon, she hears many voices, much hullabaloo in front of her cell. Some people were saying that she should be handed over to them. They'd 'make her over', then leave her. O.C. Rahman says sharply, 'She's in the custody of the Court, no one can raise a hand against her now.'

Hearing his voice, Ila sighs and closes her eyes. The special diet, the medicines, have no effect at all. It is as if every knot that holds her body together is unravelling. Then one evening, some sepoys arrive with a stretcher, and come to her cell.

In a grave voice, devoid of any feeling, they inform her she would have to go elsewhere for medical examination. Ila doesn't want to know where she has to go, why. She simply says. 'My body aches. I can't get up.'

The heavy blow of a cane lands with a thud on her head. Instantly, lightning flashes in her eyes, the desire to retaliate arises, but as they come forward as if threatening her, she gets onto the stretcher and lies down. All her processes of thought, all her powers of feeling, desert her.

She realizes that they have brought her to a house. A blue curtain hangs at a window. There is a table and a bench in the room. A torn sheet, the oil-stained pillow gives off a musty smell. Ila lies there, half conscious, somebody holds a spoon of milk to her lips, but it runs down in streams on either side of her lips. A piece of blank paper is held before her. 'Sign on this.' Behind her lowered lids, her pupils seem to detect nothing, as if a thick fog covers field and forest, nothing can be seen even at arm's length. Yet, she would have to go far away. Is the blue curtain actually a kingfisher? Drugged by fever, she finds it painful to look up, her eyelids are so heavy! All around, booted footsteps approach her. A storm rises with the sound of marching boots, blowing away the people, their homes!

The thick, harsh voice roars, 'Sign here!'

'She won't sign on her own. You'll have to make her sign.'

They raise her to a sitting posture. One of them rests his hand on the back of her neck. Another one holds her left hand, yet another pushes a pen into her right hand, curls the fingers over it, holds the curled fist over the blank page. Her head sways forward, close to the table.

Again that voice, 'You have to make her write. There's' no other way. Hold her hand by force and trace out her signature on the paper.'

Then, marks appear on the smooth paper, a name is written in shaky, uneven letters on the blank page. Ila glances for a moment at that page and realizes its not her name: it's the mace in Harek's fist or the spear of Shukra Madong, or perhaps, the thousands of arrows that had entered the body of Daroga Jafeezuddin. But the next moment, the name is transformed into a cartridge. Ila falls back on the bed, she has no strength to sit up. But still she understands that the bullet is now in her fist, there's a battle in front of her again, a battle.

When her condition deteriorates further, she is taken to the hospital. She cannot see Ayub Ali bending over her face administering injections, his forehead furrowed with anxiety, deep worry-lines standing out between his brows. The high fever has made her delirious. A nurse washes her head.

Her condition worsens rapidly. She looks pale and bloodless, the bones of her neck, her rib-cage, her jawline painfully thrust-out; the views blue in her wrists. There is no light in her gaze, as if her pupils would be extinguished any moment now.

She is brought in this state to the central jail in Rajshahi and admitted to the hospital. There are people everywhere in the female ward. She breathes deep lungfuls of air here, among humans. Women crowd around her bed, stare at her open mouthed; whisper to each other. Gathering up their courage, one or two ask, 'Did they beat you very hard?' Ila nods. 'Oh! What a state she's in!' Another says in wonder, 'Aren't they sons of humans?' A third woman twists her lips in revulsion. When an old lady, her head covered, asks her, 'How did you bear it?' Tears come to her eyes then. The old lady says, 'May Allah heal you quickly! Oh, the poor young girl! The old lady kneels, and prays. She has no teeth, her cheeks are deeply wrinkled, her vision hazy. Perhaps her life spans a century. She has left her own bed with great difficulty to see Ila, to say a few words of comfort. Ila salutes her silently, mutters incoherently, 'But whatever my condition, still. I've not told the police anything! They've not been able to get a single word out from my mouth!'

Translated by Sipra Bhattacharya from Selina Hossain,
Kata Tare Prajapati, Dhaka: Jatiya Sahitya Prakashani, 1989.
By kind permission of the author © 1989 Selina Hossain.

We reproduce here ILA MITRA'S statement which was distributed as a pamphlet throughout East Pakistan in February 1950.

How Humanity [Is] Attacked under Liakat-Nurul Amin Regime

Below is the statement of Sm. Ila Mitra made before the court at Rajshahi with regard to inhuman treatment meted out to a lady only because she holds a political opinion other than that of Liakat-Nurul Amin feudal class:

Sm. Ila Mitra in her statement pleading 'not guilty' to the charges said, 'I know nothing about the case. On 7.1.50 last I was arrested in Rahanpur and taken to Nachol the next day. The police guards assaulted me on the way and thereafter I was taken inside a cell. The S.I. threatened to make me naked if I did not confess everything about the murder. As I had nothing to say, all my garments were taken away and I was imprisoned inside the cell in stark naked condition.

'No food was given to me, not even a drop of water. The same day in the evening the sepoys began to beat me on the head with butt-ends of their guns, in the presence of the S.I. was profusely bleeding through the nose. Afterwards my garments were returned to me, and at about 12 midnight I was taken out of the cell and led possibly to the quarters of the S.I., but I was not certain.

'In that room where I was taken they tried brutal methods to bring out confession. My legs were pressed between two sticks, and I was being administered a "Pakistani injection". When this torture was going on, they tied my mouth with a napkin. They also pulled off my hair, but as they could not force me to say anything, I was taken back to the cell carried by the sepoys, as after the torture it was not possible for me to walk.

'Inside the cell again the S.I. ordered the sepoys to bring four hot eggs, and said, now she will talk. Thereafter four or five sepoys forced me to lie down on my back, and one pushed a hot egg through my private parts. I was feeling like being burnt with fire and became unconscious.

'When I came back to my senses in the morning of 9.1.50 the S.I. and some sepoys came into my cell, and began to kick me on the belly with boots on. Thereafter a nail was pierced through my right heel. I was then lying half conscious, and heard the S.I. muttering: "We are coming again at night, and if you do not confess, one by one the sepoys will ravish you." At dead of night, the S.I. and his sepoys came back and the threat was repeated. But as I still refused to say anything three or four men got hold of me, and a sepoy actually began to rape me. Shortly afterwards I became unconscious.

'Next day on 10.1.50 when I became conscious, again I found that I was profusely bleeding and my cloth was drenched in blood. I was in that state taken to Nawabganj from Nachol. The sepoys in Nawabganj jail gate received me with smart blows.

'I was at that time in a prostate condition and the Court Inspector and some sepoys carried me to a cell. I had high fever then and I was still bleeding. A doctor possibly from the Govt. Hospital at Nawabganj had noted the temperature of my body to be 105°. When he heard from me of the profuse bleeding I had he assured me, I would be treated with the help of a woman nurse. I was also given some medicines and two pieces of rugs.

'On 11.1.50 the woman nurse of the Govt. Hospital examined me. I do not know what report she gave about my condition. After she came the bloodstained piece of cloth I was wearing was changed for a clean one. During all this time, I was in a cell of the Nawabganj P.S. under the treatment of a doctor. I had high fever and profuse bleeding, and was unconscious from time to time.

'On 16.1.50, a stretcher was brought before my cell in the evening and I was told that I would have to go elsewhere for examination. On my protest that I was too ill to move about, I was, struck with a stick and forced to get on the stretcher after which I was carried on it to another house. I told nothing there, but the sepoys forced me to sign a blank paper. I was at time in a semi-conscious state with high fever. As my condition was going worse [sic], I was next day transferred to the Nawabganj Govt. Hospital and on 21.1.50 when the state of my health was still very precarious. I was brought from Nawabganj to Rajshahi Central Jail, and was admitted to the Jail Hospital.

'I had not under any circumstances said anything to the police, and I have nothing more to say than I have stated above.'

4

Re(Creating) the Home: Women's Role in the Development of Refugee Colonies in South Calcutta

Rachel Weber

INTRODUCTION

AS A THIRD-GENERATION refugee, I am familiar with the household symbols of displacement. In my grandmother's apartment, one finds packed suitcases standing in closets, food hoarded in boxes and remnants of a homeland destroyed (yellowing photos, religious paraphernalia, and so on) lining the walls. Although evidence of uprootedness is visible in the house of refugees, the psychic legacy inherited by later generations is more difficult to detect. Nonetheless, I wrangle with questions of national and ethnic identity, of security and of the home. Perhaps this is what brought me to Calcutta, adopted home of millions.

My interview subjects—early refugees from East Pakistan—have pointed out the parallels between their experiences and those of the Jews who fled form the Nazis during the World War II. They mention a shared emphasis on food, family and education, as well as a history of involvement in leftist politics. In the early 1950s, a play was performed in Calcutta whose subject was the East Pakistani refugee. The play was entitled *Natun Yehudi* (Das Gupta 1986).

But there also exist many differences between the two groups. The one which intrigues me the most as a student of urban planning is the spatial organization and physical settlement patterns of the refugees. In America, immigrants flocked to the city centre and carved out living spaces in the tenements, multi-storied rectangular blocks, full to capacity. In contrast, the refugee settlements of Calcutta sprouted up on what was marshy wasteland on the periphery of the city. The houses were built on small plots where the settlers were at liberty to create individualized structures adapted to their specific needs. They built colonies instead of settling in neighbourhoods. The very word 'colony' (enclosed and exclusive) implies that the East Pakistani refugees had a different conception and use of urban space than the European Jews in America.

The houses and colonies, which the refugees built, reflect not only the needs of a middle class population desperate for property and some semblance of a security, but also reflect a reorganization of space. The newly built environment also reflected and affected women's relations to private and public spaces. Due to spatial considerations and economic restructuring, the home took on a critical importance and various barriers which previously enforced a strict distinction between public and private spaces began to dissolve. I will examine the circumstances which led to the development of the colonies in south Calcutta and the ways in which women participated and were affected by the transformation of space.

METHODOLOGY

I have relied primarily upon interviews with refugees residing in south Calcutta. I conducted the interviews in English and Bengali, with and without the assistance of an interpreter. Some of the interviews were very casual while others were conducted in a more formal manner where I relied upon a questionnaire which I had developed and translated into Bengali. In total, I conducted 30 interviews over a period of five months. The interviews were not only physically taxing but theoretically problematic. The researcher has a dual role in that she interprets material and is also critically involved in the creation of the material itself, that is, the transcript. Particular questions prompt particular responses, and perhaps if the question had been phrased differently, it would have provoked a different response. So many variables affect the construction of the narrative—the way I present myself, the temperature outside, my status as a woman and as a foreigner. My memory also plays a large role in the reconstruction of the script. I did not use a tape recorder nor did I take extensive notes while the 'subjects' were speaking. I felt that this would only contribute to the official nature of the interview and would deter people from speaking freely.

In addition to these theoretical problems, I also faced difficulties in interviewing women. Oftentimes husbands and sons would speak for the women in their families or would dismiss the women's achievements, choosing to focus on their own lives and careers instead. One man stated straightforwardly: 'Why do you wish to speak with the women in this colony? They are all illiterate, dead or disabled.'

Colony residents were also suspicious of me as an outsider and a foreigner. As an American, I was particularly suspect because most of the residents had ties to the ruling Communist Party. In addition, the land upon which the colony of Bijoygarh is built was originally the site of the United States Army Barracks. One man asked if I had been sent by the army to investigate the occupation of the land. Many of the residents do not possess titles for their plots of land and feel they could be evicted at any moment. As such, they did not wish to disclose information about their houses or about the development of the colony to a perfect stranger.

I also interviewed many men and women who were involved in governmental and non-governmental agencies to assist the refugees, specifically refugee women. Although the majority of refugees with whom I spoke stressed the fact that they relied only upon themselves, by the late 1940s there was in place an organized system of rehabilitation to aid those from East Pakistan. Organizations such as the All-India Women's Conference (AIWC) provided job-training programmes for women, housing projects for families, and schools for the refugee children.

I relied upon various documentary sources: memoranda written to and from government agencies and refugee organizations such as the Dakshin Kalikata Sahartali Udbastu Sammelan; pamphlets and handouts from rallies; lease agreements and newspaper articles. I examined census reports and survey maps of the colonies available from the local colony committees. Surprisingly, there has been very little academic writing, in either Bengali or English, on the subject of East Pakistani refugees. Although their presence pervades Calcutta's economic, cultural and political life, the subject is not yet popular with academics, many of whose families originally hail from East Pakistan. Aside from Prafulla Chakraborty's study (1990) of refugee involvement in Left politics, entitled *The Marginal Men*, and Nilanjana Chatterjee's (1990) piece in the anthology, *Calcutta: The Living City*, I find the most compelling accounts of refugee life and their use of space to be those recorded in films, especially those by Ritwick Ghatak.

I have based much of my theoretical orientation on the works of academics and planners who are developing the field of feminist geography (Ardener 1981; Hayden 1984; Mackenzie 1986; Women and Geography Study Group 1984; Wright 1984). They propose a study of the social and economic factors which transform women's use of space as well as a study of women's perceptions and responses to changes in their socio-physical environment. Researchers in this field have focused on such diverse subjects as economic restructuring (i.e., how industrialization brings about a separation of home and workplace), housing policies (i.e., how zoning laws serve to reproduce the nuclear family), and ideological constructs (i.e., how 'model homes' or 'safe communities' are defined). They take off from where the urban critic David Harvey left off in his pioneering work, *Social Justice and the City*, exploring the ways in which spatial form and social process interact to produce maps of territoriality and identification.

SPACE AND GENDER IN BENGALI CULTURE

The relationship between spatial form and social process becomes evident when we discuss the difference between the concepts of 'house' and of 'home'. Whereas 'house' is the physical structure of residence, 'home' represents particular social relations both inside and outside the physical structure, relations which link residents to other families, to communities and to the state. The concept of home conjures up images of family, warmth, security, emotion and stability. In Bengali, there are many different conceptions of house and home reflected in the language. For example, *bastu* means one's father's or husband's father's ancestral home, normally located in a rural area and inhabited by *bastushap*, snakes which guard the family property, and status. On the other hand, *basha* implies a more temporary, rented house, normally located in an urban area. *Bari* is somewhere in between, a permanent and personally owned house which is not the ancestral home. Bengalis are by tradition deeply attached to their homes. One interview subject pointed out that the rivers of Bengal (so frequently conjured up as symbols of the lush, bountiful homeland) played an important role in separating communities and making any sort of travel incredibly difficult. Especially during the monsoon floods, people were forced to remain at home and as such developed a very strong spiritual and emotional affinity with their bastu.

What is the relationship between house and home? This is where women make their entrance as it is most commonly women who are responsible for forging a relationship between the physical and social aspects of the built environment. They are responsible for making a house into a home and imbuing it with love, warmth and the smells of home cooking. Women's domain, sphere and place have traditionally been inside the home and they have, across epochs and cultures, been associated with a private world juxtaposed with a public world of men. Both spaces carry with them certain social and economic connotations: the enshrinement of the ethic of care, morality and selflessness which supposedly exists in the domestic realm compared to the world of men where self-interest and profit reign supreme. The private/public, inside/outside, nature/culture dichotomies and the pervasive influence of these dualisms is the subject of many early feminist tracts (Lamphere 1974; Rosaldo 1974). However, as feminist academics begin to examine the subject nature of women, they are questioning the usefulness of such restrictive dichotomies used so frequently to determine women's 'place' in relation to men's. These dichotomies are neither fixed nor watertight. The positioning of a male public world and a female private world as opposites is not reflective of the permeability and interdependency which exists between the home and the world. They do not reflect the particularities of culture or of historical moment.[1]

During times of political and social upheaval, for example, the division between public and private spaces becomes radi-

cally altered: private life becomes the subject of national discourse and the home takes on a new significance as a site of political activity. The reorganization of space becomes especially
important when discussing the displacement which occurs when
people leave or are forced to flee their homelands. The act of
migration involves more than just a change in physical environment; it involves a rupturing of bonds to a place and to a place-
based identity (Buttimer and Seamon 1980). Re(Creating) the
home puts increased pressure on the domestic sphere, women's
territory, and involves an increased reliance on the strategies and
resources within the home. The boundaries between public and
private shift back and forth to accommodate this reorganization
of space. In examining the resettlement of the East Pakistani
refugees in the colonies of south Calcutta, one finds new defini-
tions of what constitutes public and private space and in the process, a redefinition of gender.

REFUGEES AND THE RIGHT TO HOUSING

In an article in the *Statesman*, Somdeb Das Gupta (1986) wrote
that 'the word "refugee" does more violence to the word "home"
than any other.' 'Refugee' is a difficult word to define and even
more difficult to identify with. Many people do not identify
themselves as refugees even though they fled from their homelands as a result of political and religious persecution. To identify with this 'caste' means to associate oneself with the
raggedness, poverty and homelessness that the word connotes.
In Bengali, the most commonly used term for 'refugee' is *udbastu*,
literally to be without a *bastu* or ancestral home. Some feel that
the word 'refugee' does not apply to those from East Pakistan
because, even though they crossed a national boundary, they
entered a region whose inhabitants shared their linguistic, religious and ethnic backgrounds. They were not considered 'aliens'
per se. This type of explanation, however, ignores the deeply felt
differences between *bangal* (East Pakistani/Bengali culture) and
ghoti (native or West Bengal culture) as it does the differences
between the dialects particular to East and West Bengal. The
refugees, for lack of a better word, constituted a very heteroge-
neous group. There were refugees who came before 1958 (at
which time the government decided that they were ineligible for

government assistance) and those who came after the Indo-Pakistan war of 1971; there were those who came from Chittagong and those who came from Barisal; there were those who were agriculturalists. I have limited myself to a group of people who came to south Calcutta between 1946 and 1951 and who would now consider themselves to be middle class. A survey published by the Indian Statistical Institute states that this group consisted primarily of non-agriculturists from the upper and middle castes and classes (quoted in Chatterjee 1990: 72). In the homes I visited, husbands held professional positions as journalists, owners of small manufacturing companies, homeopathic doctor, and bank manager. Most of these refugees had pre-Partition ties to Calcutta; sons had completed schooling or had found employment in the city. Many had relatives living there. Although the official statistics vary, it is estimated that about 35 lakh refugees came from East Pakistan between 1946 and 1950, and that after the Delhi Pact (Liaquat-Nehru Pact, signed by Pakistan and India) in 1950, 12 lakhs returned home. The 1951 Census report mentions that the enormous scale of increase in population in West Bengal by adding the influx of refugees from 1946 to 1951 amounted to fifty years normal population growth (Census of India 1951). Packed into five years, the demographic implications are staggering.

The largest concentration of refugees settled in the 24-Parganas, Nadia and Calcutta Metropolitan districts, in this order. The entire landscape of the Calcutta Corporation Area was radically altered as older, central areas swelled beyond capacity and new areas on the periphery of the city were brought under habitation. In this way the new settlers extended the physical horizon of the city beyond its original boundaries. Their social and economic impact aided in filling in the gaps between previously isolated urban settlements, forcing the city to congeal and setting in motion an outward instead of upward looking growth dynamic (Sen and Banerjee 1983).

I will not delve into the reasons why the refugees came to Calcutta. Suffice it to say that the stream of migration began around the time of Partition when communal violence and tension peaked. The Great Calcutta Killings in 1946 and the ensuing Noakhali riots set off widespread harassment, discrimination and persecution of the Hindu population. Although few of the people with whom I spoke had experienced violence first-hand, their fear of violence and a growing sense of insecurity were sufficient to precipitate a mass exodus. Fear of rape and the dishonour of women are cited as the primary motivating factor. Women were abducted, raped, sold to brothels, killed, forced to convert and marry Muslims. Writes Chakrabarti (1990) in *The Marginal Men:* 'There was a universally shared concern of Hindus for saving their womenfolk from the leering Muslims'.[2] The image of the Hindu woman bathing in the *pukur* or pond and being heckled by groups of Muslim boys is prevalent in the literature and was acknowledged frequently in the interviews. Although sexual harassment and abduction undoubtedly occurred, many feel that the figures are exaggerated and only contributed to the communal tensions and mass hysteria. What is interesting is the role of the defiled woman as a symbol for the loss of identity and homeland. *Sonar Bangla* is depicted as a woman who because of Partition was maimed and dismembered. In the interviews, I noticed an overriding concern for property and for the honour of Hindu women, and I would suggest that the two are inextricably linked in the gendered narrative of communal identity and exodus.

The refugees describe their journeys to Calcutta as tortuous. Some came on overcrowded steamers while others came through the jungle on foot. They could not carry much of their property with them, perhaps a change of clothing or a small tin trunk. One woman, in preparation for the journey, stitched taka (local currency) into the folds of her *kantha*-embroidered sari. The West Bengal government, caught unprepared for such a huge influx of people, set up a reception and transit centre at Sealdah Station. Incoming refugees were first inoculated and then were told to present themselves as a 'family grouping' to an officer from the Relief and Rehabilitation Department. The concept of a family grouping puzzled many of the newcomers as they were accustomed to living in large joint families and did not think of themselves as belonging to the smaller, nuclear units which the officer sought. Based upon the appraisal of the officers, joint families were split up into male-headed groupings and, once issued a certificate, were directed to particular types of camps: work camps for families which included an able-bodied male breadwinner and permanent liability camps for widows, children and the physically disabled. The families were given a small dole and some remained on the platforms of Sealdah for months before they went to the camps.[3]

The hastily constructed camps are described as nothing short of hellholes—filthy and overcrowded. The government initially did not view this problem as permanent, insisting that the 'displaced persons' would soon be returning to East Pakistan. This attitude was reflected in the low level of concern for the first wave of refugees. It was only in the late 1950s that the government realized that it had a responsibility to provide adequate shelter and rehabilitation schemes. As a result of the atrocious conditions in the camps, only very poor families and those deemed a 'permanent liability' were forced to remain in them. It is estimated that only a paltry fifth of the refugees were accommodated in the government camps (Chatterjee 1990: 74).

Middle class Bengalis seeking to eke out an existence independent of the government found Calcutta reeling from its worst housing shortage to date. Some were able to purchase and rent properties, and some exchanged their property in East Pakistan with evacuee Muslims. When land was acquired through legal means, the government labelled areas of refugee settlement 'private colonies'.

Others acquired property by forcibly occupying vacant lands, some owned by the government and some owned by private landlords. The process of collective takeover has been mythologized and immortalized by the term *jabardakhal* (seizure and settlement). The very act of erecting a home, even a *kuchha* hutment, was a symbolic and politically significant act for the refugees. They felt abandoned by the government and by the native West Bengalis and chose to take matters into their own hands. This is reflected in the covert and calculated pattern of jabardakhal. Informal groups of men would meet and decide upon a parcel of land, which appeared desirable. At night individual plots were marked off and shacks quickly erected, hogla leaves used to thatch the makeshift roofs. The area where the majority of refugees established hutments was completely undeveloped jungle and forestland. The 'squatters' themselves were responsible for felling the trees, clearing the land, installing tubewells and drainage systems (ibid: 73). The land was low-lying and marshy, prone to monsoonal flooding and ripe for the spread of communicable diseases. The largest concentration of pre-1950 squatter colonies was found in the southeastern portion of the Calcutta Metropolitan District, especially in the areas now known as Jadavpur, Tollygunge, Kasba, Behala and Santoshpur. Approximately 40 such colonies were established by 1950 (Chaudhuri 1980).

The houses themselves, built on small plots, were constructed out of woven split bamboo, and had mud floors and roofs of thatch, tin or tile. They consisted of a single room, which might house up to 10 people. There were few public amenities: water had to be carried by *bhistis* or water carriers as there were initially no tubewells in the area; kerosene and candles were used in the absence of electricity. As one refugee stated in an angry letter to the Refugee Rehabilitation Department, 'We who had formerly inhabited large and decent houses are now living in a busti without roads, electricity, water supply, drainage and other ordinary sanitary requirements.'4

I focused on the colony of Bijoygarh which is located in the Jadavpur area and bordered by Saktigarh, Pallisree, Sri Colony, Golf Green and Vikramnagar. It covers an area of approximately 2 square miles, and living within the colony today are approximately 15,000 inhabitants.5 The land was originally owned by the United State Army and by a private zamindar. Although the settlement of this land by first wave refugees in 1946 appears to be in line with the classic pattern of jabardakhal, there was actually much behind-the-scene negotiations with the government on the part of veteran freedom fighter Santoshkumar Dutta who had 'cut a deal' to occupy the land. There is no document to back this up but the people with whom I had spoken assured me that the then chief minister B.C. Roy had given his verbal consent to the settlement of the lands. There were secret instructions to the police not to disturb those squatters, but nonetheless there were frequent police raids and the constant presence of plainclothes policemen. The zamindar, however, had not given his tacit approval to the settlement, and there were constant confrontations with his hired hoodlums. Despite these often-bloody raids, the squatters felt that by fending off the onslaught of invaders, they had won a significant battle. In recognition of this pride, they named the colony Bijoygarh which means 'Victory Fort'.

Today the colony of Bijoygarh is divided into 11 wards, each with its own colony committee. The committees are elected by every adult member of the community, and they are responsible for overseeing land disputes and for mobilizing refugees around political issues. Within Bijoygarh, there is one college, one hospital and maternity home, four schools, one large park and a very active bazaar, all built by the refugees themselves.

Although the government to this day considers Bijoygarh and colonies surrounding it to be unplanned, haphazard in design and layout, there is evidence to suggest that a well-informed leadership was able to implement a rudimentary subdivision pattern, arranging for the allocation of plots and for land use. These colonies were preferable to 'designed' living in government camps, in the overflowing city centre, or, when the government finally took a more active role in settling the refugees, in public housing. On their own plots of land the refugees could transform their environment and their houses according to their own specifications and needs. Their needs were those of an uprooted people who did not feel assured of the permanency of their homes. Perhaps, many thought, they would be forced to move again. Partition had dissolved the bastu; perhaps the newly erected bari could also be snatched away without a moment's notice. As a result of their hesitancy to put down roots, the refugees added rooms to their hutments rather slowly, as their families and income grew.

As such, this system of plot allotment allowed for frequent upgrading and change, and reflects the refugees' desire for flexibility and control over their own lives. The houses themselves are very individualized structures and most bear no resemblance to those adjacent. Some families attempted to replicate the original bastu, building bungalow-style, single-storied houses, leaving space for gardens. They emphasize the 'village-like' ambience of the colony. One resident said, 'It is so green and peaceful here. It is possible to forget Calcutta and remember East Bengal'. Others built more modern structures, multi-storied buildings with elaborate verandah railings and pastel paint jobs. Today, more than 40 years after settling the colony, most of the houses—*pucca* and kuchha—look as if they are still in the process of construction. Building materials are visible in most of the plots as are large piles of gravel and sand.

WOMEN'S ROLE IN THE NEW COMMUNITIES

The creation of refugee colonies and the transition from the sprawling bastu with its ancestral snakes to a one-roomed bari involved a reorganization of space as well as an alteration of the emotional affiliations with the home. With this reorganization of space came a refiguring of gender and of women's relationship to public and private spaces. As Joan Scott writes, 'Massive political upheavals that throw old orders into chaos and bring new ones into being may ultimately revise the terms and the organization of gender in search of new forms of legitimation' (Scott 1985: 49). As nations and communities reconstruct themselves, there is bound to be a change in the way women are perceived, signified and deployed to serve new purposes and agendas. During this period, the new agenda was the reconstruction of the home and of the homeland. As I will demonstrate, women's role inside and outside the home changed to accommodate these new responsibilities.

In East Pakistan, houses were located in more rural, less densely populated areas. They were designed for huge joint families, sometimes housing up to 80 people. Critical in the design of the house was the *andarmahal* or separate women's quarters with its focus on the kitchen space (sometimes there were separate kitchens for vegetarian and non-vegetarian food) and on an inner courtyard. Occasionally, the andarmahal would be an entirely separate building with its own pond for bathing and washing kitchen utensils. The women's world was designed to be physically separate from the *kacharighar* or office and from the *bahir* (outside, men's living space) in general. Although the rigidity of the division between andar and bahir depended upon the individual family's desires, the women with whom I spoke rarely crossed this invisible but palpable line. Although they used the bathroom and bathed outside, they were scolded by older female relatives if they looked out to the men's quarters. Few had been outside their basti compound except for visits to relatives.

After they moved to Calcutta, they found that their space had shrunk and that their families had neither the property nor the finances to build a separate andarmahal. Most could not afford to build more than one room during the first decade of occupation. In this sense, one of the physical barriers between public and private disappeared after the move to West Bengal. Women shared their space with men, sleeping in the same room as their in-laws and brothers-in-law. They complained to me about the lack of privacy and of the permeability of the flimsy, split bamboo walls. Many became seriously ill as wind, rain and cold seeped through the exterior of their hutments. However, their exposure to the world of men brought them into contact with new ideas, with the business and political issues the men discussed. It brought about a politicization and a growing awareness of the communal problems faced by the refugees living in the colonies.

Not only was the house different in the refugee colony, but also the entire community was organized in a different manner. When the refugees describe their bastus, they speak of self-supporting, enclosed communities of family members and servants, cut off from those unrelated either economically or familially. They describe sprawling compounds with ponds, fields and large open spaces.

In contrast, Bijoygarh and most of the colonies in south Calcutta are very communal, interdependent organisms due partly to the lack of space and partly to the layout of their streets, the colonies created themselves around a series of maze-like gullies and footpaths linking houses to other houses and to the main streets. There is a multi-layered effect to the spatial organization of the settlement: certain plots have direct access to a street, but these plots are surrounded by other plots and still more plots. Therefore, one often is forced to cross though someone else's property in order to reach one's destination. The streets are not yet wide enough to accommodate automobile traffic, so most residents walk, bicycle or hire cycles or auto-rickshaws. The bazaar and the temple complex are centres of activity and are a short walk from even the farthest of the settlement.

How does this shift from an enclosed community to bazaar-centred, densely populated colony affect women? There is more interaction with the community, with both neighbours and outsiders, and there is the awareness which comes about through meeting other members of a community who are experiencing similar difficulties (Moser 1987). For instance, when the refugees first settled in Bijoygarh, there were very few tubewells. Although the women relied upon bhistis, they also had to bring water from the pump themselves. There they would meet other women like themselves and would discuss the latest rice or kerosene shortage, exchanging helpful hints and sharing their own stories. Today, most of the women employ the services of *kajer lok* or servants, but when they first settled in the colonies, they could not afford any domestic help. They experienced the inadequate provision of municipal services first hand. Although the loss of the andarmahal meant the loss of a system, which often provided women with support, friendship and intimacy, new bonds with women in the community were created instead.

Public spaces, previously off-limits to women, such as the bazaar, were now safe places for women. One woman noted, 'I had never been to the market before, but because my husband worked very awkward hours, I went to the Bijoygarh Bazaar. 'In fact, all the residents point out how safe the colonies are for women. Said one resident, 'They [women] can go outside in their nighties or wearing a white sari with a red petticoat or with loose, wet hair. You can't do that in north Calcutta.'

It was this growing awareness of the community as a community—as a colony with boundaries, under siege by the landlords and ignored by the government as well as the calculated tactics of political groups and refugee organizations—which led women to participate in the anti-eviction campaigns of the 1950s. Their participation was encouraged from the very beginning, from the time the Communist Party of India began to take an interest in the refugees. Initially the communists and the refugees were very suspicious of each other. The communists believed that the refugees were too communal and anti-Muslim and could be used as potential strikebreakers. The refugees had faith, initially, that the Congress would eventually pull through and offer them the assistance they needed. In an effort to bring the two groups together, communist Bijoy Majumdar masqueraded as a Congress supporter and went from camp to camp mustering support for a central refugee committee, eventually to be called the Dakshin Kalikata Bastuhara Sangram Parishad (The South Calcutta Refugee Council of Action). He felt that women should be the first to be mobilized, for unlike the menfolk, refugee women were more susceptible and more willing to talk against the establishment with persons who soothed them with womanly sympathy and brought them succour. The women had to face the tantrums of children who are hungry. They had to go about food gathering and borrowing money when their menfolk came home empty-handed. They were without food, proper shelter and a decent thing to cover their nakedness. They were willing to talk and listen (Chakrabarti 1990: 49).

Bijoy Majumdar convinced members of the Mahila Atma Raksha Samiti, a communist-led women's group, to make connections with the refugee women and to attempt to temper their virulent anti-communist sentiments. From 1949 onwards, the streets of Calcutta became sites for refugee-led rallies, processions and often-violent demonstrations. The burning of tram cars became an important refugee motif as police brutality and the government's inactivity spurred them on. Between January and May of 1949, the refugees began an organized seizure of land in south Calcutta which they called a 'land-grabbing movement'. Some refugee organizations carried out a propaganda campaign to provoke more recent arrivals to commit jabardakhal. These attempts were not always successful. For example, when refugees from the Durgapur camp occupied a plot of government land behind the Mint in New Alipore, the police launched a four-day assault. Newspaper accounts describe groups of women fending off the lathi charges of the police. 'The struggles of these women', writes Chakrabarti, 'gave a new impetus to the founding of colonies with greater determination and planning' (ibid: 65).

In the early 1950s, a second wave of more impoverished refugees began to pour over the border. Every day more

thatched huts sprang up in south Calcutta. The government issued notifications that the squatters must vacate lands within
15 days or face forcible eviction, but the refugees did not
budge. They were assured by the refugee organizations and
colony committees that the government did not have the power
to dismantle the 149 colonies, almost 1,50,000 people squatting
on acres of city property (ibid: 80).

Although the government did not have the power to evict
all of the refugees, the landlords in collusion with hired
goondas made many attempts. They raided the colonies frequently and razed the refugees' huts. These raids were most
frequent in the Jadavpur area where the value of land was the
highest. Women played a critical role in fending off the invaders and in defending their newly erected houses. They describe
sleeping with knives under their pillows and mattresses and
charging out of their houses armed with their bontis—knives
with a curved blade that are fixed to a piece of wood—brooms
and other household utensils. They gave shelter and food to
those fleeing from the attackers. They spread the word across
the colony when they were tipped off about a raid. A model resistance strategy was developed, based on an ancient pattern,
whereby women stood at the front of a phalanx of refugees
holding their household weapons. They met the police or the
landlord's men head-on as the refugees felt that the attackers
would be flustered by the sight of armed women. In reality, the
women were not spared because of their gender. They were frequently injured and many were killed, like the pregnant woman
hit by a police bullet in Dhakuria.

In response to the passage of the West Bengal Act XVI of
1951 (otherwise known as the Eviction Bill) which gave landlords the right to claim full compensation for lands squatted
upon by refugees, the pace and fervour of the demonstrations
increased. The newspapers describe 'all-ladies' marches and rallies and remarked that women were now a regular feature during the Tram Fare Enhancement Movement (1953) and the Food
Movement (1959).[6] Says Chakrabarti, 'The entire eviction campaign brought women out onto the street' (p 95).

Another force which brought women 'out of their homes'
was sheer economic necessity. Droves of women joined the
wage labour force in the 1950s, women who had never worked

outside the home before, and who, in East Pakistan, had never really intended to.[7] They had lived in areas lacking the service-oriented yet professional economy which a large city like Calcutta could support. Without the cumulative earnings of a large joint family and the earnings from property to maintain them, women found jobs which were suitable. They became teachers, office workers, tutors, tailors and small shop managers. Like Khuki in Ritwik Ghatak's *Meghe Dhaka Tara*, the working woman with broken chappals (symbolizing the sacrifices women made for the family's survival) became a presence on the crowded streets of central Calcutta and on various types of public transportation. Symbolic shelter was given by the state to women who chose to enter a public world: ladies' sections on public buses and trams. During this period, women also entered various educational institutions in Calcutta and today Jadavpur, home to many of the refugee colonies, has one of the highest female literacy rates in the city.[8]

HAVE WOMEN REALLY 'COME OUT'?

It could be argued that when women crossed the border between East Pakistan and West Bengal, they also, in essence, crossed the border from a highly segregated world to a public and more visible sphere. It could be argued that they took on new roles—of provider, of activist—as their homes, houses and colonies took on increasing political significance. Their 'coming out' has been hailed as a liberating experience, as having increased women's status. One man said of the women in the colony, 'Tradition, culture and customs were all left behind. In the new environment women worked outside and spoke to unknown men.' Another activist stated, 'Values changed. Women were once illiterate and backward. They spent all of their time cooking and gossiping. In Calcutta they went out on the streets.'

I feel, however, that the type of analysis, which separates spaces so rigidly and then speaks of a 'coming out' does not reflect the complex relations between women, power and space. Women do not simply cross these borders when they cross the thresholds of their houses. It is not as simple as the scene in Satyajit Ray's interpretation of Tagore's *Ghare Baire* (The home and the world) when Bimala walks through the splendidly-lit corridor into the public world of men and nationalist politics. Refugee women did not really move into public life, but rather the domestic realm expanded to include their participation in political, community and economic affairs.

First, in the interviews I found that the men were extremely proud of their wives and working daughters and readily accepted that women had been liberated by their experiences. The older women, however, were embarrassed. It was embarrassing for these daughters of doctors and lawyers to search for employment and to do domestic work without the help of servants. They did not appreciate their public exposure nor did they feel entitled to it. Instead, they saw their work and political involvement outside the home as a necessity, a sacrifice required of them. They also felt that their new responsibilities—to defend their homes, to participate in demonstrations, to work for wages—in addition to their regular household chores were quite burdensome. Many returned to the world of the home as soon as their families were comfortably situated, financially and physically. Many of the second-generation daughters do not work outside the home because, as one to them stated, 'We don't need to now'.

Second, I believe that the private world expanded to include these new roles because women's entrance into the public sphere is and was legitimated on the basis of women's domestic roles as wives, mothers and daughters. In other words, because a woman's home is her domain, it is only natural that she fight for its right to exist. Women's mobilization is perceived as an extension of their natural realm of interest and power within the domestic arena (Moser 1987: 86). The same qualities associated with domesticity—selflessness, care, morality, familial obligation—are evoked when the women speak of their participation in refugee struggles. Symbols of domesticity, of motherhood and of the dutiful daughter are prevalent in the literature and in oral history: from the use of cooking utensils as weapons to the description of the United Congress of Refugee Committees (UCRC) as the 'central mothering body'. There is nothing in and of itself offensive or problematic about the use of these 'private' symbols. In fact one can look at these women as appropriating the symbols used so frequently to oppress them, using typologies with which they have been identified in order to expand their space and secure a footing in public life. However, when women's economic and political activity is associated with women's natural domestic responsibilities, it is often, like the domestic realm in general, undervalued. Perhaps this is why it has been so difficult for me to obtain information on this when I asked about women's role during this turbulent period, I was told stories of women's abduction by Muslims in East Pakistan or that women did not do anything of importance. It is difficult to accept this position when women were such a new and vital presence on the streets of Calcutta, walking to work, marching in processions, and so on. Indeed, refugee women paved the way for future generations of Bengali working women and activists.

Refugee women found that in the colonies of south Calcutta the border between 'outside' and 'inside', 'public' and 'private' was not as clearly delineated as it once had been. In recreating their homes and their worlds, they had to take new factors into account—the demands of a displaced nation, financial necessity and the responsibilities of living within communities in the process of formation. However, equating liberation and status enhancement with 'coming out' does not take into account the way their participation was legitimized within the eyes of the community and the way refugee women from this period perceived their own actions.

NOTES

Research for this paper was completed while I was a visiting Fulbright Scholar in Calcutta during the 1991 college year. I wish to thank Uma Das Gupta, Jasodhara Bagchi, Meenakshi Chaudhuri and Sarbani Goswami for their assistance.

1. See Banerji (1991), Karlekar (1991) and Nair (1990) who have studied the complexities of the private/public dichotomy in the context of nineteenth-century Calcutta. Conversations with Sudipta Sen, Indrani Chatterjee and Samita Sen were also very instructive.

2. In addition to Chakrabarti (1990), see Sinha (1991) who reports, 'This fear [of women's dishonour] conforms to the general trend among Bengali Hindu refugees whose first concern was to find safe shelter for their daughters and nieces'.
3. Personal conversation with Nalini Mitra.
4. Letter from the Dakshin Kalikata Sahartali Udbastu Sammelan to the Chief Minister, Government of West Bengal, 9 March 1969.
5. I am grateful to Amal Ghosh Roy for these calculations.
6. In the 1950s and 1960s, West Bengal witnessed rapid political polarization and popular protest. These two movements were among the more important ones involving students from all political parties, industrial workers and women. Participants criticized the Congress government for the rise in prices, whether of essential food grains, or of tram fares.
7. See Tables B-I and B-II (Workers and Non-Workers Classified by Sex and Broad Age Group), in Census of India, 1961: 64.
8. Conversations with Jasodhara Bagchi and other members of the Girl Child Project, School of Women's Studies, Jadavpur University.

REFERENCES

Ardener, Shirley. 1981. Women and Space. London: Croom Helm.
Banerji, Himani. 1991. Fashioning a Self, Economic and Political Weekly, 26, 43: WS 50–62.
Buttimer, Anne and David Seamon. 1980. The Human Experience of Space and Place. London: Croom Helm.
Chatterjee, Nilanjana 1990. The East Bengal Refugees—A Lesson in Survival. In Calcutta the Living City, edited by Sukanta Chaudhui, vol 2, pp. 70–77 Calcutta: Oxford University Press.
Census of India, 1951. West Bengal, vol 2, 1961 (Working Paper No. 55), Bengal.
Chakrabarti, Prafulla. 1990. The Marginal Men. Kalyani: Lumiere Books.
Chaudhuri, Pranati. 1980. Refugees in West Bengal. A study of the Growth and Distribution of Refugee Settlements within the Calcutta Metropolitan District. Working Paper No. 55. Calcutta: Centre for Studies in the Social Sciences.
Das Gupta, Somdeb 1986. Once a Refugee, The Statesman, 2 March.
Harvey, David. 1973. Social Justice and the City. Baltimore: Johns Hopkins University Press.

Hayden Dolores. 1984. *Redesigning the American Dream*. New York: Norton.

Karlekar, Malavika. 1991. *Voice from Within: Early Personal Narratives of Bengali Women*. New Delhi: Oxford University Press

Lamphere, Louise. 1974. Strategies, Cooperation and Conflict Among Women in Domestic Groups. In *Women, Culture and Society*, edited by Michelle Zimbalist Rosaldo and Louise Lamphere, pp.97-112. Palo Alto: Stanford University Press.

Mackenzie, Suzanne. 1986. Women's Response to Economic Restructuring. In *The Politics of Diversity: Feminism, Marxism and Nationalism*, edited by Michele Barrett and Roberta Hamilton, pp. 97-132. London: Verso.

Moser, Caroline. 1987. A Conceptual Framework for Analysis and Policy-making. In *Women, Human Settlements and Housing*, edited by Caroline Moser and Linda Peake, pp. 2-22. London: Tavistock.

Nair, Janaki. 1990. Uncovering the Zenana, *Journal of Women's History*, 12, 1: 345-67.

Rosaldo, Michelle Zimbalist. 1974. A Theoretical Overview. In *Women, Culture and Society*, edited by Michelle Zimbalist Rosaldo and Louise Lamphere, pp. 17-42. Palo Alto: Stanford University Press.

Scott, Joan Wallach. 1985. *Gender and the Politics of History*. New York: Columbia University Press.

Sen, Asok, and Alok Banerjee. 1983. The Calcutta Metropolitan District in the Urban Context of West Bengal (1951-1981). Calcutta: Centre for Studies in the Social Sciences (Occasional Paper No. 60).

Sinha, Dipankar. 1991. Change and Continuity in a Bengali Refugee Settlement (1950-1951): A survey of Three Generations. In *Bengal, Yesterday and Today*, edited by Nisith Ranjan Ray and Ranjit Ray, pp. 98-118 Calcutta: Papyrus.

Women and Geography Study Group. 1984. *Gender and Geography*. London: Hutchinson.

Wright, Gwendolyn. 1984. *Building the Dream*. New York: Pantheon.

5

And Still They Come

Renuka Roy

PARTITION AND REFUGEES are intertwined in our minds. Hindus in their millions fled from West Punjab to India and an equivalent number of Muslims left East Punjab and north India for Pakistan: 4.7 millions each way. The tremendous sufferings, the loss of life, and the brutalities to which they were exposed defy description. An interchange of population took place in a matter of a few weeks: a two-way migration, on either side, of a magnitude hitherto unknown in history, took place. The upheaval was formidable and grim. So final and inevitable it was that it had to receive the urgent attention of the Central government. The displaced persons presented an immediate problem. Their rehabilitation could not be delayed. Immediate policies had to be formulated and implemented. But what was happening in the partitioned Bengal which had once been the scene of the Great Calcutta Killings as a result of the Direct Action Day?

The miracle of Beliaghata had spread farther, and we saw the spectacle of friendship and fraternity between Hindus and Muslims. Thus, there was no immediate interchange of population, nor even panic. We find that it was not until some months after Gandhiji's death that migration started as a trickle but grew to a rivulet and eventually swelled like a river in spate. Thus, in the truncated province of West Bengal there was at first a deceptive calm. It was not till December 1949 that it became obvious that an influx of refugees from East Pakistan had started. They came through a great ordeal. Some were mur-

dered on the way. Women were raped and many were muti-
lated or wounded. Terror-stricken, they arrived half-dead,
weary, and footsore, and as a result of their experience needed
psychological treatment. Their arrival in West Bengal and
Assam had its repercussions. Many Muslims started leaving for
East Pakistan. But with Jawaharlal Nehru as Prime Minister
and Dr. Bidhan Chandra Roy as chief minister in West Bengal,
the secular character of the state was maintained and due protection was given to the minority. On the Indian side of the border, the situation was quickly brought under control. As a
result, the number of Muslims who ultimately left West Bengal
was negligible, about half a million in all; many of them returned after the Liaquat-Nehru Pact, which assured restoration
of security and property, and thus there was no interchange of
population. The exodus was a one-way affair. The Hindus from
East Pakistan continued to seek refuge in West Bengal and
Assam in ever increasing number because the Pakistani government could not reassure them. The figures of the exodus from
both sides bear testimony to the difference of approach in the
two countries. By the end of 1956, 3.33 million refugees had
come into West Bengal, Assam, and Tripura.

During the first few years following the creation of Pakistan there was considerable reluctance on the part of the Central government to acknowledge that the displaced persons
from East Pakistan were here to stay. This was partly because
they had not come spectacularly in one avalanche, as had happened in the Punjab; and also because the early conditions in
East Pakistan, though not conducive to security, had not given
rise to wholesale murder and rapine as had again been the experience in the Punjab.

The situation, however, continued to deteriorate but the
Central government seemed unable to recognize this. After I
visited the Sealdah Station in December 1948 and found the station overcrowded with these terrified refugees, I rushed to
Delhi. As a session of the Provisional Parliament (Constituent
Assembly) was on, I submitted a short notice question on the
exodus. Mohanlal Saxena was the Minister for Rehabilitation at
the Centre. The ministry had so far concentrated exclusively on
the West Punjab refugees. He stated in reply that he had no
such information. When I persisted that I had seen the dis-

placed persons coming over from East Pakistan in their hundreds daily, and that they were congested at Sealdah, the prime minister intervened and said that the intelligence service gave a different picture. Pandit H.N. Kunzru then said that as an Hon'ble Lady Member had stated that she spoke from her own experience it was up to the government to make further enquiries. The Central government could no longer deny that a large-scale migration was taking place from East Pakistan. The unwillingness to accept the facts and the reluctance of the Central government to rehabilitate the refugees in the east is one of the major reasons why even today the refugee problem in eastern India has not been solved.

The Indian government sought in the past to contain the problem of the refugees by coming to an agreement with the Liaquat-Nehru Pact, in 1950. The main provisions of the Pakistan Pact were based on the assumption that the influx from East Pakistan, unlike that from West Pakistan, was a temporary affair. The governments of both countries would encourage the return of their citizens and see that their homes and belongings were given back to them and conditions created for them to live without fear. While the Pact was honoured in secular India and temporary aberrations were ruthlessly quelled, it was a dead letter in Pakistan from the outset. The attempts of those Hindus who had left large properties in East Pakistan and wanted to go back were foiled because the East Pakistani authorities did not help them to get back their land and the new occupants threatened their lives. Hence, they could not resettle in East Pakistan and had to return to India. Instead of improving the conditions for the refugees, the Liaquat-Nehru Pact became the source of all problems which beset the East Bengal refugees in India. Treated here as a temporary phenomenon, their rehabilitation was put off to a much later date. When it was undertaken it was in a niggardly fashion and the Indian government never came to grips with some of the major issues.

The West Bengal government for its part did not like the Pact, though it did not publicly disapprove of it, as the prestige of the Prime Minister was involved. However, when the Pact came before the Provisional Parliament for confirmation many members not only from West Bengal but also from other places criticized it. Dr. Syama Prasad Mukherjee, who was the Minister for Industries, vigorously opposed the Pact in one of his most famous speeches. Mr. K.C. Neogy, Minister for Commerce, also argued against it. They both resigned from the cabinet on this issue. Among the MPs from West Bengal there was considerable resentment and many thought of resigning too, but eventually it was decided it would be wiser to continue, as they thought they could do better from inside. Suresh Chandra Mazumdar, formerly editor of the *Ananda Bazaar Patrika*, and a few members, including me, took resort to the 'conscience clause' allowed in the Constituent Assembly days. The 'conscience clause' permitted a Congress member to refrain from voting with the government, with the Prime Minister's consent, on any issue on which he or she felt very strongly. To the credit of Jawaharlal Nehru, who was undoubtedly one of the greatest democrats of all times, it must be said that this right of remaining neutral and abstaining from voting on matters on which a party member had qualms of conscience was allowed.

But Pandit Nehru had failed to understand the reasons for the opposition to the Pact from West Bengal. He did not give credence to the belief of some members that the Pact would not be honoured by Pakistan. Panditji had made the false assumption that the opponents to the Pact were all communalists and thus the people of West Bengal were passionately attached to communal ideas. The leadership of Dr. Syama Prasad Mukherjee and the fact that he was a founder of the Bharatiya Jana Sangh confirmed his suspicions. Later events show how wrong he was because West Bengal was one of the few areas where neither the Hindu Mahasabha nor the Jana Sangh held sway. He admitted this later. In fact, he realized that the heartland of the communal parties was the Hindi-speaking region.

The only effect of the Pact was to deepen the reluctance of the Central government to recognize the influx as a permanent one. In 1950, after the Pact was signed, another large exodus of the East Pakistani Hindus began, and it continued with intensity until the end of 1951. This was followed by a lull, and then again from the end of 1952 to 1954 there was a continuous influx of refugees in their thousands. In 1956, and even in the 1960s, there were additional influxes. Even during the temporary periods of lull, the monthly migrant influx was about 30,000. This was the official figure of those who came over and were given migration certificates. As mentioned in *The Great Challenge*, a report issued by the West Bengal government in 1956, the influx was 'like the tides that rise and fall with the changing phases of the moon, the relation between the march of events in another land and the flow of migration from East Pakistan is more than mere coincidence'. The total number of refugees in the eastern region was estimated in 1956 at the colossal figure of 4.1 million while the total number of those who came into the western region was 4.7 million. Since then the numbers have gone up much higher. At times, the subsequent influx was recognized by the Union government and at other times ignored. Thus, to make an accurate assessment of the problem even from those with migration certificates, leaving aside the many others without them, has been well-nigh impossible. The report pinpoints the continuous nature of the influx as the crux of the problem.

Their number could not be assessed with any degree of accuracy and thus a precise and careful planning became almost impossible. In the eastern region all those who came were adding to the existing population and the resultant density of population in West Bengal was the second highest in the country. There was also no vacant land or property where the newcomers could settle themselves. The Muslims leaving West Bengal were much fewer than those coming from East Pakistan, and many who had fled later returned and got their lands back. Ultimately the Central government realized that the problem was not merely one of keeping refugees in camps for a temporary period but that their rehabilitation was an urgent necessity. It eventually set up a branch secretariat of the Ministry of Rehabilitation in Calcutta to help the West Bengal government.

Let us get back to the period when the Provisional Parliament was functioning. As the Union Minister for Rehabilitation, Mohanlal Saxena, had already appointed a Regional Adviser from amongst the MPs for the Western Zone, he had decided to appoint one for the Eastern Zone also, and I was selected. It was at this time that I came into close contact in my day-to-day work with Dr. Bidhan Chandra Roy, the chief minister of West Bengal. Before the influx started on a large scale, the portfolio of rehabilitation in West Bengal was held by Nikunja Behari Maity but Dr. Bidhan Chandra Roy himself took it over in 1950. To provide shelter and food to thousands upon thousands of refugees was indeed a tremendous job. No one was left exposed to die and all were provided with food. Epidemics did not break out among them because of the satisfactory sanitary and medical arrangements. A large number of refugee has contracted TB, but with Dr. B. C. Roy on the saddle excellent arrangements were made for their treatment.

The new arrivals were brought by train from Bongaon and Pertrapole border posts to Sealdah Station. They also entered south and north Bengal from the neighbouring districts. They were supplied with migration certificates at the border posts or at Sealdah Station. As large numbers came on foot, crossing the many miles of the border at various points where there were no checkposts, many could not get migration certificates. Giving such refugees official recognition posed a complex problem. I remember waiting at Sealdah Station at all hours, sometimes past midnight, when the trains came in. In retrospect, we have to acknowledge that the initial problem of meeting the refugees and channeling them into relief was undertaken with remarkable success. Invariably I found that Major P. C. Banerjee, Director of Refugee Relief, and other officers of the department were present to receive the newcomers. I can testify to the disciplined and excellent manner in which some of the relief directorate personnel worked in those days. There had been complaints against this directorate. Some of them were no doubt justified. Many of those employed there were themselves displaced persons. It is unfortunate but true that we caught some of these persons red-handed and they had to be penalized. But this does not take away the almost superhuman achievement of the dedicated officials who showed both compassion and ability in dealing with those who came to India in a miserable plight.

Unfortunately, the refugees' plight was exploited by certain ruthless persons, right from the moment of their arrival, particularly at Sealdah Station. Elaborate arrangements were made to take them away from the station and place them in camp settlements. But the refugees were deliberately encouraged to stay on the platforms. In spite of our entreaties and best efforts, this resulted in their merciless exploitation and women in particular numbered more among the victims. Besides those who came to the camps, there were many hundreds of well-to-do middle-class families who left East Pakistan and stayed with their relatives and friends in West Bengal.

Many descriptions have been given of the conditions of the poorer refugees, the unfortunate men, women and children fleeing from terror and arriving in India. But nothing can accurately describe the heartbreak and tears, the grim tragedy that was being enacted. I saw the hard and exacting work which was undertaken at all hours by those who were in charge under the direction of the Refugee Relief Commissioner, Hironmoy Banerjee, whose untiring efforts and devoted service inspired them all. Many volunteer organizations rendered dedicated service. We owe them a deep debt of gratitude. One of the reasons why it was possible to arrange accommodation for the refugees in camps and elsewhere, and to feed them, was that the government personnel at all levels had a measure of integrity and devotion to duty which seems to have gradually evaporated in later years. Looking back on those years, one is convinced that the manner in which the refugees were sheltered and handled goes to the credit of the government personnel.

Let me recall how I came to be in a position of responsibility for the refugees. Soon after the elections in 1952, Dr. B. C. Roy was preoccupied with the formation of his ministry in West Bengal. During this time, I went to him regarding some problem of the refugees because I was still Refugee Adviser for the Eastern Zone. P. C. Sen was with him at the time. Dr. Roy listened to me and said, 'I think the best thing for you would be to join my cabinet as Rehabilitation Minister.' I asked him not to make jokes at my expense. I pointed out, 'I am not even a member of the Assembly, nor am I willing to be in the Legislative Council because in the Constituent Assembly I took a stand against the establishment of a second chamber in a small state like West Bengal.' Dr. Roy then asked for a copy of the Constitution and after consulting it remarked that minister could be appointed on condition that he or she found a seat in the Assembly within six months. He told me that he was serious and assured me that I would find a seat in six months. On his asking, P. C. Sen agreed with him. I protested and asked, 'Have you consulted any other person about this?' His reply was that he had asked the only person it was necessary to consult and that was my husband. I still refused and left the place. When I rang him up the next day

and asked him what he had decided about the refugee issue that
I had placed before him, he told me, 'It appears that women like
to be advisers but not to take on any responsibility and so I have
nothing else to say to you. I made an offer to you to help me in
resolving this difficult problem.' When I told this to my husband,
he felt that I should not disoblige the old man. When I asked him
whether he had been consulted by Dr. Roy, he told me that the
chief minister had merely asked him, 'Have you any objection to
stand up when your wife comes into the room?' My husband's
rejoinder was that he would always stand up when women enter a room and the same thing was observed with his wife in
public. Dr. Roy said that then there was no problem. As my husband was chief secretary to the Government of West Bengal, this
was Dr. B. C. Roy's way of informing him. Thus, I was propelled
into this position of responsibility, which I held for the next five
years . . . . It was a great experience for me and it gave me a clear
insight into Centre-State relations at the time.

The question of rehabilitation of those who came to India
after partition was answered by an assurance given by the Indian nation that it was committed to giving them a second
chance to make their home in India. The relief and resettlement
of migrants was a direct responsibility of the Central government. The State government was authorized to incur expenses
for relief purposes in camps, which would be reimbursed by
the Central government. But in the case of resettlement of the
migrants, that is, rehabilitation that could only take place outside the camps, where the actual work had to be executed by
the State government, the expenditure was to be kept completely separate from the State finances. Expenditure could only
be incurred after the Central government had sanctioned
schemes and allotted funds for them. It led to many complications. It led to compartmentalized treatment which had an un-
wholesome effect, as it was to increase the gulf between the
refugees and the local people. In the First Five-year Plan, the
budget and the work of rehabilitation were part of the plan but
in the Second Plan, rehabilitation of refugees was placed outside the plan.

The only plan was that of giving small loans in instalments
for various purposes such as housing to agriculturists, or for
starting a small business. We pointed out to the Central govern-

ment again and again that these loans in instalments were frittered away in meeting day-to-day expenses when the refugees did not reside in the camps: there could be no question of a refugee family succeeding in carving out an independent existence by establishing a business or acquiring adequate job training with such a small sum. Instead, the regular small sums were habit-forming and conducive to continued dependence. Then an irksome situation arose for the State government when in 1954 and 1955 about Rs. 3-4 crores under the scheme for rehabilitation of the non-camp refugees included in the budget estimated was not allotted in time by the Government of India. In those days if expenditure did not take place by 31 March, the closing day of the financial year, there was no way of carrying it forward as is done at present. Thus, it happened that due to non-allotment of funds before 31 March, rehabilitation work was stalled. Large sums of money, which were in the budget estimate remained unspent. The State government pointed out to the Centre that the time-lag between the allotment and the placement of funds through the Reserve Bank of India accounted for the delay and the subsequent shortfall in expenditure during the financial year. Allotment received in the last two or three days of March could not be dispatched to various colonies and rehabilitation centres in time. Yet in 1956 and 1957 the Union Minister for Rehabilitation, speaking in Parliament, squarely blamed the State government for the shortfall in expenditure. What was worse, rehabilitation of the refugees was further postponed owing to the delay in the allotment of funds.

In the years 1956 and 1957, before the allotment and placement of funds took place the money was advanced by the State government as soon as it was sanctioned. This resulted in preventing any shortfall in its disbursement, and the refugees received their loans and grants in time. But as the Union Minister for Rehabilitation, Mehr Chand Khanna, pointed out to me, it was not proper or legal for a minister of the State government to have followed such a procedure. Fortunately for me, as the Chief Minister was equally involved, the matter was not pursued further. I have mentioned this incident because I gained an insight into the relationship that could exist between the Centre and the State and in what a helpless condition the executing authority in the State could be placed.

Another point on which I had disagreed with the Central government at the time was regarding the expenditure on the huge temporary camps, such as those in Dhubulia and Chandmari. When hundreds of thousands came together perhaps, it was essential to establish such camps. As soon as there was a respite, when I took over as minister, the State government pointed out that huge sums spent yearly on mere repairs where the displaced persons were kept over the years without any occupation, crippled them psychologically and made them unfit to be rehabilitated. We pointed out that the urgent need was to keep those refugees in smaller centres where they could be provided with some kind of occupation. Even if this employment caused some expenditure at the outset, this would be more than recompensed by placing the refugees on the road to rehabilitating themselves. If the larger camps, which were centres of exploitation, were closed down, there would be a saving of a huge sum of money on their annual repairs. We could utilize this amount in providing occupation in the worksite camps. With the concurrence of the Union Minister for Rehabilitation, Ajit Prasad Jain, the State government was allowed to start a certain number of worksite camps. But after Mehr Chand Khanna took over charge of that ministry, this was completely stopped.

In and around Calcutta the non-camp refugees had settled on their initiative on whatever land was available. But according to the Government of India's direction, they were not given rehabilitation assistance. When Ajit Prasad Jain was minister at the Centre, an amendment to Article 31 of the Indian Constitution (compensation for properties) was made which enabled the government to take over land for the resettlement of refugees and for which compensation rates were formulated by Parliament and not by any court of law. This went through and at the time it was not challenged before the courts. In pursuance of this, a movement to regularize the squatters' colonies was undertaken by the West Bengal government during my tenure as minister. Towards the end of 1956 after acquiring the lands on which the refugees squatted, we gave *arpan patras* (title deeds) to the squatters and they were helped with loans to settle themselves. Unfortunately, in the years that followed, this practice was not continued and even where settlements had been made, some of them failed to continue. Fairly recently, about 1974, it was decided that regularization of squatters' colonies would be continued.

The State government wanted to mix up the camp and the non-camp refugees on the settled lands because we believed this would help those who had always been in the camps to learn from the others. This was frustrated because of the unimaginative policy of the Central government, which was reluctant to give loan facilities to the non-camp refugees on the same basis, as the policy of the government of India was that the camp refugees must have priority. This might have seemed correct in theory but was not practical because the displaced persons who had lived in camps for years during the period when there was wishful thinking that they would go back, had lost their initiative. The State government felt that the only way for these colonies to become successful rehabilitation centres was to mix up the residents with the non-camp refugees who had initiative and would be able to give leadership and direction.

When the overcrowding in West Bengal assumed impossible proportions in 1954, a decision was made to send the displaced persons to the neighbouring States. Arrangements were made for the displaced persons to be sent to Uttar Pradesh (Naini Tal), Bihar, and Orissa, and to other places. There was great reluctance on the part of the refugees to go farther than West Bengal, which was understandable but not practical. But some elements, including the political parties, played on their fear. This was unfortunate because the political parties should have taken the issue with the Central government in regard to its policies which needed to be reversed and for which they could have led the demand. Instead, both in the Assembly in West Bengal and in Parliament, where the members from West Bengal led the way, there were concentrated attacks on the Government of West Bengal. It is not that the attackers did not blame the Central government at all, but their main target was the State government for allowing the refugees to be sent to places outside West Bengal. Thus, instead of insisting on the right of the displaced persons to settle anywhere in India, they located them in West Bengal.

Logically this meant that these politicians should have insisted on much better amenities in an overcrowded economy. They could have given full support to the State government's plea for considerable expansion of civic amenities in Calcutta, for setting up a proper township with adequate rail and road connections. Instead of allowing the Centre to give loans in a niggardly fashion, they could have stressed the need for generosity on the scale that was displayed in setting up a city such as Chandigarh for the refugees from West Punjab. The State government's entreaties for funds to establish new avenues of employment and long-term schemes for reclamation of land could have received their backing and thus rehabilitated a large number of refugees in West Bengal. But the role played by the opposition party politicians of West Bengal at the Centre and in the State Assembly was negative and did not help increase the facilities for a large number to be accommodated in the state. If adequate arrangements were made outside West Bengal, would it not have benefited the refugees if these politicians had supported these measures instead of opposing them even before they could make headway, which is once again what they did? For instance, in Betia, in Bihar, good cultivable agricultural land had been found and plots given to a number of refugees from East Bengal while others were kept waiting in camps as plots were being developed. But owing to the agitators who included the members of the opposition political parties who visited these people in the camps, some of the refugees were persuaded to return to West Bengal. At this stage, along with the Minister for Rehabilitation of Bihar, I visited the settlement at Betia where the agriculturists had been placed and found that the land was far more fertile and far more healthy than at any place in West Bengal that could have been given to them. Afterwards, I went to the Bihar camps and described the position to the refugees and was able to persuade those who were still at the camps to wait until land was made ready for them. On my return to Calcutta when I went to report to Dr. B. C. Roy at Writers Building, I found that the opposition party members led by Jyoti Basu, and a sprinkling of other were seated around him. Dr. Roy asked me to give an account of what I had seen. I did so and appealed to the opposition parties to visit the rehabilitation sites and to consider the real interests of the refugees awaiting rehabilitation in this matter. They did so and the result was that the rest of the refugees of Betia were able to settle down there.

Another place where the displaced persons from East Bengal were settled well and are flourishing today are the Andamans. I remember that when the first batch went to the Andamans the Refugee Relief Commissioner accompanied me to see them off. Officials were hard put to persuade them to go. This was because of the prejudice against the Andamans, which were associated with the prison, where so many of the terrorists and others, who defied the British government, had been confined. Their reluctance was understandable. Fortunately, the first batch was received by the commissioner Upen Ghosal himself and they were treated so well and placed so quickly on suitable rehabilitation sites that they wrote back to their friends and relatives to join them. Although in Calcutta agitation still continued against settlement, the refugees invited by those who had gone before wanted to go on their own. The numbers for whom rehabilitation had been planned by the Government of India were soon exhausted and I asked for more to be sent, but the Government of India in the Home Ministry suddenly came up with a technical reason for not sending more than the prescribed quota. Its plea was that persons from Kerala and other places in India had also to be accommodated in the quota fixed for outsiders. This seemed to be most unreasonable to Dr. Roy and to the thoughtful Indians that at a time when the country was facing a constant rush of displaced persons into the eastern region we should have to worry about theoretical quotas. We were at first able to persuade the Home Ministry where Dr. Kailash Nath Katju was in charge, to send some more refugees from East Pakistan. But gradually this was stopped. The refusal of the Union Home Ministry to increase the quota for the refugees from East Bengal in an island environment ideally suited to a riverine people appeared to be proof of the unsympathetic attitude of the Central government.

The branch secretariat of the Union Ministry of Rehabilitation in Calcutta had worked well at the initial stages. However, at a later stage when Mehr Chand Khanna was the Union Minister for Rehabilitation, we discovered that it became a means by which further delays took place and the State government's problems were compounded. It became the fashion of the Central ministry to blame the State government whenever it could. A study made by the Union Ministry of Rehabilitation reflected its attitude to the refugees from East Bengal. It compared them with the refugees who came from West Punjab to East Punjab and said that the former did not pay back their loans whereas the latter did. It did not mention the fact that the loans given to the displaced persons in the Punjab were set off against the evacuee properties they received in exchange. This naturally made a profound difference. Displaced persons from East Bengal were not only given loans in small instalments which were frittered away on day-to-day living, but it was also not possible to resettle them on such minuscule sums. Even those who could settle somehow were not a position to repay the loan. Had the money been given as loans in one instalment, the position of refugee rehabilitation in West Bengal could have been vastly different. The Government of India published summaries of the expenditure spent on refugees from West Punjab and East Bengal (Tables 5.1, 5.2, and 5.3). The great disparity in the amount spent on rehabilitation could not be merely put down to the absence of evacuee property compensation in the eastern region.

TABLE 5.1: Number of Refugees Arrived in India
and Admitted to Camps

Month	Number of refugees	Admitted to camps
July 1955	22,957	15,661
August	13,820	9,983
September	9,371	4,526
October	13,761	6,564
November	11,335	4,209
December	18,903	7,656
January 1956	17,011	5,201
February	42,360	14,802
March	45,167	22,198
April	18,039	6,523
May	24,657	8,992
June	24,734	6,214
Total	262,115	112,529

TABLE 5.2 Comparative Expenditure on Displaced Persons
from East Pakistan and West Pakistan for 1954-1955

Expenditure head	Displaced persons from West Pakistan	Displaced persons from East Pakistan	Total
Grants	65.78	29.13	94.91
Loans	23.26	22.48	45.74
Housing	55.74	16.47	72.21
Establishments	(1)18	0.14	(1)32
Miscellaneous	0.01	—	0.01
Total	145.97	68.22	214.19
Loans by RFA	7.42	2.07	9.49
Grand Total	153.39	70.29	223.68

Source: *Summary 1954-1955*, government of India, Ministry or
Rehabilitation

TABLE 5.3: Comparative Expenditure on Displaced Persons from
East Pakistan and West Pakistan for 1956-1957

Expenditure head	Displaced persons from West Pakistan	Displaced person from East Pakistan	Total
Grants	75.38	48.91	124.29
Loans	25.53	27.67	53.20
Housing	59.69	29.77	80.46
Establishments	1.66	0.33	1.99
Miscellaneous	0.01	—	0.01
Compensation	53.12	—	53.12
Adjustment Transport from/to capital outside revenue account for compensation	14.83	—	14.83
Total	230.22	106.68	336.90
Loans by RFA	7.13	3.17	10.30
Grant Total	237.35	109.85	347.20

Source: *Summary 1956-1957*, Government of India, Ministry of Rehabilitation.

Another point which had been overlooked but which had
already taken place in the early years of migration was that
many refugees were placed in colonies or lands unsuitable for

occupation. When I took over as minister, there was a respite in the influx for a few months in 1952 and so an attempt was made to resettle the refugees according to whether they were agriculturists or non-agriculturists on land suitable for their occupation. However, we faced every conceivable opposition from the Centre and it was difficult going.

When Ajit Prasad Jain was Union Minister for Rehabilitation, I was able to convince him on significant points and achieved results. For instance, in regard to the permanent liability (PL) camps (Permanent Liability—a curious name that was dubbed to the women and children without male guardians to protect them), although he was doubtful, Ajit Prasad Jain agreed to let me set up training and production centres for the women through which they ultimately would be able to fend for themselves. As for the children, whether in the PL camps or outside, the West Bengal government could proudly claim that it was able to provide education and training for them. Schools—primary and secondary—vocational training centres for men as well as for women, and a number of colleges known as sponsored colleges were set up through which these people learned to become useful citizens. Social welfare organizations of both men and women played a great part in helping towards the success of the educational and training institutions. Women's organizations such as the All-India Women's Conference, the All-Bengal Women's Union, the Nari Seva Sangha, Deshbandhu Balika Vidyalaya and others undertook the training of a large number of women. The Ananda Ashram, which came from East Bengal and found a home in Calcutta, also participated in taking larger numbers under the guidance of the courageous Mother Charusila Devi. To the Ramkrishna Mission in particular we have to be grateful. Rahra Home for Boys and Narendrapur and other educational centres sprang up and played a vital role in educating the children of the displaced persons.

We must acknowledge that the successful attempt in providing opportunities for the children of the displaced persons compared well with the staggering figures of illiteracy, lack of education in the state and in the country as a whole. We can proudly claim that every refugee child was educated in schools and none was left unlettered in contrast to the ordinary child in West Bengal.

I had made a last desperate appeal to the Central government that if nothing else could be done for the refugees who came after 1956, they should at least be treated on the same level as the Burmese refugees. They should be provided with adequate sums of money to rehabilitate themselves anywhere, provided they found land at their own initiative in the Union of India.

Summing up in retrospect, we find that as no interchange of population took place all at once after Partition, as in the western region, it lulled the Central government into complacency. The Liaquat-Nehru Pact added considerably to the difficulties, for it was only honoured on the Indian side. As there was no vacuum created in eastern India and no evacuee properties for the displaced persons who came, their rehabilitation was a much more complex problem in an overcrowded economy. The reluctance of the Central government and the niggardly and half-hearted help to the refugees from East Bengal were the further obstacles to successful rehabilitation (see Tables 5.2 and 5.3 for comparisons with the refugees from West Pakistan). Wherever successful rehabilitation became possible, as in Naini Tal and the Andamans, it was restricted and then stopped owing to such technicalities as allotment of quotas. Then again the refugees were sent to uninhabitable areas for settlement, such as Dandakaranya. What little development took place was done by the refugees themselves. As soon as large schemes for irrigation and electricity were accepted in Dandakaranya, the refugees were induced deliberately to leave their settlements by vested interests who wanted the lands for their own use. No town like Faridabad was built for them, nor were any extra amenities given in the crowded city of Calcutta or in areas such as Tripura to accommodate the refugees. The contribution that the early migrants made to the economy of West Bengal and Assam was ignored and went unnoticed in view of the ever-increasing number that followed. Moreover, what the critics of the refugees from East Bengal and of the State government forget is the nature of the influx: it was continuous and unpredictable and the immediate need for providing relief meant that there was a much smaller opportunity to plan for rehabilitation, quite the opposite of what happened in the western region. Indeed it must be emphasized that no proper planning was possible in an overall sense for the refugees who continued to come. No accurate estimate could be made of what the numbers of refugees would be from month to month. For instance, in July 1955 there were 22,957. In August 1955 there were 13,820, while in December 1955 there were 18,903. (see Table 5.1). It was only after the Bangladesh Liberation War in 1971 that there was a short respite and we found that those who came to India then actually went back. Even today they still come and from Tripura we have the latest report [1980] that even the Mogs of Chittagong who had remained there for such a long time are being compelled to cross the border into India.

After facing so many odds in my endeavours to rehabilitate the refugees, I was convinced that it was not right for me to occupy a ministerial chair without the requisite authority to solve this challenging problem. Although Dr. B.C. Roy was extremely reluctant, I was able to persuade him to allow me to go to the Lok Sabha when the elections came in 1957. I was then of the opinion that it would be possible for me to convince Parliament and persuade the authorities to appreciate the gravity of the problem of absorbing the displaced persons from East Bengal in West Bengal. This was because I was under the impression that the atmosphere that prevailed during the Constituent Assembly days still continued. But when I came to the Lok Sabha I found that things were vastly different. Gone were the days when we were concerned with objective policies and their implementation. Sectarian and group interests had become paramount and who should go to what committee and delegations at home and abroad seemed more important that how developmental work proceeded or how refugees could be absorbed into the economy of India. I, therefore, felt frustrated in my endeavour to focus attention on the refugees from East Bengal who, I was convinced, had not received a fair deal and whose problems are still with us.

NOTE

We are grateful to Rathindra Nath Roy, the son and literary heir of Renuka Roy, for permission to reproduce the chapter 'And Still They Come' from her book, *My Reminiscences*, Delhi, Allied Publishers, 1982; copyright 1998 Rathindra Nath Roy.

6

Uprooted and Divided
Meghna Guha Thakurta

I AM NOT a historian by training. Hence, imagine my surprise when I found myself researching into family histories of the 1947 Partition of Bengal during my first sabbatical from Dhaka University where I taught International Relations! The reasons for taking up such a subject, as I discovered later, were manifold. First, it took me a long time to realize that my family and I, like every other citizen of the current state of Bangladesh, were directly and indirectly a byproduct of Partition to the extent that even our daily struggles sometimes evolved around it.

Second, as noted by many scholars, even after two generations the migration across borders continues. It is still debated and deliberated among family members, perhaps not for the same reasons, but from circumstances, which arose from the same event. Third, as a feminist scholar, I realized it is not enough to declare that the personal is equally political in one's academic work but that it is necessary to confront it in living out one's own life.

The result is my current research on Understanding Population Movements through Reconstructing Family Histories: The Case of the Bengal Partition. I will try to outline my intervention in the following way: (a) to delineate both the discursive and situational context of the Bengal Partition; (b) to explain why I have chosen family histories as the method by which to research this area; and (c) to outline some of the findings by using illustrations from the case studies.

Until recently, apart from the well-known historical accounts, writings on the partition of the subcontinent have mainly been centred on fictional literature and autobiographical narratives. There has also been a tendency to focus on the communal and violent nature of Partition and the mass exodus accompanying it. That was more the case of the Punjab frontier where forced migration took place. Along the Bengal border, things were different. For some families, it was a matter of conscious choice: for example, those families whose members were in government service and were given the option to take up equivalent work on the other side. Some families, however, had to decide in a very short period of time, so that people who exercised the option also had to reach a hurried decision which they later regretted.

For others, the decision to migrate was taken almost overnight, especially if the family was directly or indirectly hit by any one of the communal uprisings, which followed Partition. But for most families the decision to migrate was deliberated slowly and in waves, within the circle of the family, a process which continues even today. This has created a curious effect on the social makeup of the region resulting in a 'diaspora' of families—Hindus, Muslims, Biharis, Chakmas, Garos and so on—separated and divided, living on either side of the lines chalked out by the Radcliffe Award, each part engrossed in its own struggle for survival or achievement and yet connected by ties, emotional, imaginary and real.

This is not to say that the Bengal Partition occurred without violence or was not stricken by communal forces. Violence is not always to be measured by external acts of murder, loot or abduction, reports of which are also found in pre-and post-partition Bengal. However, these occurrences might have been more sporadic on this side. What is crucial to note is that violence also typifies a state where a sense of fear is generated and perpetrated in such a way as to make it systemic, pervasive and inevitable. Thus, during the nine-month occupation of Dhaka by the Pakistani Army in 1971, what General Yahya Khan called a 'normal and peaceful' situation, people went about their daily chores in dread and fear, not knowing when a tap on the door could mean death or, even worse for women, rape.

In the many communal riots, which preceded as well as

followed Partition, it was the *fear* of being persecuted, the fear of being dispossessed, the fear of not belonging that caused many to flee rather than actual incidents of violence. In many cases, this fear was deliberately generated, by leaflets or newspaper reports, by rumours or mere example (seeing your neighbours leave). Interviewing migrants across the borders, one is astounded by the large number of people who said they had not witnessed an act of violence, but had fled because of rumours that a mob was coming their way, or that the next village had been set ablaze, or even by idle chatter which made them believe that this country no longer belonged to them!

It is also not necessary that actual incidents of violence always cause people to flee because there are many who remain (given the choice, of course). Fear is sometimes less derived from actual acts of violence than from perceptions of violence. People stay for many reasons and nowhere are those reasons more rich or varied than in the case of the Bengal Partition as the case histories demonstrate.

Bengal enjoyed open borders for a long period of time. It was not until 1953 that passports were introduced and only after the 1965 Indo-Pakistan war were visas required. Rail and air communication also stopped after the 1965 war and only very restrictive overland communication was maintained. People across the border, both for trading as well as other social reasons, persistently defied these restrictions. So much so, a whole network of underground operators who helped people cross borders without a visa or passport grew steadily, a method often colourfully termed in the local language as *gola-dhakka* passage (taking you by the scruff of the neck and pushing you across).

The Bangladesh Liberation War in 1971 and the consequent mass exodus of people fleeing from persecution interrogated the same borderlines and boundaries. Despite all this porousness, 'illegal' trade or smuggling has been a primary concern for successive national governments. Such 'border incidents' or skirmishes between border forces have also captured front-page news. This phenomenon reached its peak in contemporary times when economic migrants by the thousands, Hindus and Muslims, have crossed frontiers in search of better means of livelihood.

But as far as Partition is concerned, there has been a further silencing of the processes at work, apparent in the writing about the Partition of the two Bengals. Although fiction and autobiographical writings have dominated the Partition discourse on both sides, the voices of Hindu migrants from East Bengal have been more prominent than Muslim migrants from West Bengal. The reason for this is of course an open question, which awaits further research.

One of the important distinctions between the two 'migrant' groups has been created by the political conditions in the country to which they migrated. For Hindus the experience of dispossession and nostalgia for their 'homesteads' (*bhitabari*) has been very pronounced and glorified in their writings. For many Muslims of a particular generation the journey to Pakistan was like a journey to a 'promised land', an image which later became tarnished as Pakistan entered its most repressive stage under the Ayub regime, the brunt of which was borne by the people of East Bengal.

In the oppressive atmosphere of a martial law regime whose favourite occupation was 'India-bashing', it was understandably difficult to write, much less be nostalgic, about one's homeland in India. There is therefore a reticence, even now, among Bengali Muslims to talk of their *desh* (ancestral home as it is referred to in Bengali) publicly, if it happens to be in India. In recording family histories, however, one succeeded to a certain extent in overcoming this barrier, for nostalgic memories of childhood, growing up, family ties and accompanying emotions find a space where one can talk about them freely without the direct intervention of nationalist politics.

There is yet another phenomenon, which distinguishes East Bengali Hindu reminiscences of Partition from those promoted by the Muslim migration from West Bengal. This is the Bangladesh Liberation War of 1971. Memories of 1947 or Partition have often been superseded by memories 1971, or movements which led to 1971, because in the quest for a Bengali identity many Bengali Muslims had to rethink their positions. Thus when memories of Partition are revived, they are either blocked or coloured by memories of 1971.

Many Muslims came to the east from West Bengal and Bihar in the hope of finding their promised land, though not all of them believed in the Muslim League ideology. Many progressive cultural activists and professionals came from Calcutta,

102 The Trauma and the Triumph

not spontaneously, but with the ambition of constructing a new
nation that would give shape and colour to their dreams. But
for most, this dream was short-lived. The repression of Bengali
identity and the imposition of a new cultural identity of Pakistan, the imposition of martial law, generated spontaneous resistance from the people whether in the form of the Language
movement of 1952, or the anti-Ayub demonstrations of 1969,
culminating in the Liberation War of 1971 for an independent
Bangladesh.

Though in the nationalist writing of history these events
appear in a linear schema, the personal histories of those involved in or affected by these movements were far from linear.
These events foreshadowed the contradictions of identity which
individuals had to confront in their personal lives as they contested the different notions of nationhood in the political arena:
one based on the Bengali language and the other on Islam. This
is why, even in present-day Bangladesh, narratives of the Liberation War are still a site for contestation between rival nation-
alisms: Bengali and Bangladeshi.

I now explain my choice of family histories as a method of
research. Dominant historiographical trends construe the 1947
partition of the subcontinent as a product of the colonial state
as well as a landmark in the progressive march towards achiev-
ing modern nationhood. In subsequent years this nationhood
came to determine questions of citizenship and social exchange
and to define personal identities for the people occupying the
newly defined territories of India and Pakistan.

A major critique of this view has come from the subaltern
school which maintains that there exist groups like peasants,
women and others whose voices have remained silent or
marginalized and who may possess a notion of community different from, even in opposition to, that of the nationalist project.
My focus on family histories uses the subaltern perspective, both
as a point of departure as well as a springboard from which to
explore the problematic of looking at the social history of a
people who, though disempowered by developments beyond
their control, have at the same time struggled hard to retain an
element of control in their effort to adapt to the new situation.

Family histories provide us with a conceptual tool through
which such processes could be better understood. I wish to

emphasize the importance of looking at family histories because they enable us to: *(a)* look at Partition from a site that is intermediate to, but not wholly exclusive from, larger structural forces on the one hand and individual decision-making on the other, and *(b)* to locate Partition and what it represents in the temporal scale of generations since family histories are about intergenerational exchanges. To focus on the family, as an important intermediary site, is to see how memories of individuals and generations are constructed and negotiated and how personal identities of gender, class or nation·are formed, conformed to or contested and confronted.

I have studied the case histories of two families: one a Muslim family from Barasat, West Bengal, and the other a Hindu family from Barisal, East Bengal. In the latter case it is my own family. However, I am not the prime narrator here, but my aunt who was a witness to Partition. In both cases the interviewees are men and women who crossed the border in 1947 or afterwards as a result of the fallout of Partition.

The structures of both families are of course different. While the family from Barasat was land-centred and hence patrilineal and location-specific, the family from Banaripara was not dependent on land—it capitalized on education and the service sector. But many of the marriage alliances, which took place, were with the landed gentry, and these alliances were used for resource polling within my family.

In the first instance almost everyone married into the same district or at least neighbouring ones, in West or East Bengal. Apart from the members who migrated to Bangladesh and one who settled in another village in West Bengal, most of the family lives in the natal village, though they have separate households. In the second instance, marriages took place with families in other districts, but located essentially within East Bengal. However, as the members of the Hindu family were not directly dependent on land, and the ancestral home existed mostly at a symbolic level, even for the previous generation, the residence pattern was scattered.

But a general trend emerged where the inclination was to move towards the urban centres: Mymensingh, Dhaka, Calcutta. Though this was prompted by the need for white collar jobs, the gravitation towards the metropolis was not always through patrilineal ties, but often by using connections through marriage. Thus, many cousins in the Hindu family grew up in their *mamabari* or maternal uncle's house. All this was a pre-partition syndrome. When Partition occurred, each member of the family took his own decision.

Calcutta was the mega city and metropolis of British India, and hence the focal point of migration. Urban migration had increased in the 1940s, especially during and after the famine of 1943. Dhaka and Mymensingh in the eastern parts too had their attractions. The Muslim family from Barasat, though land-centred, also lived in the vicinity of Calcutta. This determined their mindset when the option to move came up. Both concerns of property and living in the vicinity of Calcutta with educational and employment opportunities for their children became important considerations.

The Hindu service worker had, however, started his/her migratory trend towards Calcutta long before everyone else, both in relation to education and employment. As the second case shows, this was true for them as well. This pre-partition migration, like any other urban migratory trend, used family connections and contacts to establish a 'chain' which enabled other members of the family to follow. But when Partition came, this 'chain' was stretched to its limits and often broke down. At this precise juncture, migrants became refugees. Too many people were coming in at short notice and family resources were often inadequate to bear the burden. Many 'fictive kinships' and extra family alliances too were made at this point.

The findings of the case studies are organized into four subthemes: (a) Communal identity and the decision to migrate; (b) The construction and deconstruction of the nation; (c) Resource base and social mobility; and (d) Gendered interpretations of the family, community and nation.

COMMUNAL IDENTITY AND THE DECISION TO MIGRATE

In both families the actual decision to migrate was taken at the height of the communal conflict. In both cases it was the post-partition communal riots which created the context. For the Muslim family it was the 1964 riots, for the Hindu family it was the 1950 riots.

In 1964, Barasat was affected by Hindu-Muslim riots. At that time the family (let us say, Minhaj's family) consisted of J. Ali, the father, his wife and their nine children, of whom Minhaj was the seventh. Out of the nine children, three elder sisters and three brothers remained in Barasat. Only Minhaj, his younger sister, Arjoo, and his elder brother Momtaj subsequently migrated to East Bengal, now Bangladesh. The areas surrounding their village were hit hard. People fled their homes to take shelter in the fields. When the Indo-Pakistan war came in the wake of the riots, it was no surprise to see many Muslim families supporting Pakistan in the war. Minhaj recalls that during the war they listened to BBC radio in the mango grove out of earshot, and joyously cheered for Pakistan. People began calling them Pakistan-panthi, followers of Pakistan. They felt cornered.

In the meantime families around Barasat were gradually sending their children away to Pakistan. But Minhaj's family refused to budge. There seemed too much at stake: their property, for example. Moreover, by this time everyone in the family was comfortably off, each with his own side business, mostly shopkeeping. That they had their own high school in the village was mentioned as a plus point. Besides, no one wanted to go to a 'backward place' like East Pakistan, leaving behind their property. So the general feeling was to keep an open mind about it: *Dekha, jacchi jabo* (Let us see and then decide).

Minhaj's elder brother had already accompanied his uncle to East Pakistan for reasons that will be discussed in the next section. But in 1967, Minhaj's father instructed him and his youngest sister Arjoo to join their elder brother in East Pakistan. Why? And why Minhaj and Arjoo out of the remaining six brothers and sisters? The answer to the first question was supplied by Minhaj's father himself. 'Your brother lives in a foreign land, so you must go in case he needs help.' One needs a family member in times of crises.

At that time Minhaj had passed his school finals and was seeking admission to Bangabasi College and and then to Surendranath College in Calcutta. To his family, it seemed that Minhaj, an extrovert from childhood, was 'mixing too much with his Hindu friends.'

The threat of the Naxal movement also pervaded the air. So with his three elder sisters married off, and two older brothers to look after the property, Minhaj was the best possible choice to 'send away'. Arjoo, the youngest daughter of the family, eleven years old and unmarried, was chosen for reasons of security. After the 1964 riots, it was no longer considered safe to keep an unmarried girl at home. Hence, Minhaj and Arjoo reluctantly left West Bengal to join their brother in Pakistan.

For my own family, living in Dhaka the decision to migrate was prompted by circumstances created by the 1964 Hindu-Muslim riots. Here is how my aunt Tapati and my uncle Jyotsnamoy described the situation. At that time the family consisted of Sumati, the widowed mother, and her four children— Jyotirmoy, Arati, Jyotsnamoy and Tapati. Jyotirmoy, the eldest son (my father), was the sole bread earner and had just started his teaching career at a college in Dhaka. He had also married Basanti (my mother) who was a headmistress in a girl's school.

After the riots Arati, the elder sister, married and settled down in Bihar and Sumati together with the two younger children, Jyotsnamoy and Tapati, migrated to Calcutta. Jyotsnamoy and Tapati are still alive.

The riots started in late January 1950. Quite suddenly, rumours of the killing of Hindus were heard in Dhaka. Arati was teaching at Basanti's school and was already on her way when news about the riot broke. Jyotirmoy was stopped in time from going out and Basanti too stayed back. Only Arati was out on the road. Jyotsnamoy tried to catch up with her on a bicycle but did not succeed. Arati did not reach her destination. She too learnt of the riots and got down at a friend's house. The friend's house was attacked by an unruly mob and they barely managed to escape by the backdoor. They took shelter in the neighbouring house from where they could hear the mob debating whether they should charge in and kill everyone or not. Suddenly the mob was called of by someone, and later everyone took refuge at a Hindu police inspector's house which had virtually become a refugee centre. Since there was no safe way of communication at that point, Arati and others who took shelter like her spent the whole day and night in terror, their whereabouts unknown to their families. It was not until the next afternoon that Arati was found and brought back home.

This incident had a radical effect on the family. Arati's

wedding was to take place as planned, in curfew-ridden Dhaka. Only close relatives and some friends were to attend. Their houses were guarded by young students and friends who formed brigades, keeping watch on the roofs at night to ward off any assault. After the wedding Arati was to go to her new home in Giridih, Bihar, with her husband. Tapati and Jyotsnamoy would accompany her to Calcutta. The decision to migrate was made almost overnight! But Jyotirmoy and Basanti decided to stay. Tapati was too young to understand why. She just mentioned that her eldest brother was persistent in his refusal to leave and would not give a clear answer.

However, much later his friend and political colleague K. K. Sinha said his memoirs:

> He [Jyotirmoy] always ended by saying that the intellectual horizon of the young Bengali Muslims in East Pakistan was undergoing a revolution ... A new generation was rising and it was that which sustained his confidence and faith. The new intellectual elite that was rising was much more virile, much more creative and much more open-minded and flexible and he felt that he was sharing the joy of this emergence of the new rising sun.

Jyotirmoy was a follower of M. N. Roy's Radical Humanist Party and believed that he should stay in his homeland (whatever be its nomenclature) and work for his country and not subscribe to the communal frenzy which by then seemed to have taken over most of the middle class Hindu families. But due to the peculiar circumstances arising out of the 1950 riots, he failed to communicate his confidence to most of his family members. Only my mother shared his beliefs and remained with him.

We therefore see that despite the prevailing current of affairs, each family member was negotiating notions of communal identity for himself, according to his own perception of security. Minhaj's family members carefully weighed their well being with their perceptions of security just as my family debated the idealism of my father vis-à-vis the practicality of siding with the mainstream. In both families, however, the fate of the younger women of the family (the unmarried girls) was decided for them.

THE CONSTRUCTION AND DECONSTRUCTION OF THE NATION

Just as communal identities were negotiated within the family, notions of nationhood too were constructed and deconstructed therein. In Minhaj's family the construction of Pakistan as a homeland for Muslims was quite a popular idea and one which was earnestly believed in by his eldest uncle, S. Ali. In fact, in 1947, S. Ali opted for Pakistan because he, like many others of his generation, believed that Pakistan was the homeland for all the Muslims of the subcontinent.

Minhaj remembered that he had grown up in an atmosphere where the politics of the Muslim League held sway. In addition to taking his family with him, S. Ali asked his nephew Momtaj, then a schoolboy in his teens, to accompany him to the 'promised land'. His father did not object because at that time the whole family was in two minds about moving, and it seemed that S. Ali was merely taking the first step.

But following their arrival in East Pakistan, the political atmosphere in the country gradually started heating up with the demand for autonomy for East Bengal. Campuses were hotbeds of politics. Minhaj had got involved, if only marginally, in student politics. After his arrival he was asked by friends to join the New Student's Federations, the branch of the Muslim League which had supported the Ayub regime.

But in 1969 he was won over by the Bangladesh Chhatro Union, the student's wing of the Communist Party, which had a fairly strong base at Jessore. The 1969 anti-Ayub demonstrations in the eastern wing of Pakistan had left little about in anyone's mind, including Minhaj's family back in Barasat, that the concept of Pakistan as the homeland of Muslims was foredoomed to failure.

In the case of my family only my father seemed to retain a non-nationalist vision. He did cherish a concept of the homeland, a sense of rootedness in his birthland and a commitment to stand by democratic ideals. He met his death at the hands of the Pakistan Army in 1971 when he was accused of possessing an identity which he had always resisted, that is, of being a Hindu. His professed identity of a humanist was not to be found anywhere in the vocabulary of Yahya Khan's barbaric regime.

On the other hand, my grandmother, uncle and aunts who, haunted by a sheer sense of insecurity, had migrated to India did not have any convictions about nationhood. Some of them felt for their birthland but they never ceased to coax, cajole and pester my parents to migrate to India or any other country. The trauma of the 1950 riots remained, and their vision was still tainted by it.

For them, Muslims in the abstract were still the Other and by that definition they themselves were Hindus. Like many Hindu families in West Bengal, they used the categories of Bengali and Hindus as synonymous, thus excluding Muslims from their sense of nationhood. Most of these families until recently were oblivious or chose to remain oblivious of the Bengali nationalist movement across the border in East Bengal until the 1971 Liberation War.

RESOURCE BASE AND SOCIAL MOBILITY

In both narratives, the importance of the resource base of the family has featured time and again. This has been the prime factor in the process of decision-making: to move or not to move, whom to include in the family while constructing marriage alliances and kinship networks or breaking joint households into single ones. Indeed, education, employment opportunity and favourable marital alliances can open up horizons for an individual in a new place. But what is important to remember in the context of Partition is that these are also political spaces, which enable an individual to contest and protest the feeling of otherness, which he/she faces in a new place.

After migration when Minhaj entered college, he first joined a student's party that was aligned with the Muslim League. But later he found assimilation easier when he associated himself with the strong demand for a Bengali identity. The concept of 'homeland' embedded in Minhaj's consciousness was under constant threat. It was threatened by communal uprisings in the homeland itself when he was construed by the dominant community as the Other. It was also threatened when he failed to identify with causes and movements in his new surroundings.

It is important to see at what point in one's life migration takes place. Life cycle is an important element in both narratives. It makes a difference if there is a primary breadwinner among the migrant's family, on whom one can fall back on during crisis. A lack of skills and adequate qualification can be a disadvantage as in the case of Jyotsnamoy, whose schooling was interrupted by Partition and who as the only male member had to look after the practicalities of getting the family settled.

Even after he raised his own family, he had to struggle hard to give his three sons a good education. Therefore, the family always stated that if Jyotirmoy (the sole breadwinner at the time of Partition) had come to Calcutta, the family fortunes would have been different. Their conjecture is not without basis. In fact, this also runs contrary to general migration patterns, where it is the breadwinner who migrates first and then 'pulls' in the others.

GENDERED INTERPRETATIONS OF THE FAMILY, COMMUNITY AND NATION

My methodological intervention aims to reveal the gendered narratives in family histories. Since in both the families interviewed, I found women who were unmarried at Partition and as a consequence were forced to migrate for reasons of security, this task was made easier for me. Arjoo, Minhaj's sister, was barely twelve when she was forced to leave her mother for the security of East Pakistan where her elder brother lived.

The incident is related in her own poignant words:

'Everyone got panicky. I remember some outsiders came and put fire to some houses in Kazipara, a nearby village. I panicked. At that time, my mother and I were alone in the house. I ran and hid in the sugarcane field for an hour. My mother didn't go with me. Being the youngest in the family, I used to be the only one to go to the Kazipara primary school. The rest of the family had attended the village school. But after the riots, my father put pressure on me to go and stay in East Pakistan with my brother. Both my mother and I resisted at first, but my father said he would stop my education if I didn't listen to him. My mother then laid out the options and said that either I go or my education would be stopped. I was determined to get an education, so I went.'

About community relations she said: 'I have found memories of my school at Kazipara. I still maintain contact with some of my friends. I had mostly Hindu friends. I remember no signs of discrimination but there were differences. For example, I remember we had a crazy teacher called Ganesh. Hindu girls used to say *aggey* while answering to the roll call while Muslim girls said *ji*. Once my Hindu friend said ji instead and Ganesh sir immediately reacted. "You are a Hindu," he said, "Why should you say ji?".'

Arjoo's perception of nation or homeland was mediated through kinship and marital relations. She got married to someone whose ancestral home was in Jessore. It meant double dislocation for her. Not only did she feel herself an outsider in East Pakistan or Bangladesh, she was also an outsider in her in-law's house.

She relates her experience as a new bride: 'I felt the difference because I came from West Bengal although I was not openly told about it.' She said there were differences in their dialect and hers. Her in-laws used to tease her and called her 'khuni' (murderer) because she spoke in her local dialect 'jaboney khabony'. She sometimes could not understand her mother-in-law when she asked her to come down from the roof (*ulla aia*); Ulla was the name of her village.

Arjoo feels proud of her natal village in Barasat. She visits it often, though sometimes she has to fight with her husband for that right. When her husband asks her why she goes there so often, her response is that as long as she has the strength she will go. 'Once I lose my strength I will automatically stop.' She visits with her children, a boy and two girls. Once when she took her boy there he was surprised when he got down at Barasat. He remarked, 'Mom! But we have only come to Jessore.'

Tapati on the other hand felt more insecure in her perceptions of family, community and homeland/nation. This was perhaps due to the disturbing and traumatic experiences of her adolescence and adult life. Tapati's miseries did not stop with Partition. In 1957 she married and began to live in a joint family, which soon broke up. The year 1971 brought the tragic news of Jyotirmoy's death at the hands of the Pakistan Army, but what was most tragic of all was that in 1980 her husband died of a heart attack, leaving her to fend for herself and their two unmarried daughters.

In her own words, 'I could never find a secure home. I lost my father when I was barely some months old. Throughout my life, I have been compelled to leave one home for another. Even now, that is my reality.' Tapati has no nostalgia about her homeland, some memories perhaps, but she *never* glorifies them. Her life has been too unsettling and she still relives the trauma in her everyday life. She is afraid whenever she reads in the papers that the Tenancy Act could be revoked, withdrawing the rights of the tenant. She quakes with fear that the house she is living in might suddenly collapse because it is built on uncertain foundations. Her only concern is the security of her daughters and herself.

The Bengal Partition compelled divided or migrant families, whether of Hindu or Muslim origin, to render different narratives according to different orientations in their resources base: whether land-based or service-oriented, or located near or linked to a mega city like Calcutta. Likewise, individuals within families speak with many voices given their resource base, life skills, age and gender. Questions of migration and mobility not only link up to the events of Partition but also to the quest for education, employment and the sustenance or breaking-up of marital and kinship ties.

Family histories of Partition, therefore, make a strong statement about social transformation. They reiterate that families are open to change, transforming themselves and thereby changing social reality. Times of transition are trying as such changes, brought about suddenly, create havoc and an upheaval that continues to haunt one into another century.

7

The Nowhere People[1]
Urvashi Butalia

FOR MOST PEOPLE who live alongside it, the border between
India and Bangladesh is a chimera. Flat, green fields stretch over
a wide terrain. Dotted across them you can see men and women
bent over in work, a stray goat or cow lazily grazing alongside.
It is difficult to tell from their appearance which side of the
border the human beings, or indeed the animals, belong to.
Somewhere between one field and another lies an imaginary line
that marks the territorial boundaries of two nations: there is no
fence or barricade to give it materiality. Every now and again a
small, triangular concrete pillar, dirtied and worn, a number and
an arrow etched onto it, announces the international boundary.
In the normal course, there is no one to stop you walking across
this so-called border.

Even the occasional watchtower is not manned, except at
night, as if to say that border crossings in darkness are somehow more of an offence than those attempted in daylight. Or, if
you want to cross 'legitimately' (that is, still without a passport
but with the confidence that you will not be troubled once you
are over the other side) there's a tout, popularly known as the
'borderia', who helps you cross for a fixed fee (Rs 800, approximately US $20).

The guardians of the border, the Border Security Force
(BSF), turn a blind eye to such crossings because the borderia
ensures they get their cut. The most difficult crossings are those
you make at the properly set up border—which is not really a

border at all—inside airports and railway stations and bus ter-
minals, for here you need passports, visas and official stamps.
For the residents of small enclaves called chitmahals, however, the border has other meanings altogether. Abu Bakar
Siddique is one such resident. In 1994 his home, on Indian territory inside Bangladesh, was raided and burnt along with 700
other houses. The people of the area call this the *agnikand*—the
great fire. Abu lost everything and decided to cross the border
into India where he and others were lodged in a rehabilitation
camp for some months.

One day, while waiting at the bus stand in Jalpaiguri with
his wife and children, Abu Bakar was arrested on charges of
being an illegal immigrant—a Bangladeshi inside India. He was
jailed, and then released on bail. Abu Bakar's plea that although he had been living inside Bangladesh he was technically
an Indian, for the territory he lived on belonged to India, cut
no ice with the police who refused to believe that such a thing
could be possible. The case went to court and, until the time of
writing, the courts had still to rule on it.[2]

Standing in the village of Berubari in India I could see, in
the middle distance, the hamlet where Abu Bakar and many
others like him had lived. This, by a quirk of history, is a piece
of Indian territory inside the Bangladesh border—a chitmahal
(known as Salbari). There are 128 such Indian chitmahals inside
Bangladesh. They cover 20,95,707 acres of land. Bangladesh has
95 chitmahals inside India which cover 11,00,000 acres. A few
of these, such as the Angrapota and Dahgram chitmahals, covering 56,15,85 acres within India, were connected to the
Bangladeshi mainland by a corridor known as, the Tin Bigha
corridor in 1992. People who live in these enclaves are, even today, stateless people, without an identity, without documents,
without any rights or privileges. For all intents and purposes,
they do not belong to anyone.[3] India does not want to have
anything to do with its citizens who live in chitmahals inside
Bangladesh[4] and vice versa. In Bangla, a 'chit' means a frag-
ment, something that is part of a whole, but not integrated into
it. 'Mahal' is land from which revenue is collected. The Indian
chitmahals that now lie inside Bangladesh were once the property of the maharaja of Cooch Behar prior to Indian independence. In 1947 when the British finally left India after two

centuries, they created two countries, India and Pakistan, out of one. In order to partition the country they brought in a little-known lawyer, Cyril Radcliffe, to demarcate the boundary between India and what was to become Pakistan.

At the time there were in India a number of princely states—states ruled by kings and princes that had not come under British rule. Now that a sovereign nation was coming into being, these small principalities were given the option of joining one of the two new republics or remaining independent. On the Bengal/East Pakistan (now Bangladesh) border, two such states, Cooch Behar and Rangpur, stayed out of the option to 'merge' with the newly-created nation-states, and when the boundary was finalized, it left one, Cooch Behar, on the Indian side, and Rangpur, on the East Pakistan side.

Three years later, both decided they no longer wished to remain independent, and each chose to stay with the country inside whose borders it now was: Cooch Behar came to India and Rangpur chose Pakistan. This was all to the good, except that each had been, over time, conquering territories from the other and these territories, chitmahals, remained, theoretically in the possession of the conquering state, housing its subjects, but located in the 'other' state.

The result? There were small enclaves (for that is what they were) of India inside Pakistan and small enclaves of Pakistan inside India.[5] At first, it did not matter too much for very few people actually believed that the drawing of a boundary on a piece of paper would have any direct impact on their lives. The residents of chitmahals had, after all, lived within different sorts of boundaries for generations—owing allegiance to one ruler, but located inside the geographical space of the other, further demarcated within enclaves that belonged to 'their' ruler. But then, India and Pakistan introduced passports and visas, and established the technicalities of 'national' boundaries, and their troubles began.

The residents of Indian chitmahals in what was then East Pakistan and is now Bangladesh suddenly found themselves surrounded by people, usually hostile, of the other country who saw them as fair game. They began to live in terror of attacks, of murder, theft and rape. And worse, they had no recourse to law, nowhere to turn to for help. If they were robbed, if the women were raped (and this is a common occurrence), they could not go to the police, for that would mean crossing the border into India to file a report and getting the police to cross the border into Bangladesh to take action. How can the police of one country take action against the people of another country?

Many, like Abu Bakar Siddique, are landowners and live in constant fear of losing their lands. Often, they are forced to hand over their documents. The land registration office is located in Haldibari, inside the Indian border. It is here that fraudulent sales are registered, with one person posing as the owner and another as the buyer. Once this is done, the actual owner is presented with a fait accompli and his lands are taken over. If the owners resist, there's a simple next step that is followed: gangs of hooligans are hired to terrorize residents and burn down their homes.

For the women, things are worse. They cannot even afford to venture out of their homes. If they do, they will almost certainly invite rape or abduction—or both. And once they have been taken away and raped, there is no coming back, for now they have crossed the borderline between purity and pollution, they are tainted by their contact with the 'other'. If the women are able to marry at all, it is often the case that they have to find someone who is not from the area, someone perhaps who is not familiar with their history.[6]

'That's why we came away,' says Milan Burman, a young woman from a chit called Dahala Khagrabari. 'It wasn't safe even to go out to the fields to relieve yourself [to shit]—any time they saw a young woman, they would simply whisk her away. Sometimes she was returned and sometimes not. And if they were sent back home, often the families would not want anything to do with them—they saw them as polluted.' But what happened to these women? Milan doesn't know. Neither do women like Minara Begum and others from the neighbouring chits. 'Perhaps they went into prostitution. What else could they do?'

Milan and her husband lost their lands to raiders in the chits and came away to India nine years ago. 'We crossed over stealthily,' she said. 'If they'd come to know we were going, they would have killed us.' Milan's parents and other members of her family still remain in the chits but she has no communication with them: 'There are no postal services there you see, so how can we remain in touch?'

Clearly, for the residents of the chitmahals, the international border between India and Bangladesh is not the one they fear, it's the border between their small hamlets and the outside world. It is here that danger lies. 'We live in constant fear of crossing this border for once we are out, we can be arrested for being illegal immigrants into Bangladesh! Even when we need to go to a doctor or a hospital, we have to go under cover of darkness. And if the doctor finds out where we are from he'll keep us waiting till he has treated everyone else, and only then look at us. Sometimes they just turn us away.'

For several months in the year the river Balasone that runs through North Bengal in India is dry. Fugitives from Indian chitmahals, who make it across the border and settle on the river's rocky banks, earn a meagre living by breaking stones collected from the riverbed. 'Eight hours of breaking stones,' says Sushil Chandra Ray, once a rich farmer in the Salbari chit in Bangladesh, 'earns you some eight to ten rupees a day. This is our life now. We make do. We've lost everything, but at least we have peace. We can walk out into the city, and know that no one will raid our homes or rape our women in our absence. The most we have to fear is ordinary crime.'

ADVERSE POSSESSION

If chitmahals gave rise to one kind of problem with the establishing of the border of the new nation-states in 1947, lands held in what is known as 'adverse' possession created quite another. Simply put, these are territories that belong to one country but are in the control of another, often the leftovers of wars and conflict, but in the case of India and Pakistan (and later, Bangladesh) many of these are the legacy of Partition and Radcliffe's boundary.

In Berubari village in India, Jagadish Babu,[7] walks me through the BSF checkpost to one edge of the village. 'Look there,' he says, pointing to one side, 'that is Bangladesh, and where we are, that's India.' We move a little further and stand by a tree at one edge of a small, winding road. 'This tree is in India,' says Jagdish Babu, 'and the one across the road, the banana tree, is in Bangladesh.' We get into a car and drive down the small road. Some distance away, a thin cycle path cuts across the road—you can barely see it in the dust. 'That,' says Jagdish Babu, 'is the boundary that demarcates Bangladesh and India.' He laughs and tells me a tale that the villagers of Berubari enjoy telling. 'You see how this border curls and winds,' he says? 'Which person in his sane mind would draw a boundary like that? You know that Radcliffe? What did he know about anything? He was so confused by what he had to do that he decided, forget it. I'll just get drunk! The bastard drank all night, and then in the morning he woke up and picked up his pen, and naturally he couldn't draw a straight line! So he went this way and that—and botched the whole thing up. And of course we have to live with the consequences!'

Jagdish Babu has reason to complain, for while the creation of chitmahals was not something that could be laid at Radcliffe's door, the situation in which Berubari village finds itself certainly can. The village lies in an area that is known as 'adverse possession lands'.[8] These are pieces of land that should, if the boundaries had been drawn geographically, been part of one country. But because the boundary in this case was a political rather than a geographic one (and perhaps because Radcliffe was drunk!), these lands fall into another country.

The southern part of south Berubari Panchayat in Jalpaiguri district, for example, borders the river Panga. There's little to distinguish this area from the rest of Berubari (which is made up of 23 villages), and not only the people of Berubari, but also those of this small piece of land which, oddly enough, falls into a 'different' country, feel they belong to the same area. If Radcliffe had drawn the boundary more carefully, this kind of problem need not have arisen. But then, once it was drawn, the people were caught, unsuspecting, in the game of territories and nationalities. In 1958, the then prime minister of India, Jawaharlal Nehru, signed an agreement to return this territory to erstwhile East Pakistan (this is popularly known as the Nehru-Noon agreement). But the residents of Berubari protested. They formed a resistance group known as the Dakshin Berubari Pratiraksha Samiti, and one of their key slogans was: *Rakta dim, pran dim, Berubari chharim na* (we'll shed blood, we'll give up our lives, but we will not let Berubari go).[9]

Unlike the residents of the chitmahals, however, people who live in adverse lands are not denied facilities, rights and privileges. The state too is aware of their existence and has tried to address the problem. The Nehru-Noon Treaty was part of this effort, as were the visits to this area by political leaders subsequently.

'We did not ask to be made into another country,' says Jagdish Babu. 'Why should we accept their decision just because some strange Englishman drew a crazy boundary? The residents of Berubari have been vociferous in their resistance to transfer of what they see as 'their' land to another country. The Samiti has mobilized public opinion, they have appealed to the government and, at one time, they even sent a petition signed in blood by 40,000 residents to the then Indian President, Dr. Rajendra Prasad, appealing against the planned transfer. Moreover, they filed a public interest litigation in the Calcutta High Court raising objections to Nehru's plan to transfer South Berubari to East Pakistan. The court ruled in their favour, and the government then appealed to the Supreme Court. But here, too, the Samiti's luck held, for the Supreme Court ruled that, according to the Constitution, the prime minister of India did not have the right to give away any territory controlled by India. For this, a Constitutional Amendment was needed.[10]

In 1974 the prime ministers of India and Bangladesh, Indira Gandhi and Mujibur Rehman, signed another accord—this time after a constitutional amendment had come in (although the Nehru-Noon Treaty had still not been ratified by Parliament)—but the people of Berubari refuse to accept this too. They have their own solution to offer: 'Various political parties have spoken of an exchange of territories,' says Jagdish Babu, 'but this will mean an exchange of citizens as well. Why should we do this? No government,' he goes on to say, 'has the mandate to ask its citizens to change their citizenship. Instead, all they need to do is to demarcate the border in a more rational way, draw a straight line instead of this drunken one, and our lives will be very much simpler.'[11]

His words are echoed by others. Abdul Rajjak, Bimal Barman of Chilahati, Anisuddin, Mafizul and Mohammed Alam of Nautari Devottar had this to say: 'There is no need to disturb us. We are happy living here. Our sons and daughters are married in this area, their children are studying in schools close by. Haldibari has a good market for selling agricultural products.' But what of the troubled question of nationalities? The members of the resistance group return a unique answer. It is precisely on this question that they are fighting, they tell you. 'Have you seen the pillar in the market where it is inscribed: "We shall give blood and life, but there is no question of leaving Berubari."' That's what nationality and nationhood is all about for the residents of South Berubari Gram Panchayat and those of the rest of Berubari—not about a crazy boundary, but about where they feel they belong, and where they have shared their joys and sorrows, where they have grown up and grown old, where they have lived and died.

More than half a century has passed since India and Pakistan came into existence. By drawing a border that was based not on geographical features but on religious difference—Hindus on one side and Muslims on another—they thought they were solving the problems that exist between the two communities in India. But borders are never intractable, and for people who live alongside them, they can be easily transgressed—as the evidence of the 'borderia' on both sides shows. And yet, borders bring with them other problems—as those of the people of the chitmahals. The international border means little to them, except as a place that might promise relative safety. But home lies inside another border—the chitmahal—and this is the border that constrains them, one they cannot easily move out of, and one that has become the more intractable with the creation of an international border between two nation-states. It is this border too that denies them their rights as citizens, denies them a nationality, denies them an existence. For all intents and purposes, the people of Indian chitmahals inside Bangladesh do not exist: the enumeration teams of the Indian census have never visited them. Thus they do not exist statistically. They have no passports or identity cards. They cannot vote in the Indian elections. 'You're talking of borders and nationality,' they say, 'We've never had any doubt about our nationality. We're Indians. The problem doesn't lie with us; it lies with the Indian state. For the state we're the nowhere people living in no-man's land.'

NOTES

1. This essay grows out of 'The Violence Mitigation and Ameliora-
    tion Project', run by the Oxfam (India) Trust. Arindam Sen is
    coordinator of the sub-project that deals with the issues de-
    scribed in this essay. I am grateful to Arindam Sen for making
    me aware of this particular problem, and for accompanying me
    on my visit to the areas I discuss here. He has been particularly
    generous with his time, and knowledge and much of the mate-
    rial in this essay is based on his pioneering research, and his
    admirable work among the residents of chitmahals and adverse
    possessions. It is rare to find people to whom the cause is so im-
    portant, that the research they do becomes part of that, and is,
    therefore easily made public, rather than held close to the chest.
    Arindam is such a person. Any errors in this essay are, of course,
    mine. I would also like to acknowledge the Association for
    Citizen's Rights for the Residents and Oustees of Indian
    Chitmahals as well as the Dakshin Berubari Pratiraksha Samiti.
    Interested readers may find two particular documents (other
    than those cited in the course of the essay) useful. These are:
    Arindam K. Sen, *Tales of Nowhere People* (Kolkata: Centre for De-
    velopment Activities, 2001); and Arindam K. Sen, 'Marooned:
    The Chitmahal People' in *Humanscape*, November 2002.
2. Recently, Abu Bakar Siddique has been released by the order of
    the Jalpaiguri District Court.
3. Theoretically, and from a rights point of view, the residents of
    Bangladeshi chitmahals are citizens of Bangladesh, and those of
    Indian chitmahals are citizens of India, but in practice, they are
    often ignored by the two states, hence this statement. Their own
    sense of belonging may, in fact, be very different from the
    writer's.
4. Interestingly, Bangladesh has shown more interest in its
    chitmahals than India. Indeed, given that Bangladesh fought for
    the Tin Bigha corridor for twenty years before it succeeded, and
    two more corridors are still on its list of demands, they have
    been more interested in getting access to 'their' chitmahals. The
    Indian state has shown no such interest. I am grateful for this
    information to Arindam Sen.
5. In the 'original' princely states, chitmahals were small enclaves
    within the territories of Cooch Behar and Rangpur, which be-
    longed to the rulers of the 'other' territory. After India and Paki-
    stan were created, and the two states merged with the different
    nations, these enclaves came to acquire a different meaning, for

now they belonged to the two nations, rather than to the two principalities.

6. I am grateful to Arindam Sen for this information.

7. Jagdish Roy Barman, leader of the Berubari movement and a state level leader of the Revolutionary Socialist Party (RSP).

8. There are 43 Lands in Adverse Possession (LAPs) which belong to India and are in the control of Bangladesh on the India-Bangladesh border and India has 47 such territories which belong to Bangladesh.

9. See Arindam K. Sen: 'Untold Tales of Nowhere People', a publication of the 'Violence Mitigation and Amelioration Project', Calcutta, Oxfam (India) Trust, 2000. See also 'Dakshin Berubari Simanto Samasya O Samadhaner Path' (The Border Problem Concerning South Berubari and Its Solution), pamphlet published by the Dakshin Berubari Pratiraksha Samiti, n.d.

10. This was eventually done, but the transfer was not implemented because by this time, relations between India and Pakistan had deteriorated considerably, and the will to implement had gone.

11. In recent years, and particularly since a number of incidents took place on the India-Bangladesh border in 2001, the two governments have put more effort into finding a solution to the problem of adverse possession. The trouble, of course, is that any solution must be not only about territories, but also about people.

8
Tripura: The Aftermath
Meenakshi Sen

INTRODUCTION

The influx of the Bengali-speaking Hindu minority from East Bengal to Tripura began well before Partition. The Manikya kings of Tripura invited high caste Bengalis as teachers and administrators for the first time in 1280. This was followed by a steady migration from East Bengal, which also received royal support. While the services of educated Hindu Bengalis were needed to run the administration, the hardworking peasantry of East Bengal, both Hindu and Muslim, introduced wet-rice settled agriculture in the state.

Bengali migration gathered momentum from the beginning of the twentieth century. Hence, even on the eve of Partition, the indigenous tribals, barely 50 percent of the total population, did not constitute a decisive majority (Table 8.1). This gradual process of demographic change in favour of Bengali settlers accelerated sharply when Partition in 1947 prompted a massive exodus (Table 8.2), and within just four years, by 1951, the tribal population came down to 37.23 percent. Moreover, the end of princely rule and the advent of parliamentary democracy following the incorporation of Tripura in the Indian Union also marginalized the tribals in the sociopolitical sphere.

The inevitable domination of the Bengali Hindu migrants in the economy and body politic of post-Partition Tripura not only led to the deprivation of the indigenous tribals but also to

TABLE 8.1 Decadal Variation of Population and Percentage of Tribals

Year	Total Population	Percentage Variation	Total Tribal Population	Percentage of Tribals
1874-75	74,523	—	47,523	63.77
1881	95,637	28.33	49,915	52.19
1891	137,575	43.85	70,292	51.09
1901	173,325	25.99	91,679	52.89
1911	229,613	32.48	111,303	48.47
1921	304,347	32.59	171,610	56.37
1931	382,450	25.63	203,327	52.00
1941	513,010	34.14	256,991	53.16
1951	639,028	24.56	237,953	37.23
1961	11,42,005	28.71	360,070	31.50
1971	15,56,342	36.28	450,554	28.95
1981	20,53,058	31.92	583,920	28.44

TABLE 8.2 Year-wise Influx of Displaced Persons into Tripura

Year	Number of Displaced Persons
1947	8124
1948	9554
1949	10575
1950	67151 (upto February)
1951	184,000
1952	233,000
1953	80,000
1954	3,200
1955	4,700
1956	17,500
1957	57,700
1958	3,600
Hereafter, from 1959 to 1963, registration of refugees was discontinued.	
1964-65	1,00,340
1965-66	13,073
1966-67	1,654
1067-68	12,299
1968-69	3,120
1969-70	4,334
1970-71 (upto 24 March)	5,774
Total	6,09,998

Source, Tables 8.1, 8.2: Census Reports

the estrangement of the migrant Muslim population which was as high as 40 percent in the 1940s. Many Muslims decided to cross over to East Bengal to avoid persecution. At present, the Muslims account for even less than 5 percent of the population. Thus the 1947 Partition affected the three communities—Bengali-Muslim settlers, Hindu-Bengali migrants and tribals—in distinctive ways. In this article, based primarily on interviews, the impact of the division on the women of the three communities is examined.

THE MUSLIM WOMEN OF TRIPURA

During the reign of the kings of Tripura, the efficient and prosperous farmers were mostly Bengali Muslims. They were the best in civil construction and in the decorative arts. They comprised 35 percent of the state's population before Partition. No one had heard of Hindu-Muslim riots when Tripura was ruled by the kings. The exodus of the Bengali Hindus from East Bengal increased sharply with Partition and this new pressure of refugees prompted many Muslims to migrate to the east. Because there were no apparent hostilities between the two communities, the Muslims could take their time about leaving. They exchanged their property with the Hindus who were migrating from East Pakistan and left gradually. As they left for East Pakistan, their land was slowly occupied by the Hindu Bengalis. The Muslims, at the same time, could go and settle down comfortably in the land acquired in East Pakistan, in exchange with the property of those Hindus who had left for Tripura.

Later, in the sixties, this 'exchange' stopped. Muslims trying to settle across the border on the other side could not do so because of the 'mastans' or lumpens who terrorized them. They had to come back to Tripura and had to move away to the poorer regions of the state. Even there they were attacked and uprooted. Thus for them danger lurked on both sides. In fact, the unfair treatment meted out to the Muslims during the rule of the then Congress regime, in 1964 in particular, was shameful. From Sonamug to Amarpur, the raids covered all the Muslim populated areas of Tripura. Under cover of night, truckloads of Muslims were picked up like animals and summarily dumped across the border. Children were separated from their mothers, husbands from their wives. Many families suffered during this period. No document recording their plight exists today.

Against this backdrop, I will record the story of Akia Begum and Kulsum, two Muslim women who during that period had experienced the pain and trauma of survival against all odds. From their experiences we shall learn how the lives of the present Muslim women evolved.

Akia Begum was the wife of Dudu Mian who was the royal mahout employed by the kings of Tripura. Akia was the mother of my housemaid Kulsum whom she had adopted. She was born into a family of prosperous farmers. However, when she was left an orphan as a child she was brought up by her mother's family. They were prosperous farmers too and lived in Anandnagar. When they got married, Dudu Mian held a job at the palace. He drew a regular salary and received lots of tips and gifts from the king. When he presented his wife to the queen, Akia remembers that she was given a pair of gold earrings and silver anklets.

When the king was dethroned, Dudu Mian lost his job. As per the treaty between the Government of India and the maharani of Tripura, he was supposed to get a pension. He did not get one. He could not produce any paper to prove that he had been in the service of the king. Idan Khalifa, the tailor who used to make all the royal clothes, suffered the same fate. Dudu Mian accepted his fate quite philosophically and converted himself into a daily labourer to earn a living. He still had the brick house to live in, the house presented to him by the king. When the well-to-do and educated Muslims had left the country to settle in East Pakistan in the fifties, after exchanging their property legally with the Bengali Hindus willing to settle in Tripura, Dudu Mian did not accompany them. He chose to stay on in Tripura because in his own words, 'I just could not think of leaving. This is my own land!' Perhaps Akia could not really guess at the size of India or the world. To her, her motherland meant her familiar courtyard, her kitchen garden, the shaded path through which Dudu came home in the late afternoon. Yet because of her love for all these things she never stepped out of her homeland. She never even visited Bangladesh.

When the refugees started to encroach on their land, they had to give up their brick house. The papers of ownership of this house were in the name of the king and hence they could not sell the property. People just took away their home. They moved on to Shivnagar to live in a cottage made of split cane. This was the time when the Congress regime launched its eviction drive against the Muslims, who lived out those days in constant fear. When the police trucks came at night, they used to hide in the homes of their friends and neighbours. Who were these friends? They were the tribals of Tripura who had always been on good terms with the Bengali Muslims. Those days of horror passed, yet Dudu Mia and Akia could not prolong their stay in Shivnagar.

'Why? Did the people threaten to beat you up?'
'No. It was something subtle which made us feel unwanted. We would be abused at the slightest pretext. . . . People started to encroach on our land too . . . '

They left with the feeling of insecurity common among minority communities. Thereafter, they built a hut of mud and cane at Aralia, on the banks of the river Haora. Luckily they could sell their house this time, albeit for a pittance. Those days, poor Muslims were flocking to Aralia to build makeshift homes and huddle together to gain some small measure of relief from insecurity. This place is known as Sheikhpatty even today. This is where Akia spent the last phase of her life.

Akia's brother-in-law, in the meanwhile, had gone to settle in Bangladesh. He was cheated of his property and had to come back home. He came back with a young widow and her child. This child was Kulsum. He married the woman and had two children, Renu and Idris. When he died of tetanus, his widow built a fresh hut for herself and left the children with Akia. Thus the childless Akia came to be the mother of three children. Dudu had voiced his displeasure at her adopting Kulsum. He said, 'Renu and Idris are our own flesh and blood. But Kulsum does not belong to our family.'

'I am not your flesh and blood either. I have no blood ties with either Idris or Renu. Yet if I can be your wife and the "Bari-Ma" of Idris and Renu then I can be a mother to Kulsum too,' was Akia's firm reply. From then on Akia became the mother of Kulsum. Abject poverty kept Kulsum away from

school. The other girls used to talk of catching a boy and settling down. This was the atmosphere of the place. In Akia's
words, 'I was born into such a good family. And this is what I
had to see during my latter days. Yet Kulsum could sew well.
The Waqf Board had given her a sewing machine.'

Even as Akia struggled to educate Kulsum to the best of
her abilities, her natural mother got her married off to a married man in Bangladesh. She did this with the help of her brothers who had settled there. While giving birth to a stillborn child
in Bangladesh Kulsum lost the use of her limbs. What use could
a crippled wife be? Her husband smothered her breath one
night with a pillow and buried her. When Akia heard of this,
she experienced the death of her second self.

Illiteracy bred of poverty and unhealthy environment, the
death of one's hopes and dreams, life torn by anguish and
pain—this was the ultimate truth in the lives of Muslim
women after Partition. The Republic of India could have em-
braced them into her fold. Yet no one had thought of doing
so. The world of Akia and Kulsum was filled with darkness,
only darkness.

HINDU BENGALI WOMEN OF TRIPURA

My first discussion on Hindu women was with the chairperson
of the Women's Commission and CPM State Committee Member,
Manjulika Basu. While her original home was in East Bengal, she
had settled in Tripura well before Partition. Her father was a
lawyer. She told me that in their circle it had become customary for girls to be educated, although from childhood they were
also prepared for marriage. In her words,

> 'However, after becoming a schoolteacher I could persuade
> my family that I would not marry. Moreover, I was in active
> politics. For such women a degree of change and a special
> state of mind were inevitable. Partition brought us no loss.
> Jobs were available for the educated. The arrival of the refu-
> gees did not immediately change this ... But the state gov-
> ernment and the people of Tripura made them feel welcome
> with open arms. The tribals extended all help. No matter

what interpretation is given now, it is a fact that many clever and cunning Bengalis deceived the tribals at that time. Seeing their helplessness, the latter allowed them [refugees] to stay on their land, but after conditions improved, they could not remove the Bengalis. Or they accepted a small amount of cash, signing with a thumbprint, unable to comprehend the implications.

'The refugees had to work hard no doubt. Specially those who went to the hilly jungle areas. Uncultivable land had to be made cultivation-worthy ... Even women had to labour hard. But most of the land had belonged to the tribals.

' ... women were easily rehabilitated in Tripura. ... Tribal people were the grassroot supporters of the CPM. Dasarath Deb, CPM leader and later chief minister, made every effort to ensure that no hatred was born among the tribals for Bengali refugees. Women benefited by being easily rehabilitated, and were able to join the mainstream.'

Basu testified that the Congress had extended every help to the migrants by allotting land reserved by the maharaja for the tribals, by land acquisition, by using reserved forest, and even by forcibly deporting Bengali Muslims in 1964. The CPM also extended all possible assistance. In fact, in Tripura, compared to other regions of India, the refugees were rehabilitated with comparative ease. At least they were not forced into trucks for deportation to Dandakaranya. It is true that women had to suffer as a result of the massive displacement but they also struggled to establish themselves. The social restrictions of East Bengal were not operative in Tripura where they could move freely outdoors and obtain education and jobs.

The same opinion was held by Anjali Barman. Just after Partition Anjali's father had bought land and built a house in Krishnanagore, Agartala. But they did not go there immediately. They crossed over in 1954. They had lived in Poula village in Brahmanberia (East Pakistan), where there were no riots. But carnage took place in villages nearby and they were a witness to it. Recalling those days she said, 'I saw cartloads of dead bodies. It was no longer a safe place for girls to grow up in. We, brothers and sister left. Father was a lawyer, so he stayed back. I passed Matric in East Bengal and Teachers' Training. I got a job in a school as soon as I came to Tripura. There was no shortage of jobs. There were jobs available for the educated. No educated girl remained idle. The girls of our community were all educated.' Her father came to Tripura after learning that employment was available and got a good job too. Anjali Barman is a realist. She said Partition and Independence were due to happen together and they did. There was no point in wondering what would have happened otherwise. But the women who came from East Bengal benefited, rather than otherwise. Those who went to the villages in the hills suffered initially, but settled down later. That is until the extremist attacks started. Extremism has brought calamity into their lives now. She also stated that in 1954 Krishnanagore was full of tribal houses, though now these belong mostly to Bengalis. 'I can still see those houses where the tribal owners allowed the helpless to stay. Now the land and houses have been taken over by the shelter-seekers.' In short, no one disputes the fact that the Bengali migrants, themselves displaced from the east, were responsible to a large extent for the internal displacement of the tribals in Tripura.

Anjali Barman is not a refugee in the real sense. So, to find out how actual refugee women managed at that time, I went to the Two Hundred and Fifty Colony. As the name suggests, two hundred and fifty widows and deserted women were rehabilitated there by the Congress government. Thus there is no male name for any house in this colony. Wearing the white saris of widowhood, the widows in Naliniprabha's house came forth with their memories. Seventy-year-old Subashi Das said that they came from East Bengal and found shelter in Arundhuti Nagar Camp. A son had been born earlier, the daughter was yet to be born, though expected, when her husband expired. He was a farmer. She recalled,

'I came here with father, brother and brother-in-law, to the camp. After one and a half years I was sent to Ajay Nagar. For one and a half years I learnt weaving. Then I was settled in this colony, with son and daughter. My father and brother-in-law went elsewhere. Land and house were given. A samiti [society] was organized. There was training for

weaving, tailoring and catering. We produced police uniform, peon uniform, bed sheets, shawls and did catering for
colleges and police camps. All of us were shareholders. We
took wages. There was profit ... This is how I brought up
my children. My son has passed the Higher Secondary Examination. He has a government job. My son-in-law is also
a government servant. I got a good groom for my daughter
so I did not keep her in school beyond class nine.'

It is more or less the same story with Pushparani Pal,
Naliniprabha Deb, Niharbala Kar and Bindubasi Seal. They all
came to Tripura between 1948 and 1955, except Bindubasi who
arrived in 1942 when the maharaja reigned, not as a refugee but
as a widow and a dependent. 'When I heard there was such a
colony, I came, hoping for a means to live. I lied a lot to Ashwini,
the clerk, and managed to get a card, a refugee card. Now I can
tell the truth,' said Bindubasi, smiling shyly. Naliniprabha came
to Khowai, to her brother's house, as a widow. Her brother was
active in the Communist Party. A party leader helped her to find
accommodation in this colony. The rest had come from refugee
camps. Some wove, some tailored, some cooked canteen food as
per the orders of the Samiti.

'For the first one and a half years we received dole for
food and clothing. That stopped later when we started earning. It was all jungle here. As if we were Sitas in exile with
Lab and Kush,' said Naliniprabha. 'We had to enter our huts
pushing through the jungle growth with our hands. Finally we
were self-sufficient. Some of our sons and daughters are MA,
or BA. In every family there is at least one government job-
holder. Some have all their children employed. All the sons-
in-law are employed, or in business, and are doing well ... It
is the Samiti which has been our saviour, which has provided
everything. But now the Samiti is in the hands of the younger
women who do not work properly. There are no orders.'

The struggles of the members of this Samiti, of Two Hundred and Fifty Colony's widowed refugees, prove that with
adequate government help, uneducated refugee women, by
their own efforts, could achieve a better life after overcoming
initial difficulties and problems. I think that the impact of Partition on the lives of the refugee women can be best understood

from the testimony of the widows of Two Hundred and Fifty Colony. No other detail or commentary is required. They went through the trauma and are modest in their triumph.

THE TRIBAL WOMEN OF TRIPURA

The tribal women of Tripura are those whom Partition affected in the most adverse manner, while at the same time the abolition of the system of royalty and bringing Tripura within the ambit of the Indian Constitution brought new opportunities of transformation into their lives.

The refugee rehabilitation policy of the government and the tremendous pressure of the helpless, uprooted people of East Bengal who searched for a place to live in Tripura led to the dislacement of the tribals who were deprived of the jhum (slash and burn cultivation) land. In the villages of the plain and even in the towns and their suburbs, the land began to pass in many ways from the hands of the tribals into those of the refugees. There is no industry in Tripura. This perhaps was the reason for the tremendous pressure on the use of land. Shifting cultivation became impossible. The extent of jhum land decreased and the tribals who had been deprived in many ways since the era of the kings, became increasingly marginalized, as a result of unequal competition with the advanced and skilled Bengali peasants.

Women always occupied an important place in tribal society. Jhum cultivation, including planting seeds, clearing the soil, weeding, transplanting the seedlings, reaping, trenching, was chiefly carried out by women. In the new circumstances, these landless, pauperized women were transformed from peasants into agricultural labourers. Even today, the majority of agricultural labourers in Tripura consists of women. What is to be noted is that all women working in the countryside of Tripura, whether Bengali or tribal, were denied equal wages. All this created an adverse reaction in the lives of the tribal women who were further exploited.

Simultaneously, those forest lands which had been placed under reservation for the tribals were utilized to provide rehabilitation for the refugees. As a result, the tribals faced an unequal competition in the forest as well, which was their source of firewood and food in times of scarcity. It was chiefly the job of women to gather sticks for firewood and soon they were hard hit by the drastic change. Anyone visiting any tribal village will be able to see that these women are never idle. Either they are busy with jhum cultivation or a few of them together are planting seedlings in the plain or drawing jute from the moistened trees. A tribal woman is also busy collecting food or firewood, with a child tied to her back. All this is done in the intervals of housework. 'Rest' is a word unknown in the lives of these women. They form an indispensable part of the production system of the tribals. Partition however transformed these busy and productive women into agricultural labourers. Later they became unemployed in large numbers. Nowadays tribal women plagued by unemployment, come down to the plains to work in the brick kilns or carry heavy loads. They do not hesitate to participate in any kind of work. The struggle for existence has driven them to the very margin of life.

The picture, nevertheless, is not all black. The abolition of the princely system, parliamentary democracy and autonomous councils for tribals—these measures, after all, have been carried out. There is little doubt that the Indian ruling classes have constantly neglected Tripura in every way. In the entire north-eastern region, there is no state as neglected as Tripura. Still the link with the mainstream of Indian democracy has brought some benefits, even in the lives of tribal women. In truth, Bengali–tribal coexistence and a mixed culture are indispensable parts of the lives of the people and the reality of Tripura. It is perhaps natural that shifting cultivation, jhum and the like should come to an end as a result of contact with more advanced methods of production. This change should come about slowly, keeping pace with the broader social evolution. In the present situation, correct government policy and bringing the tribals back into the mainstream of national life through various projects are essential. Even among tribal women, an eagerness for change, for education, is being created. When the late Anurupa Mukherjee opened schools and hostels for dropout girls, the long queues of girls, waiting with their luggage to enrol themselves, was a proof of their enthusiasm.

A final point has to be made. The contact with the so-called 'advanced culture' of the Bengalis has also brought about a transformation in the values of the tribal people. The tribal women of Tripura have been greatly influenced by this factor. They, who once occupied a very important place in the family and who could be often sought in marriage only at the cost of a bride-price, are now being subjected to dowry-related culture. The tendency of men to take second wives under the fig leaf of customary law is on the increase. As a result, women are being oppressed. In this context, it might be mentioned that bigamy among lower class Hindus still exceeds what is to be found among corresponding classes in Muslim society. As a result of imitating other social groups, tribal society is witnessing an increase in dowry demands and dowry-related oppression. The advantages of the changed Hindu Marriage Law of 1955 and the changed Hindu Succession Law of 1956 have not been extended to tribal women. On the other hand, the influence of the family life of bigger social ethnic groups has led to a deterioration of their previously honourable position. In the same manner, the royal dynasty of Tripura had previously taken over the superstition of sati or widow burning from the Indian princes. And, very strongly, the custom had spread even among the tribals of the hilly regions of Tripura.

CONCLUSION

Partition, then, functioned as a blessing and a curse at the same time for the women of Tripura. While it provided opportunities to many Anjalis (Hindu refugees from East Pakistan) to establish themselves with dignity, it led to the cruel deprivation of Akias (Muslim women) and tribal women. Above all, the hegemonic re-settlement of the Hindu Bengali community following its displacement in East Bengal caused the displacement of the Muslims and the tribals in this State. Thus conflicting though interrelated narratives of displacement, exdous and marginalization constitute the 'gender' experience of the 1947 Partition in Tripura.

NOTE

We are grateful to Subir Bhaumik for his inputs and the two tables.

PART II

Interviews and Reminiscences

9

Partition and Associated Memories
Nalini Mitra

INTRODUCTION

Nalini Mitra (1909-2002) lived in Dhaka as a child and as an adult until 1950. She witnessed how the atmosphere of communal amity in Dhaka changed drastically in the second half of the twenties. Because she was a working woman, a college lecturer and a dedicated social worker, she did not cross over to West Bengal before 1950. After migration she worked as the principal of an industrial home at Chunar, U.P., where displaced women of East Pakistan were given vocational training. Thereafter, she became the director of the Refugee Rehabilitation Department of West Bengal Government. In this dialogue, she recalled her days at Dhaka and described the situation which had compelled her to leave her beloved city. (Interviewed by the Research Team, School of Women's Studies [SWS], Jadavpur University, who addressed the interviewee as Mashima or aunt; in the interview she is referred to as NM)

DHAKA: FROM THE QUIET TWENTIES TO THE TURBULENT FORTIES

SWS: Mashima, let us start with your life in Dhaka. As we know, prior to 1926, Dhaka experienced communal amity. The atmosphere was, by and large, friendly and cordial. Would you narrate your experiences of those days?

NM: We were happily settled in Dhaka. Our lifestyle, during those days, was simple yet peaceful—no tension, no ill feelings. The area where we used to live was Armanitala. Everybody knew everybody else out there. On the whole, the ambience was tranquil and friendly—marked by deep fraternal feelings.

SWS: Well, this in short, gives us a picture of life in Dhaka in the early 1920s. How did this change 1926 onwards?

NM: Before going into that topic, let me tell you a few things. A huge procession led by the nawab of Dhaka used to be taken out during the Janmashtami celebration, every year. Muslims, spontaneously participated in it. Dhaka University, a prestigious educational institution of undivided Bengal, was the centre of cordial and amicable relationship between Hindu and Muslim students. As you might know, the cardinal principle behind the foundation of Dhaka University was the Divide and Rule policy of the Imperial Rulers. The Muslim students enjoyed a privileged position: they were blessed with facilities like stipends, scholarships, etc. But not a single trace of animosity or jealousy tainted the relations between the students of the two religious communities.

However, around 1926, a particular incident in the university indicated that things were not the same any longer, that the situation was gradually beginning to change. The Hindu students during the annual functions used to decorate the dais with earthen pots. Suddenly, around the middle of the 1920s, Muslims started objecting to such decorative pieces. They said that such a display was indicative of Hindu hegemonic domination. It all started after this.

SWS: Could you recall the period from 1926 to 1947? How rapid was the deterioration?

NM: Riots broke out for the first time in 1926. But these were not severe. The riotous mobs were armed not with knives and choppers, but only lathis (harmless when compared to later days). Nobody dared to venture out alone. The Hindus could not pass through the Muslim majority areas. Any untoward incident there was bound to have its repercussion on the other side. Interaction with the Muslim families with whom we were very close, lessened. We lived in a Muslim majority area. Whenever riots erupted, many right-thinking Muslim gentlemen of our locality tried to mediate. But alas! To no avail. Their pleas fell on deaf ears because there were others who instigated the mob. In fact, the schism between the two groups widened. The situation deteriorated rapidly between 1926 and 1930. Yet even then, we never ever thought of leaving everything and crossing over to this side. Nor did we ever dream that such a day would eventually come. By this time we had shifted to our own house near the university, where my husband was a professor. But alas! The good old days did not last long. Amidst the rapidly deteriorating situation, especially during the Muslim League regime, we were left with no other option but to abandon everything and cross over. Even many of the right-thinking, secular-minded Muslims, under fundamentalist pressure, were forced to hoist the star and moon flag in their homes.

SWS: The exodus began in 1946. But your family stayed back in Dhaka till 1950. What was the single most important factor that ultimately prompted your decision to leave?

NM: We had tried our level best to prevent Partition. Why should not the general masses be taken into account, we argued. Under the leadership of Leela Roy,[1] we organized a signature campaign against the dissection of the country. However, after Partition became a reality, our efforts were redirected towards preventing the exodus of the Hindus from East Bengal. Leela Roy set up a women's organization named 'Purba Pakistan Mahila Samiti' (East Pakistan Women's Organization). She became the president while I was chosen vice president. We organized processions and marches in different localities, we raised the slogan: 'Hindu Muslim bhai bhai' (Hindus and Muslims are brothers).

SWS: Did you do any relief work while you were in Dhaka?

NM: During those tumultuous years, we were forced to sell our house near the university. We moved over to a rented house in Wari with our infant daughter. Trouble started on 8 February 1950. From a Muslim gentleman who had very kindly escorted my little daughter home after her evening school, I came to know that a riot had broken out and that irate mobs, armed with weapons, were heading towards our locality. Many in our neighbourhood, in search of a safe haven, gathered in our home. Everyone waited with bated breath. Any moment the rioters could come in and massacre all of us. Two young Muslim magistrates in our locality showed exemplary courage and saved us from the jaws of death. Armed with rifles, they fired some blank rounds and diverted the rioters into another direction. The whole of February continued like this. In March we were forced to take the painful decision of leaving our motherland.

SWS: The next phase started with your decision to migrate to Kolkata; what were the problems, that you faced on the eve of departure?

NM: Well, we were reluctant to cross over at the initial stage. My husband used to say, 'We have so many dependants here. If we abandon them and cross over for our own safety, their mental strength and confidence will be shattered'. But the situation worsened rapidly. It became increasingly difficult for me to pass through a locality of Bihari Muslims on my way to college. My daughter was only four years old. For reasons of safety, I could not entrust her to the care of an ayah and leave for my work. My unusually prolonged absence prompted the principal of the college to drop by my home. I explained the whole situation to him. He offered a solution which astounded me. He asked me not to put sindur on the parting of my hair. This so-called simple solution, he felt, would save me from all future harassment. I put my foot down. If necessary, I was willing to resign from my work, but how could I stop putting sindoor? It is our tradition, an auspicious symbol, so many sentiments are associated with it. Ultimately it was decided that I would bring my daughter to college. Our college remained more or less untouched by all the unsavoury incidents happening outside. However, gradually the trouble that was brewing outside, began to seep in and vitiated the atmosphere of our college. One day, as I was sitting in the common room, some obscene remarks were directed towards me. At that instant, I realized that it

would no longer be possible to stay in my beloved motherland. How could one live in such a filthy environment?
Even the murder of Mahatma Gandhi was given a ghastly
communal overtone. Unfortunately, I, too, had to sometimes, speak in their favour. What else could I have done?
Since we had to stay amongst them and they were the
majority, how could we opt to be different?

My younger brother was very close to many of the
ministers. He assured us that he would make arrangements
for our safe passage to Kolkata. Those who migrated at
that time carried a lot of cash and other valuables since
there was no upper ceiling. Our only resource was the
money that we got after selling our house (the one near the
university). We transferred the money to our bank account·
in Calcutta. This house in Alipur, that you now see, was
constructèd with that money. Thus, in a sense, it carries the
legacy of our days in Dhaka. Obtaining air tickets was the
greatest hurdle that any migrant had to face at that time.
Families camped at the airport for days with all their belongings, in hope of tickets. I told my brother that if he
could arrange for our air tickets, I would leave. My husband refused to leave immediately since he had to wrap up
some urgent work, but promised to join us later. This just
left the three of us: I, my young daughter and her maid.
But, unfortunately, only two air tickets could be arranged—
for me and my daughter. We arrived safely. A few days
later we were joined by our husband. He had also left hurriedly.

SWS: What reason did he cite for his hurried departure? Why
could not he stay there for a few more days?

NM: On his arrival, he said that one of his students (I cannot
disclose the name) had informed him that in a secret meeting in New Delhi (where Nehru, Patel and other front-
ranking Indian leaders were present), it was decided that
just like Hyderabad, East Bengal, too, would be 'taken
over' and merged with the Indian Union. My husband was
informed that the process of taking over had already been
initiated and it could no longer be safe for him to stay
back, as more violence was expected in the future. How-

ever, that plan was ultimately abandoned.

SWS: Well, Mashima, after so many years when you now look back to those days in Dhaka—fraternal feelings followed by communal carnage—what are the thoughts that cross your mind?

NM: For us, the decision to leave was taken quite suddenly. We could only pack a few books in the hold-all. The rapidly deteriorating situation made us realize that it would no longer be possible to stay back in East Bengal. In fact, we were too anxious to cross over to this side of the border. But even then, after so many years, my heart still weeps for Dhaka. How can I ever forget my motherland? I still crave to go back there.

NOTE

1. Leela Roy (*nee* Nag) (1900-1970), was born in Sylhet, now in Bangladesh, and educated at Bethune College, Kolkata, obtaining her MA from the University of Dhaka. In 1923 she founded the Deepali Sangha of women revolutionaries, and in 1926 the Deepali Chatri Sangha, the first organization of women's students in India. In 1939 she joined Sree Sangha, a revolutionary group run by Anil Roy, whom she married in 1939. She edited *Jayasree*, a journal for women, and later *Forward*, the Forward Bloc Party journal.

10

Noakhali's Victim Turned Activist
Sukumari Chaudhuri

INTRODUCTION

Sukumari Chaudhuri, about 75 years old, lives alone in her house at Santoshpur in the Jadavpur area of Kolkata. She has experienced it all. She lost her first husband in the Noakhali carnage in 1946. She crossed over to West Bengal from Debipur in Hajigunj in 1950, following another outbreak of communal violence in East Pakistan. Thereafter she lived in Sahidnagar, a jabardakhal or forcibly occupied area, for five years. She received vocational training at Nari Seva Sangha, worked at Bengal Lamp, was in the forefront of the workers' movement and married again. Her second husband was a political activist. Differing strands are entwined in her life: a portrait of Lenin adorns her verandah while she herself loves to hear Ramkatha. (Interviewed by the Research Team SWS; The interviewee is referred to as SC)

SWS: The locality where you live [Santoshpur], although it is in Kolkata, somehow seems to be outside the metropolis, it is so lush and green . . . when did you shift here?
SC: The plot of land was purchased in 1974, we shifted in 1978. Prior to that we used to live in a rented house. My mother-in-law, who was very finicky and fastidious about cleanliness, was facing a hell lot of problems there. Well, you do understand what these rented houses actually are. Thus, left with no other option, we had to move into a half-fin-

ished house. Construction was completed only after we had shifted. Since then, I have lived here.

sws: You live all by yourself. Your daughter or grandson visit you only twice a year. How do you spend your time? What do you think about? Do you spend your time reading or jotting down your thoughts?

sc: No, I don't. The only books that I read, when I feel like doing so, are those about Gods and Goddesses. Previously I used to visit the holy shrines nearby. But now I no longer do so. There are regular sessions of Ramkatha recitals held in the house across the street, and I go to listen in the afternoon.

q: Do these Ramkatha recitals help you to find peace and solace?

sc: Well, I do not know. I like to listen to the recital, that's all. Once I start doing so, I gradually become oblivious to the surrounding material world. But after the session ends, it is back to the household chores as usual.

sws: Did your husband, too, migrate from the other side? When?

sc: Yes. He came over after Partition. I have heard a lot about the violence of those days from him. Those cries of 'Allahu Akbar'. The search for jobs began only after he crossed over to this side. Because of Partition, government servants were given the option of taking up jobs on either side of the border, according to their choice. His father (my father-in-law) got a posting in Assam in the Railways. He (my husband) stayed with him for a while. His father arranged a job for him also. After some time, he (my husband) left Assam. Coming over to Kolkata he took up a job in a grocery store. In those days, an earning of four or five rupees per day was more than enough. Gradually, through his network of friends and acquaintances, he began job-hunting earnestly. His meshomoshai [maternal aunt's husband] perhaps had a share in Bengal Lamp. It was he who persuaded the proprietor of Bengal Lamp to induct my husband.

sws: Well, we have come to this topic of Bengal Lamp. Could you recall the agitation carried out there? How did you get involved?

SC: My husband had been working in Bengal Lamp one to one and a half years before I joined. This was around 1953-54. With the festive season drawing near, there was an agitation for the payment of Puja bonus. Female workers at that point numbered around 150 to 200. The picture had been quite different in the initial years, we were hardly ten at the beginning. Gradually, refugee women trained and helped by Nari Seva Sangha and other government organizations were inducted. We used to fix filaments. The male co-workers worked on the machines. Later girls also shifted to machine work. The bulk of these workers hailed from East Bengal.

Our salary was very poor. In 1955, our agitation for the payment of bonus sharpened. Matching shoulder to shoulder with their male counterparts, refugee women participated wholeheartedly in the agitation. This was a great morale booster for their male colleagues. The agitation was spearheaded by the undivided Communist Party of India (CPI) which was active and helpful in our colonies also.

SWS: We have heard a lot about your radical image, heard that you once thrashed a policeman . . .

SC: Well, I leave it to the judgement of a third party to assess whether I was radical or not. The fact is that the strike continued for long—about six months. My husband had gone off to Sunderbans to collect rice and paddy for the workers and their families. That strike was finally resolved through the mediation of some kind and learned persons. The workers immediately resumed their duties.

SWS: But that particular incident when you defiantly opposed the police?

SC: During the agitation and the strike, the proprietors used touts to spy on us. Refugee women of Bijoygarh Colony and Nihsha Colony joined us in our collection drive. I informed them about these touts. The girls always responded positively to my calls. Once the police hauled me up in a van and started off towards the thana. I threatened the police officer and told him that I shall drag him to the pond. There was a pond nearby, perhaps it still exists. The police officer replied, 'You are like my daughter.' These police officers were known faces to us as in the days of gherao and strikes they came to collect reports. I tugged at the officer's belt and threatened that I would throw him into the pond. Ultimately, the police van was steered through the entrance of the thana into the compound. I was there, so were our leaders. In those days I used to jump out of the van and block the path of the police.

SWS: This resistance that you put up—with the majority of the womenfolk hailing from East Bengal—where did you find the mental strength to do so with such determination?

SC: The bulk of those who participated in the agitation belonged to East Bengal, they were refugees. But what is perhaps most important is that they lived in abject poverty. For them it was a struggle for existence—a fight for sheer survival. The girls from the different refugee colonies came to work. Only a few of us were recruited from Nari Seva Sangha. The number of women refugee workers was increasing every day. Once we started a strike in protest against chargesheeting a male factory-worker engaged in the manufacture of lamps. The factory remained closed for three to three and a half years. I was already married at that time. This was my second marriage. My second husband and I worked together at Bengal Lamp and fought together to uphold the rights of the workers.

SWS: Let us now turn to the past. Will you tell us more about that tranquil village in Noakhali, where your father-in-law's house was located, or your memories about the riots?

SC: During the riots in Noakhali, although the Muslims were on a killing spree, many of them also helped us in a number of ways. In many cases, the young Hindu women along with their children found refuge with their Muslim neighbours. Not only did they valiantly protect, shelter and feed them, they were at the same time very polite, courteous and amicable. In fact, they enjoyed a cordial relationship with many of their Hindu neighbours. Along with my mother, my jethima [father's elder brother's wife] and other girls of the family I spent a night with a Muslim family. We were able to return only when the situation limped back to normal.

One of my elder sisters lived in Chandpur town. My

brother-in-law used to work in the railways. We were sent there. The rest left their home and took refuge, according to their convenience. Many turned towards the direction of Kolkata. I also came over to my elder brother's place in Kolkata. My kaka [father's younger brother] was based in this city, he lived in Baithakhana Road. We arrived at Sealdah Railway Station via Goalando and on our arrival were registered as refugees. From there my elder brother escorted us to his house. All these happened during the Noakhali carnage. That was around 1946-47.

We remained in Kolkata for around one to one and a half months. But we had to return to East Bengal since my mother was still based there. On my return, I received the dreadful news that my husband [first husband] was no more. I started crying inconsolably. From Kolkata, I had returned to my parents in Hajigunj and not to my in-laws' place. The name of the village was Debipur. I stayed in Debipur for nearly three years after that. In between I went only twice to my in-laws' place. Once, to perform the last rites of my husband. Both my husband and my father-in-law had been mercilessly hacked to death. My father brought me back from my in-laws' house. The second time I went there was to collect the money being distributed by Gandhiji's camp and stayed there for nearly a week.

sws: What prompted you to cross over to West Bengal?

sc: Rioting in Barisal started in 1950. The situation turned grim once again. My boudi [brother's wife] was still at Debipur, while my elder brother was in Kolkata. He sent my younger brother to escort my boudi to Kolkata. My parents, too, realized bitterly that it was no longer safe for me to stay in East Bengal. Moreover, in Kolkata I could get myself a job as a nursing assistant or something similar. The elders of the family—kaka, jetha (paternal uncles) and my father—after much deliberation, decided to send me over to Kolkata. We followed the same route to Sealdah Station via Goalando. There was no question of any relief this time. We reached my elder brother's house. Since then, I have been living here in Kolkata permanently. The jabardakhal colonies or the squatters' colonies on land forcibly occupied by the refugees had already been established when we arrived in Kolkata. I myself have seen how the nefarious agents of the landlords tried to evict the refugees from the empty plots and how the heroic land-grabbers resisted them with all their might. Using ordinary kitchen utensils, like ladle and chopper as weapons, the womenfolk staged defiant battles. Our leader was Sandhya Banerjee. She used to lead the women out of their homes and organize protest marches. Under her instructions, we organized many agitations and withstood teargas and brutal lathicharge of the police. For five long years I stayed in one such jabardakhal colony, Sahidnagar.

Then, I joined a government-sponsored course offered by Nari Seva Sangha. In fact, this organization helped me to get a job at Bengal Lamp. Nari Seva Sangha and many other such organizations were engaged in the rehabilitation of the refugee women from East Bengal; to help them stand on their feet and become self-sufficient. Even Muslim girls came to Nari Seva Sangha for vocational training. But I never felt any hatred and animosity towards them. Our teachers, like Bina Dasgupta, were all made of a different stuff altogether. They taught us to be secular and tolerant.

sws: Do you harbour any ill-feeling towards Muslims?

sc: (With conviction) No never. Maybe, if I had lived in a conventional Bengali middle class family, there might have been some traces of ill-feeling. But I am very fortunate that I never really led such a life. Education, politics, Communist Party meetings, Left movement, trade union work, all these helped me tremendously to lead a very disciplined and organized life. Then there was my factory life. Our leaders—the way they explained things to us—saw to it that all ill-feelings were nipped in the bud. Even today Muslim guests from Bangladesh regularly come over and stay at my place in Kolkata.

sws: Those visitors, who come from Bangladesh, they know very well that it was because of the ghastly riot that you had to leave everything and cross over to safety on this side of the border. Do they sometimes question you about this?

sc: No, they have not till date done so. Because of my sincere down-to-earth behaviour, they have not found even a single trace of enmity or animosity. Hence, they never felt like raising the issue.

SWS: Well, do you yearn to return to East Bengal? What are the specific memories, if any, you fondly associate with East Bengal?

SC: I am left with no such specific memories. Everything that we possessed on our father's side had to be sold off. There is practically nothing left that may be called 'ours'. My husband often longed to return. I have never nursed such false hopes. Moreover, I have become aged and infirm. To tell you very frankly, my only wish nowadays is to immerse myself in religious activities. Everybody should accept that there is one supreme controller of our fate and destiny.

Only once, years ago, in the 1960s I went to Comilla with my late father. It was then in East Pakistan. We had to go through a thousand and one complications to get a passport. Moreover, the journey itself was fraught with high risks and grave dangers. The way they stared at us ... We were trembling. Once in Comilla, we had to report to the district court with our passports. My cousin was always tense: what if I were kidnapped. Things were that bad then!

I have virtually no memories left of erstwhile East Bengal. My only wish is to spend the rest of my life in religious pursuits.

11

Becoming the Breadwinner
Bithi Chakravarti

INTRODUCTION

When Bengal was torn apart as a price for India's independence, millions in East Bengal turned homeless. Waves of migrants began pouring in through various entry points in Assam, Tripura, West Bengal. Refugees camps became overcrowded very fast. Some refugees had relatives with whom they could stay temporarily. Later they had to plunge into their grim struggles for survival. Bithi Roy, whose married name is Chakraborty (BC), was barely 14 years old, when she had to leave her ancestral home at the time of Partition. Born on 19 March 1933, in a nationalist zamindar family in Dhanata village of Sarishabari in Jamalpur subdivision of Mymensingh district (now in Bangladesh), she recalls how as a young girl she was suddenly uprooted from her secure and comfortable childhood and thrown into harsh reality. Moreover, as the eldest child, she had to bear the entire responsibility of her family: parents, three brothers and three sisters. Her trauma as well as triumph left a lasting impression on Gargi Chakravartty (GC) who interviewed her.

ELDEST SISTER TOILED FOR THE FAMILY

GC: Do you remember your childhood days, particularly at the time of independence? Let us begin with your childhood in East Bengal.

BC: I can recall everything. I was not too young when we left our village. In fact, the communal tension started much earlier with the Great Calcutta Killing of 1946. Earlier there had been no such tension or conflict between the Hindus and Muslims in our locality. But with all those news of riots and killings in Calcutta reaching the village through radio and newspapers, a sense of distrust and fear started growing between the two communities.

I can recall how our elders got panic-stricken. They could feel the storm approaching. My personal domain was affected. I was a student of Sarishabari Girls' School, and at that point suddenly I was barred from going to school. I was not even allowed to step out of the confines of our main house (*khasbari*). I was a young girl and so the elders became all the more careful and worried about me. The pressing fear was that Hindu girls would be abducted.

GC: Was there any specific incident which created such panic? Any assault, abduction, plunder?

BC: Rumours began to float that our house would be attacked. Soon we found our house surrounded by the Ansars. They were supposed to protect us, but actually they played a very destructive role. It is true that a number of girls of Hindu families in nearby areas could not be found. Some of these abducted girls were often sent back after three or four days. [A streak of silence. With a little pause and hesitation, she continued in a hushed voice.] I still remember a specific case. The girl belonged to a well-off family, used to study in my school. Yes, her name was Jyotsna. Her house was attacked, most of the family members were killed and she herself was kidnapped and gangraped. Later she became a complete lunatic.

GC: Was this just before Partition?

BC: Yes, in 1946. Let me recall another incident, Ghetu, my neighbour, used to work with my jethamashay [elder paternal uncle]. His wife was travelling with his son to Calcutta in the Surma Mail. The son was butchered and the wife stabbed to death. The particular train shuttled back with the stabbed body of Ghetu's wife. There were several such cases. This means violence and bloodshed began well before Partition and the more we heard about it, the more we felt nervous.

GC: When did you finally come to this side, to Calcutta, and how?

BC: It was in December 1946. My mamu (eldest maternal uncle) used to work in the military. A Muslim clerk, Panna, managed to secretly send a telegram to mamu with the news of our departure. So, accordingly, mamu arrived at Sealdah Station with a military truck. My youngest aunt was dressed up in borkha and I was clad in a bride's dress. When we came out of the train, we found thirty-seven of our family members were the only ones to get off. A dreadful silence engulfed the entire station. Calcutta seemed to be deadly quiet at that time. Slogans like 'Allah ho Akbar' from one side and 'Bande Mataram' from the other could be heard at a distance.

GC: But was that your final return from East Bengal or like many others did you go back to East Bengal again?

BC: Yes. We went back in 1947. Jethamashay was seriously ill, down with cancer. He wanted to breathe his last in his ancestral home. We were there once again when Pakistan's first Independence Day was celebrated on 14th August 1947. We wanted to stay back in our ancestral home. But the situation deteriorated, terrible riots broke out. Fortunately, a few Muslim students guarded us six brothers and sisters and brought us safely to Mymensingh town. There it was decided that I would be put in a school hostel in Mymensingh, but the day when I was about to leave for the hostel, riots started all over again. So the plan had to be changed. Finally, in the beginning of 1950 we returned to Calcutta and initially stayed with my young aunt. That was our final exit, our leaving our native land, our final displacement.

GC: Did you restart your studies in Calcutta, in totally new surroundings?

BC: My studies had gone to the dogs. No school for four years. Finally in 1950 I got admission in Binapani Pardah School. I was in deep waters, it was extremely difficult for me to cope with an advanced syllabus. Thankfully, in those days maths was not a compulsory subject for girls. I passed School Final in Second Division and later did my Intermediate from Victoria Institution and BA from Vidyasagar College. I had a strong desire to go for higher studies. But in the mean time, the entire responsibility of my family fell on my shoulders because I was the eldest. Though in course of time, I could manage to complete Special Honours and MA in Bengali.

GC: Now begins the second chapter of your life. Isn't it so? Bithi as the provider and bread-earner of the family, the eldest refugee sister caring for all?

BC: Yes. My father became seriously ill. When I finished my BA, he told me I could study BT provided I get a scholarship. I did get a scholarship of Rs 90 as I stood second in the admission test. As soon as I completed BT, I took up a teaching job. Though I had got a bank job, my mother did not allow me to take that. At that time with father ill, I, a new earner and five brothers and sisters, we could not rent a room anymore in Calcutta city. So we shifted to Rahara in North 24-Parganas. My chotomesho [younger maternal aunt's husband] helped me a lot during these very hard days. The room we rented used to be the shed for the landlord's cows. Small windows, stuffy and sultry. No facility of drinking water, only a shallow well. [At this point—a pause. Bithidi was recollecting the grandeur and spacious rooms in her ancestral home in Dhanata: a house with 121 acres of land.]

My monthly salary was just not enough. So, apart from teaching which fetched me Rs 90 per month, I took up tuition. At night, when I used to come back from Calcutta to Khardah station, the adjoining areas were dark and dreadfully quiet. I felt so frightened that I used to rush back home. Years passed in this way.

GC: Tell me something more about those days, some more details about your family members. How did they struggle, the entire uprooted family?

BC: That was a period of terrible hardship. I never discussed my problems with anybody. The day I used to get the salary I would straightaway visit our landlord to pay the rent. Then I collected rice and salt. Sometimes, I had to borrow money from Sabitri Ghosh, a well wisher who is still alive, to get the ration. That money, however, I did return to her in due course. But that was not enough. There were times when our chulli was simply not lighted. My sisters Bulu and Mithu simply drank plain water before going for examination. All of them stood by my side, took up tuitions to bear their own educational expenses. My immediate younger brother, Khokon, gave up his studies and took the job of a worker in Durgapur. The second brother, Tapan, followed him and joined the Central Drug Research Institute as a cleaner. While returning from his office he tried to see whether our kitchen light was on or not. If it was on, it indicated that rice was boiling, food would be available. There were days when we all starved. My youngest brother Bablu (born after Partition), five or six years old, used to hug me and ask: 'Didi, have you brought some muri [puffed rice]?' I did bring muri for him and for my sick father. My school headmistress called me on Sundays on the plea of some official work. Later I realized that she wanted to give me a proper meal. I can never forget these kind and sensitive gestures.

GC: When did you get married? How long did you have to wait?

BC: I knew Dr Chakravarti for a long time. Since 1954 we had developed a deep understanding. He had been very supportive throughout those struggling days. He also had his responsibilities, looking after fourteen members of his family. He too was a victim of Partition. He, however, could go abroad for further studies on his own merit. At one point, he proposed that I go abroad and settle down with him, assuring me that money would be sent to my family. But I refused. I wanted all my brothers and sisters to get properly settled before I could get married. I am grateful that he waited for me. We married only in 1967 when all my brothers and sisters had got jobs and our family started having a decent income. Henceforth, things moved towards some sort of stability.

Bithidi has bought a small two-storey house in Rahara. She is still frail but there is a glow in her face. At the twilight of her life she is with her old husband, a son and a daughter-in-law. There are thousands of Bithis in West Bengal who struggled with admirable determination following Partition. Many emerged victorious.

12

Opposed to the Exodus
Nibedita Nag

INTRODUCTION

While members OF the minority community crossed over from east to west in thousands in the year of Partition, some determined activists of the Communist Party did just the opposite. They either stayed back in East Pakistan or crossed over from west to east to preserve their bases and organizations in the new country. They challenged the tyrannical might of the then East Pakistani government and suffered torture and imprisonment for years. Activists like Nibedita Nag, Asita Sen, Nirupama Gupta, Juiphul Roy belonged to this opposite current. Though their valour and sacrifices have gone mostly unrecorded, they enrich the gender-aspect of the Partition Narrative with a new depth and dimension. Writer and activist Nibedita Nag (NN) recalled those days of struggle in East Pakistan in an interview with Subhoranjan Dasgupta (SD).

SD: After Partition of the country you moved in the opposite direction—you went to East Bengal from West Bengal. Why?

NN: The then Communist Party directed us to go east. In those turbulent days our strength and position were adversely affected because many members of the Party who belonged to the Hindu middle class community in East Bengal were compelled to cross over to West Bengal (India). In order to fill this big vacuum some of us went back to our bases in East Bengal and tried to retain our organizational strength there. We dedicated ourselves to the cause of Communism once again in East Pakistan and, perhaps, it would not be unfair to claim today that the Left movement as it exists now in Bangladesh has grown out of our own struggle. At that time, that is, in 1947, I was 29 years old and I had gone back to Dhaka to work as an activist.

SD: You and other comrades worked tirelessly from 1947 to 1955 in East Pakistan, you challenged the hostile rulers. Could you recollect those days?

NN: Just before we left for East Pakistan, my husband, Comrade Nepal Nag, had said, 'I think that the East Pakistani government will be quite oppressive. We have to work in extremely difficult conditions.' He proved to be right. After my return to East Pakistan (my son Sujoy was then two years old) I became the Principal of Narayanganj Women's College and in 1948 we, leftists, organized a conference of the Dhaka District Mahila Samiti. In 1949 we followed up with a much bigger conference of East Pakistan Mahila Samiti. Begum Sufia Kamal, Monorama Basu, Juiphul Roy and I were the architects of this conference held at Mymensingh. Obviously, the government did not like our activities and it forced us to close our office in Dhaka. In November 1948 the Communist Party of East Pakistan was declared illegal. We had to go underground. But the police succeeded in raiding some of our communes and arresting our leaders, who were not given the status of political prisoners. This led to a massive protest and the imprisoned communists began a hunger strike.

The Students' Federation and the Mahila Samiti organized a protest march on 11 September 1949 to express solidarity with those imprisoned. But before we could reach the venue where the meeting was to be held, the police pounced on us. Eleven women and about forty students were arrested. Once inside the jail we began our hunger strike. The police resorted to nasal feeding, which we resisted. All we took was water with a little salt. At times the attempts to force-feed us turned so brutal that our noses bled. We were also compelled to enter the lockup before 6 p.m. One evening we refused to do so. The police retaliated by beating us mercilessly. Bhanu Devi of Khulna was our leader in the jail, and she inspired us to fight on. We spent the time reading books, discussing political issues, and teaching comrades who were illiterate. We recited poetry and organized play readings.

SD: From 1947–1955, you and other comrades spent your days and nights in and out of jails. How did you manage to evade the police?

NN: Well, we used to hoodwink the police by adopting different roles. The families of workers and peasants gave us shelter and when we were living with them we turned ourselves into workers or peasants. When large middle class joint families helped us, we promptly became the sons and daughters of those families. When Muslim families who were closely linked with our struggle or sympathetic to our cause welcomed us, we adopted Muslim names and customs. In fact, many of us lived for months as Muslims in such households, none betrayed us. Even in those days the government had announced rewards ranging from Rs 5,000 to Rs 10,000, but no one betrayed us with an eye on these rewards. I recall one specific incident. I was hiding in a village as a member of a Muslim peasant family when the police raided the house. The situation was critical and, at the last moment, I swapped places with the daughter-in-law who had just given birth to a child. I lay in the *aturghar* [the room set aside for the birth] beside the newborn and deceived the police.

I still recall with gratitude the help we received from workers, peasants and the middle class. They gave us money, clothes, bedcovers, blankets. Once when the workers of Dhakeswari Mill came to know that we had no quilts, they sent us what we needed. Grandmothers and aunts gave us utensils. Indeed, after the exodus of the Hindus, we depended on our Muslim friends.

SD: How would you evaluate the political significance and impact of your struggle in East Pakistan?

NN: We did contribute to the historic Bhasha Andolan [the Language movement] in a significant way. To a large extent we provided the ideological base of this movement. Even later, the leftist parties of East Pakistan played a crucial role in the liberation struggle of 1971, and these parties and their leaders emerged out of our movement. There is no denying the fact that Partition dealt a severe blow to the Communist Party in East Pakistan, but our intervention prevented its eclipse. We kept the flag flying and then others took it up.

We did the right thing by moving in the opposite direction, that is, by going from west to east. Had we not done so and preserved the hold of the Party under the most oppressive conditions, the progressive movement in East Pakistan would have died an early death. We do know to what extent we, the banned communists, contributed to the Bhasha Andolan of 1952.

SD: Your and your comrades roles have been recognized and applauded. You have been honoured with the *Bhasa Sainik Padak* [medal for participation in the language struggle].

NN: I never imagined that this honour would be conferred on me for my activism going back to the 1940s and 1950s. When I recollect those days of struggle—those were the best years of my life—I feel happy and elated.

13

Noakhali 1946: Working under the Guidance of Mahatma Gandhi

Ashoka Gupta

IT WAS TOWARDS the end of Ashwin (mid-Sept-mid-Oct) in 1946. We were in Chittagong. Gradually, through word of mouth and newspapers we heard heart-rending stories coming of Noakhali. I was extremely anxious about the abducted and molested girls there. It was a time of intolerable tension, of feeling so agitated and restless, and yet not knowing what to do to help them.

On 20 October, under the guidance of Nellie Sengupta, the then president of the All-India Women's Conference (AIWC) Chittagong Branch, the women of Chittagong formed a committee that would engage in relief and work for the recovery and rescue of the abducted women. From 26 October onwards, every seven days, this group went into the villages of Noakhali to investigate about the abducted women, undertake general relief work in the railway stations and listened to the descriptions of horror from the humiliated villagers. They prepared a list of the affected villages.

Mahatmaji reached Chamuhani on 7 November. We approached him for guidance because we had not been successful despite our efforts. Sucheta Kriplani from Duttapara, Renuka Roy from Calcutta, and many more women workers of the AIWC and other organizations from different districts were gathered at Chamuhani. We sat together with Mahatmaji and with his guidance came up with a plan of action. We decided first of all to allocate a worker who would cover a particular police station. Her work would cover all the villages under its jurisdiction. Thus she would acquaint herself with the actual situation in the area and be able to find out about the abducted women. This was my first meeting with the Mahatma.

Following Mahatmaji's guidance, we started working at the Lakshmipur police station (PS). For about a month we examined the various problems of the people of these desolate, burnt and plundered villages. Alongside, we also assessed the extent of damage. Food, clothes and medicines were distributed. But when the villagers were called upon to return to their villages, they refused. On whose assurance would they return? Would they be safe? Meanwhile, Gandhiji had changed his plans. He camped alone at Srirampora village, Ramgunj PS. He called for volunteers who would be able to live in these isolated villages. He told us, 'It is at your assurance that the villagers will come back.' Gandhiji's fellow workers spread out into the different villages. But how could I go and live in the villages? I had my family, my children, the youngest of whom was still very small. I could not risk taking her with me and exposing her to the dangerous situation in the villages.

I wanted to keep my little daughter with me so that I did not feel compelled to return in a hurry. My husband told me, 'There is no hesitation on my part as far as you are concerned. But to take the little girl with you will affect your work and you will also be very worried.' I answered, 'As it is you are burdened all day with your work. You must take care of the two older children too. If I leave the little one here, at night you will spend sleepless hours looking after her. She will be missing her mother. This will be a source of tremendous strain. So let her come with me and stay with me.' Ultimately, after discussing the matter with Gandhiji, it was decided that my daughter would come with me. But I was not permitted to go home. Whenever my husband got a little time during the holidays, he visited our camp. At times he would come with social workers like Sanjibprasad Sen from Chittagong to visit Thakkar Bapa's camp in Char Ruhita.[1]

Our interview with Gandhiji before we went to Tumchor village has been well documented in Nirmal Kumar Basu's writings and my husband's translations in his reminiscences. I would like to state here what Gandhiji's directions were. He told us:

> 'We must ourselves go and live in the villages. Before urging the villagers to return, we must show them the way. We must live in these villages with our small children and be prepared to face any situation even if it is dangerous. If you are not prepared for this, then you cannot ask the villagers to return. You will have to be their source of strength and courage. Till you are successful in your mission, there cannot be any talk of return. Therefore, think carefully before you decide to come forward for the work.'

Phullurani Das (wife of Professor Ranendra Kumar Das) and I explained to Gandhiji that we had come to him after much deliberation and thought. Gandhiji then explained to us the future course of action and the various problems that we might face in these villages. He told us:

> 'Learn to love human beings. Do not harbour any malice in your minds. Work fearlessly and mix well with the villagers. Stick to the path of truth, only then you can hope for success or else you will be disappointed. If any one of you lives in the villages with fear then the villagers will realize that these people are scared.'

He said:

> 'You will go to the villages deserted by its inhabitants. Seeing you, they should have the strength to come back to their villages. You should go to the villages where the inhabitants are all Harijans. They are still living there with broken spirits. You will have to save them from the fear and despair that has enveloped their lives. Many of them have said that they were not tortured or hurt. But I know that is not true.'

The Mahatma went on:

> 'Times are extremely difficult. I had imagined a very frightening and difficult situation. But the present crisis at

Noakhali has surpassed my imagination. I hope that this ter-
rifying situation will change very soon. But we must prepare
ourselves. Only the future will tell us which turn the events
will take. I still hope that life would return to normal, the
nightmare of the riots will be wiped out. Muslims in general
would change their minds and attitude. Until the simmering
ash of the fire has settled and until we achieve some degree
of success in our endeavour, I will not leave Noakhali.'

He added,

'People say that my coming to Noakhali has created the
problem. That is not true. I came here because there was a
problem. You must know that the events of Noakhali were
casting a dark shadow on India's future. But, however, difficult the path seems, I will not be without hope. I will hope
for peace and amity.'

At that time we did not understand what Gandhiji meant when
he said that the events of Noakhali are 'casting a shadow over
the future of India'. In those days we could never dream or fore-
see that India would one day be divided. But a visionary like
Gandhiji was perhaps able to see what lay ahead and must have
been in deep despair. If he were alive today he would have been
even more shocked and distressed by the present condition of
the country. I quote from Dr. Maitreyi Bose's report which
covers the period before Gandhiji's arrival on 7 November 1946 :

I arrived in Chandpur on 30 October 1946. On the same
night, I attended to a labour case on the station platform.
The refugee woman who had come from Raipura (PS) (Dist.
Noakhali) by a country boat was in great pain and was
about to give birth. The RWAC (Royal Women's Auxiliary
Corps) volunteers and the Red Cross Centre promptly re-
moved her at my request, first to their room and then to
Elgin Hospital by jeep where she was confined immediately.
After this incident, I had talks with two groups of refugees:
one from Raipura consisting of 60 men, women and chil-
dren and the other from Begumganj PS near Noakhali. The
Raipura people were completely helpless. The Begumganj

group, not altogether destitute, was proceeding to Muzaffarpur. The condition of the refugees at Chandpur station was simply appalling. The Station Master, station staff, the RWAC and above all the Red Cross were doing all they could under the circumstances. I slept in a railway coach provided very kindly by the Red Cross. Next day I attended a meeting of the Relief Co-ordination Committee at the SDO's bungalow. I explained my special mission to the SDO and Major Littleboy, who was in charge of the military operation at Chandpur. I told them clearly that I wanted to see for myself the living condition and mental state of the people after mass conversion and specially to enquire as far as possible about abduction and forcible marriage of women and young girls. Both promised to cooperate and help as much possible. Then I requested the major to keep his military police (MP) in check. I had witnessed the night before their rude and unsympathetic behaviour towards the refugees. At first, he was a bit ruffled, but later on, he calmed down and I found a very good friend in him during my short stay at Chandpur. He promised to talk to his MPs. I did not know whether my requests resulted in any improvement. Later in the day I visited some of the relief centres and talked to representatives of various relief organizations.

On the morning of 1 November I proceeded to Raiganj via Faridganj in a military launch kindly placed at my disposal by the major. Early in the afternoon, we reached Faridganj PS (Tipperah Dist.) and the relief camp there. Faridganj was a small place with insanitary conditions. There was a military post and an RWAC centre. There were about 5,000 or 6,000 thousand refugees. They all complained of the bad quality of rice and said they suffered from bowel problems. As we had stopped there for a short time, I had no opportunity to visit any of the surrounding villages. I made a special point of asking some of them about abduction but could not get any definite information. One and all complained of the breaking of *sankhas* (the white shell bangles that married women wore) and the wiping off of sindur. Quite a number admitted they had been converted.

By the evening we reached Raipura. On the way, we saw only two homes burnt down. Devastation was not widespread, at least, so it seemed from the launch. At Raipura, we put up at the two-storey house of the Pal family, which stood undamaged. But the family temple was completely dismantled and its furniture broken. The house was deserted, only a few employees of the merchant remained. The army was stationed in the house. The next morning (2 November) I went round the Raipura market and surrounding homes and met and talked to the local people. The market, which was very big, was almost deserted, as a high percentage of shops and stalls belonged to Hindus. Two big *akhras* (Vaishnava place of worship) with their deities and belongings were completely destroyed and looted. Two huge mansions, consisting of several semi-detached houses, within a few yards of the PS were burnt down. One of these families was given shelter by a Muslim neighbour at the risk of his own safety for three days. Now this family is living under some temporary sheds constructed on their own plinth. Here also I got no news of abduction. They told me that there was talk of forcible marriage but it ended in talk only. Until the army was posted in the village all the males were made to go to the mosque for namaz. There was some attempt by the local Muslims to give them relief, but as soon as the army arrived relief was stopped and they were not called to the mosque for prayers.

Later in the morning, we proceeded in country boats towards Ramganj PS. After some distance, we got out of the boats and proceeded on foot. The first village we passed through had the name Karoa or Karpa—No. 5 Union. Here mass conversion was complete and houses were torched. Men, women and children ran out to meet us and the women began to cry. All of them were eager that the army should be posted there or at least patrol the area at short intervals. I collected some burnt pages of the Gita and some handwritten *Chandi*. The next village was Chandipur—a Hindu majority village—very rich and fertile but devastated. Some families were still living here somehow. The army had been posted and there was a refugee centre, sheltering about 4000 people. Mr. R. Gupta visited the village on 3 November. RWAC was opening a medical centre soon.

By 4 p.m. we reached Ramganj PS after walking six to seven miles. At Ramganj there were about 10,000 to 12,000 refugees and even more were continually pouring in. Ramganj was a big place and conditions were better there than at Faridganj but still there was a limit to its capacity. There was a military post and an RWAC centre. On 2 November R. Gupta went towards Dasghara to investigate. About 300 refugees followed him to Ramganj. Though he had an armed Inspector of Police and several armed guards with him, his party was attacked thrice by a big crowd. According to the inspector, whom I met the next day, they had to fire on the mob repeatedly and approximately 30 hooligans were killed.

We proceeded to Lamchar on the 3 November afternoon and reached the village in about two hours time. Barring three big pucca buildings almost all other houses had been burnt down. These people had very bravely defended themselves with whatever they had and there was no conversion here. Two or three young men risked their lives and came to Ramganj to inform the police station and get armed help. They lay hidden in mud and water during during the day and took two days to reach Ramganj. Lamchar village was lucky enough to get armed help the day after the terrible incident in Karpara at Rai Saheb Rajendralal Roy's house.[2] There were three refugee camps in the three undamaged houses sheltering two to three thousand people. There was a military post in the village and an RWAC centre was to open within a day or two.

Later in the afternoon we visited the scene of devastation at Karpara, which had, perhaps, no parallel. Rai Saheb's house, a big well built pucca building, was completely destroyed. The big rafters were reduced to charcoal. What happened here is well known. Four women related to the family had been abducted and had not yet been traced. One of them was seven months' pregnant, and another was a young girl aged about eight. A young married girl of a neighbouring family was also missing and yet untraced. This information was given to me by reliable people. We later drew up lists of names of young women and girls, as young as nine, who were abducted, molested or forcibly married, giving as much detail as possible. Some of them were restored to their families.

Three hours before we visited Karpara, there was an attack on a party of refugees who were going to Lamchar with military escort and 25 volunteers. The military had to open fire twice: once at 12.30 and later at 2 p.m. When we were passing Karpara on our way to Lamchar we did not notice the attack or the shooting because of the dense vegetation. I talked to the police inspector and the subedar at Lamchar who had fired the shots. Karpara remained totally unprotected and its people were in grave danger.

We returned to Ramganj in the evening and proceeded to Hajiganj the same night. No more incidents occurred.

Pressing needs are

(i)   Search parties for abducted women.
(ii)   Forming volunteer corps, patrol areas with armed guards.
(iii) Posting of more military personnel.
(iv)   Reassuring people that they are still Hindus.
(v)   Reestablishing them in their own homesteads by putting up huts as soon as possible
(vi)   Making arrangements for reaping the aman crop immediately and giving it to the rightful owners.

As Gandhiji had warned us, Noakhali cast a shadow that stretched to the partition of India. Like many who were fighting for a free, independent India, we could not believe what was happening.

OUR LAST DAYS IN NOAKHALI BEFORE PARTITION

Gandhiji was not in favour of partitioning India. In the last prayer meeting held on 28 February 1947, in Haimchar, Comilla, on his way to Bihar, he told us that he would like to come back to Noakhali to complete the task he had undertaken: the cause of Hindu–Muslim amity. His four-month stay in that part of East Bengal which had witnessed the mad days of loot, arson, conversion and killing of peaceful neighbours was coming to a close. The next morning he was proceeding to the riot-affected areas of Bihar where communal frenzy had taken toll of innocent lives of the Muslim community. One could see that he was deeply moved and grieved. He felt that his physical presence in Bihar at that moment would halt the madness for retaliation and restore peace, and ultimately good sense would gain strength. He hoped that we would carry on with the task entrusted to us and would not leave our work at that stage in Noakhali. Scores of workers like us, who remained in Noakhali in those days to spread Gandhiji's message of love and peace and worked for the rehabilitation of the utterly destitute people who lost their hearth and home, had to face a challenge. With him there, it had been easy. His promise to return to Noakhali was a great source of encouragement for us.

But the restoration of peace in Bihar was followed by a series of riots in Punjab and the country was facing a terrible crisis. Gandhiji moved from Bihar to Delhi. His prayer meeting message remained unheeded. In the affected areas people ignored the appeal for a change of heart. Nobody was willing to listen to his lone voice of appeal! The situation was going from bad to worse as the decision to partition the country was about to be announced. We in Noakhali were shocked to hear the declaration on 3 June 1947 over the radio. Naturally, we were not prepared for such a drastic decision. We faced a situation when all the work done during the past few months in restoring communal harmony was shattered by the declaration to partition the country. Our workers were heartbroken! The subsequent history is known to all of us, but nobody could visualize or predict the exodus of humanity from both ends of the same country on such a massive scale where the two communities had lived side by side for centuries. I can still hear the sad voice of Gandhiji telling us in Noakhali: 'It is like a bad dream—a nightmare. Unless you work hard, our Motherland will face a disastrous fate.'

NOTES

1. A. V. Thakkar Bapa, General Secretary of Harijan Sevak Sangh, and a member of Gandhiji's team at Noakhali.
2. Rajendralal Roy, zamindar, had trusted his Muslim subjects who were peasants. When the latter attacked his house, he came down to talk to them. They beheaded him and then impaled his head on a spear and brandished it in the village.

14

Partition: A Diary

Suhasini Das

INTRODUCTION

Suhasini Das (born 1915 in Jagannathpur village in Sunamganj district, East Bengal) is a legendary figure. Social worker and Gandhian activist, she refused to cross over from Sylhet to India in 1947. Before that she had taken part in the Non Cooperation and Quit India movements. Later she worked tirelessly for the cause of secularism, Bengali nationalism and the rights of tea garden workers. Revered as 'Mother' in Bangladesh, Suhasini Das experienced the incorporation of Sylhet into East Pakistan in 1947 following a referendum. In her diary she kept an account of those tense days and nights. Kumkum Chakravarti has translated a part of that day-to-day account which recalls the tragic drama and suspense of Partition.

14.7.1947

The results of the referendum have been announced. The District of Srihatta [Sylhet] is to go to East Bengal. We must accept the decision of the majority. I did not know whether it would be proper to go out. I stayed at home the whole day. At night I talked with the neighbours. They were all worried that the [Muslim] League could be planning some mischief. They were especially worried about protecting the womenfolk.

18.7.1947

We met at the home of Purnendu Kishore Sengupta at Puran Lane.[1] Quite a few people had come. A Central Committee was formed consisting only of women volunteers. The publicity and volunteer departments were made over to me. The Chairperson was Nalini Chaudhury. We were told to move from home to home to make sure that folks stayed on in the new state. If we did not stand by them now, we would have betrayed their trust. What is politics but the welfare of the people?

19.7.1947

We met people and told them that they should stay on in their homes without fear. The law and order situation was worsening. The exuberance of the Muslim League at the creation of Pakistan sounded like threats to the minority community.

20. 7.1947

Today, all of us, men and women, met at Chauhatta. We all spoke the same words. The news from the villages was not encouraging. No one could imagine that one day we would be facing a situation like this. The beautiful relationship between the Hindus and Muslims was deteriorating day by day. The Muslim League was going about telling people that only Muslims would be welcome in the new nation. The others were dispensable.

22.7.1947

In every locality of the city of Srihatta, the volunteers had proper communication channels in place. Today we had a meeting at Telihaore. I noticed a change in the morale of the people. They were not feeling secure. They did not know what to do and could not decide on a possible destination. They had never thought on these lines before.

23.7.1947

I moved throughout the city today and organized the volunteers. In case of any untoward incident, they were trained to do what was necessary to save lives and simultaneously inform the other members of the organization. At dusk, I called the people from Jamtala, my locality, and had a meeting in my home.

25.7.1947

No one would understand the mental agony which the Hindus suffered at this time. How could anyone happily leave behind his home where his forefathers had lived for years? I was deeply distressed today. The people of the weaver community were moving away. I went there to instil some courage in them. I don't know whether I will be able to convince them anymore. I found out from certain families that people were leaving the villages and crowding into the cities. They would have felt assured if members of the Muslim League had promised protection to them. The League members are not interested in doing so.

26.7.1947

Panic is spreading wide. Our work has increased. It was decided to continue with our work of convincing people of their safety till the 30th July.

01.8.1947

I joined a discussion in the Girls' School. The faces had lost their smiles. I felt more and more troubled. We discussed the present situation.

03.8.1947

Today a meeting of the Congress Committee was held. The leaders discussed all possible situations. The Britishers were deliberately fostering discord between the two communities. This rift could become permanent.

05.8.1947

I travelled to all parts of the city today and met many people.*
Every person seemed to be troubled.

07.8.1947

I went to the dentist's house today and found many people of
the locality gathered there. They were determined to leave in a
few days. When I tried to persuade them to stay back, I was
rebuked. They started abusing the Congress Party too. They were
holding the Party responsible for this tension. Why did they
agree to a popular vote? Why didn't they stop this?

13. 8.1947

When I went to the Girls' school today I found that they were
all leaving. When people close to me decided to leave Sylhet,
tears flooded my eyes. I would never meet them again! People
were leaving Pakistan in search of safe havens elsewhere. The
empty houses stared back at us in despair. The houses which
had been well lit only yesterday were pitch black today. Some
thieves were freely looting these empty houses. Nobody
stopped them.

14.8.1947

I met the women living in my neighbourhood, Jamtala, and at
Mirza Jangal and Taltola today. Our country had become independent at last! I could not see happiness on any face. I found
out that many had left already. The ones behind were living in
constant panic. I told them that if there was any trouble, they
should all converge to the same place. The safe zone would be
made known by blowing conchshells.

15.8.1947

I did not go anywhere today. I spent the day fasting and spinning yarn. Today in the morning I talked with Liladi. She had
come to see me. I met Binode Babu in the evening. I got some

news of the outside world then. Independence Day was celebrated in a lifeless manner here.

16.8.1947

Today is the first day of the newly created nation of Pakistan. At night I met Durgesh Kumar Deb and Nikunjabehari Goswami. I spent the whole day doing my own work. I must stop more people from leaving the city. We are here now and will be here tomorrow too. This should spread some assurance among them.

17.8.1947

The stillness of the city makes everyone an alien. Nobody is talking today. Everyone seemed to be assessing the situation silently. I went to the house of Charushila Deb in Mirza Jangal. I met Sumati Majumder, Liladi, Shobhadi and many others there. They were all worried about the future. When Durgeshda came at night, we heard everything.

19.8.1947

I went to the office of the Mahila Sangh today. We decided once again to continue working as before. I went to the house of the woman leader Kiran Shashi Devi. I noticed a strange lassitude among the volunteers today. They were perhaps all worried about the future.

30.8.1947

I left at 9 a.m. to visit the Shamsher Nagar Tea Garden. The people here too were tense. From there I went to the Kanihati and Chatlapur Tea Gardens and held meetings. I told the people to continue staying on in their own land. I told them to keep their minds pure. Most of the labourers were drunk. I told them to give up these bad habits. I spent the night at the Chatlapur Tea Garden.

31.8.1947

I left Chatlapur at 5 a.m. to reach another ashram far away.
People in the villages too were leaving. The minority Hindus
who owned prime land were the worst hit and they were being
threatened so that they would leave.

5..9.1947

After a few days of work outside, I returned to Sylhet today.
Although no major mishap had befallen people here they were
still tense and anxious.

6.9.1947

I joined the Ladies Meeting today. I attended the meeting at
Meerabazar in the afternoon.

24.9.1947

I accompanied Prabhat Choudhury and Bani at 11 a.m. when
they left by steamer for Rajanagar. We have a wing of our organization there. We had to stay there for sometime to encourage
the people by our presence. We could not afford to take it easy
and while away our time at home. We had to dispel the fear
which had settled down in the minds of the people.

26.9.1947

The subdivision of Sunamganj was also tense. As we went from
house to house people plied us with anxious queries.

28. 9.1947

In the evening, we went to the village of Janpur. Everything
seemed disoriented there.

6.10.1947

At noon we left for Sunamganj. As it was getting late we stayed
on there. Many people came to us to discuss the current situation. They wanted to know whether it would be safe for them
to stay on.

28.10.1947

I returned to my home after a long time today. What could I do
but go around to provide some kind of assurance to the people?
Till death comes, I must continue with this work.

18.12.1947

In the evening I travelled to Kula Ura. I was anxious to hear
the news from other areas. We heard that in Habiganj, in the
Harijan area, some robbers had plundered all they could lay their
hands on and driven these poor low caste people away. The
government did not do anything to remedy the situation. These
people were suffering. We decided to go to them.

22.12. 1947

In the morning we left for Habiganj. We had rehabilitation work
to do there., Today we only gathered information. We have
found out that the minorities have been harmed in a deliberate
and planned manner.

24.12.1947

In the afternoon we reached the village of Bamoi. Many came
to us to complain of their lot. It seemed that after seeing us, a
new force of life was surging through them. The poor people of
Namasudrapur had suffered terribly in the hands of the miscreants. The source of their livelihood was fishing but as they had
lost their fishing nets along with their homes they were slowly
starving to death.

25.12.1947

We spent the whole day in the village of Masudpur. The people
here too were suffering. The Congress leaders are trying to supply these people with spinning wheels and thread for weaving
fishing nets.

26.12.1947

I went to Noagram today. Again, I was sorry to see the plight
of the people. We had brought very little relief material with us.
We assured them of more help later. If we could get their will
power back, they would survive!

27.12.1947

The rehabilitation work at Bamoi has begun. We helped the
people there. Houses were repaired.

28.12.1947

We left for Gopalpur at 2 p.m. The village was in a sorry state. I
love to work with people. The villagers came forward to help us.
We were staying at the camp and were at the mercy of the miscreants here. Although they were moving about freely, before us, we
could do nothing to them for fear that they might attack us too.

29.12.1947

We reached Bhumapur this afternoon. The villagers were happy
to hear that we had come to help them. They trusted us and
poured out their woes to us. Many of them had lost their crops
and gardens. Their only sin was that they were Hindus. If the
Hindus left, the Muslims would be able to grab their land easily.

31.12.1947

In the morning we went to the village of Uchail. Although the
roads were long and we were very tired, we forgot our pain
when we saw the enthusiasm and happiness on the faces of the

villagers. We told them to rebuild their homes. We tried to teach handicrafts to the womenfolk.

01.01.1948

In the morning I had gone to Agapur. I visited practically every house there. At night we had a meeting. I feel that the pain of the people here has been alleviated by our presence. They told us in detail about the property they had lost.

2.1.1948

In the evening we sat together with the people of Bamoi. Many Muslim brothers too attended this gathering. Those who disliked the wrongs being perpetrated by their brothers, assured us of all possible help. We tried to teach the illiterate village women. There was no opportunity in this village for the women to become literate.

6.1.1948

People from Gopalpur and Nidhanpur came to collect relief material from us. Nikunjabehari Goswami is working very hard to give them these things. Many people who had lost their belongings were living in the clothes they had on for days on end. They were very happy with the clothing we could provide to them.

7.1.1948

We provided relief material to Noagaon today. People are beginning to trust us. We have been distributing clothing, medicines and providing basic education to these people and they have drawn us close to their hearts.

11.1.1948

We distributed relief material to Khora Khoi village at night. I spent the night there and came back to the camp at dawn. I could feel the restlessness of the people. They had lost all hopes of living in peace in the future. Because the government remained unconcerned, the miscreants were gaining in numbers and becoming more daring.

16.1.1948

I went to the west of Bamoi village today. I had got the volunteers to stitch 20 blouses for the women. I wanted the women to learn to do this kind of work instead of sitting idle. That is why I want to teach them sewing.

20.1.1948

I traversed Masudpur this morning and distributed coupons for relief material. In the afternoon, some of them came to collect their clothes.

21.1.1948

We took along bolts of cloth to Bamoi. The women have already learnt to sew!

31.1.1948

After Noagram and Masudpur, we came back to camp and heard of the death of Gandhiji. One day, I had left home to follow the ideals of this great man. I had worked with him closely and was fascinated by his very simple manner of living. About one and a half years ago, we had met him in Noakhali. He had given up everything for his country and this was his reward! Our volunteers were feeling sad at this news. We prayed for the eternal rest of his soul. We promised anew to devote ourselves to the service of man, as he had taught and inspired us to do.

NOTE

1. Purnendu Kishore Sengupta, freedom fighter and founder of Rangirkul Ashram, close associate of Suhasini Das; Nikunjabehari Goswami, editor of *Janashakti*, freedom fighter and social worker; others mentioned were social workers and Gandhian activists who worked with the author.

15

Sonarang

INTRODUCTION

The Bengali newspaper, Jugantar (now ceased publication), published reminiscences of refugees and migrants who had left their villages in East Bengal following Partition. These evoked a deep response in West Bengal and helped to create an atmosphere of sympathy in the 1950s. Journalist and writer Dakshinaranjan Basu strung these recollections together in the volume Chhere Asa Gram (Villages Left Behind) which was published in 1953. This book is out of print. We present an extract from these reminiscences which recalls the rhythm of life in Sonarang village. Eloquent and emotional, it underlines the tragedy of Partition.

> It is difficult to eat, to sleep,
> My mother's face keeps getting in the way.
> How can we talk of them?
> They are far away and yet close.
> I do not eat or sleep any more
> They, those boys have taken away all.

These are the words of a long forgotten poet of the past. Yet strangely, his grief is ours, today. We, who have left the land of our birth behind, can find no peace anywhere. No matter how hard we try, the face of our Motherland comes to mind all the time. Memories will not release us from the pain which comes from this bond with the past. Her wild boys have taken her away from us. We are living in a foreign land. We do not know when we will be able to go back home to our Mother.

I remember our small village Sonarang often. Hope and dismay are entwined in the deep corners of my mind with memories of the past. I suffocate in this city life, confined within four walls. There is no freedom here, no generosity, no escape from drudgery, no gaps through which the mind can stray and find solace. The vast open stretches of land around my village beckon to me constantly. I cannot see that open invitation in this concrete jungle of Calcutta. The strings of my heart have rusted. They will not be able to play beautiful music anymore. I can only sing off key and out of tune.

The history of my village is one of peace. Even today, you can see the flags of Buddhism flying high there. Relics of a long forgotten Buddhist age are still available. The late Hariprasanna Dasgupta, the village bard, used to tell us the stories of those wonderful days when the Tathagata's words of peace were repeated in this village. During the monsoons, under sheets of spreading silver water, the golden temples of Tathagata, play with each other. It is as if Mother Earth spreads out her wings to protect the forgotten past. It is because of Tathagatha, the greatest of her sons, that India could attain supremacy in the eyes of the Chinese and the Japanese. His words of peace cannot be ridiculed by tyrants anymore. The tokens of his presence are now under water. I remember the first time I visited the tiny museum at Dhaka. I saw the statue of Buddha there— placed reverentially on a high mound. My head had automatically bowed at his feet. I could hear within me the words of Kabiraj Goswami.

When the flood of love broke its banks,
It engulfed all—animals, insects, and all forms of life!

The eternal peace, love and compassion of the Buddha could not save my Bangla, my Motherland. The power of his love could not submerge within it the pointless anger and jealousy of Man. Our souls could not transcend our hearts and disappear into the far skies in an aura of lust-less, greed-less love. Why do we feel defeated even before taking the first step? How low will humans fall to satisfy the cravings of their senses? Can no one utter Buddha's words today? 'You are burning in an eternal fire of lust and anger. Free yourselves from that.'

That statue of Lord Buddha had been found when a pond was being dug in my own village! I do not know whether that statue is still there in Dhaka Museum. The millions who had sat at his feet to learn about Love—where are they today? Is my Buddha now resting in peace? In all lands and over the ages, tyrants raise their heads. Will they ever realize the errors of their ways? Can they shower love on the people they have wronged? I do not know whether I am wrong. Yet I will patiently wait for that happy day when there will be peace among all men.

Every time the steamer anchored at the jetty, on my journey to Sonarang, a strange thrill took possession of my senses. Golden dreams touched my heart with joy and I could feel the presence of Sonarang close by. My dreams would be broken by the calls of the boatmen speaking in their own dialect.

'Come Sir, come to my boat. Where will you go?'

I headed straight for the white haired old boatman with my luggage and clamber on.

'I will take you home, sir. Pay me what you want.'

I would stretch out my limbs and relax in the boat.

'Do you know where Sonarang is?'

'What do you mean Sir? I have come from that village only a while ago.'

So, since he knew the way, I could relax completely. I stretched out on my back and stared at the sky. Only a boat could take me to my village. The founder of the village too must have come in a boat singing in joy! Cutting across untamed jungles of cane and hijal, boats have unerringly come and gone for years—never losing their way. I wonder how all of them missed spotting the devils lurking within those innocent forests.

You cannot ride in a boat and keep quiet. So, I started to chat with the boatman.

'Uncle, I am hungry. Can I buy some food somewhere?'

His face turned sad. 'Why didn't you tell me this earlier? We have just left behind a small marketplace. Never mind. We will reach another small such place soon. I will buy you muri and chire from there.'

I will never forget the genuine concern behind those words. I felt that he was a member of my own family. Yet today? Where are these simple folk? Those sympathetic men full of concern have disappeared then from the face of this sad earth? Or are they scared to show their true nature because of traitors and spies within themselves? The death of beauty is a sad day indeed for a country. Why did this evil death flap its black wings and come to settle on our beautiful land?

That day, after sharing the repast with the old boatman and drinking the pure waters of the river, I had found a strange and wholesome peace. The breeze of the river Padma, her waters, had tied our hearts together. That Padma still flows. But how is it that she is silent when she sees brother betray brother? Can she not bring all of us together? Her waters have now become a fit symbol for the tears we have shed after Partition. Padma, also called 'Kirtinasa', is said to be a destroyer of creation. Yet, do we bother to remember the times when she had brought brother close to brother and tied their hearts together? Man himself is the worst destroyer in history. Who has killed humanity? It is Man himself and not Padma. In my sleep, her waves break helplessly on the shores of my heart in silent hurt. Why don't these waves lash at the hearts of others too?

Different emotions evoke different inspirations in man. The Padma which inspired Rabindranath Tagore and flooded his mind with pure poetry also helped bandits to ply her waters and reach their destinations to rob and plunder innocents. She has then inspired great poetry and also cruel plunder? How do both these actions arise from the same source? Goodness cannot leave human hearts for good. There will be an end soon to this temporary madness.

When I see the smoke of chimneys in the city, I am reminded of the old boatman smoking his hookah. The smoke arising from the hookah must have formed into an evil genie and entered his heart. Who will kill this evil genie? Can we not force him back into his tiny bottle?

Deft strokes of the oar would propel the boat forward. On both banks I could see trees and more trees. Like the hair on the head of a yogi, twisted roots came down to the water to soak up nourishment. The tree looked like a still sage, it prayed endlessly while staring at the horizon far away. I cannot forget these images. Let those trees remain in peace. Let them teach humanity the art of giving. Let them bring peace and happiness back into this world.

Groves of cane spotted the countryside beyond. It is impossible to come to Bikrampur and not see these groves of cane. In their gentle care, many animals and birds nested in peace. The first sweet notes of dawn come from these cane groves. The ghughu cries mournfully from within her slim branches in the stillness of the afternoon. Baby storks would cry plaintively at night. Water hyacinths too fight for supremacy with the cane here. Why are they so bent on choking the life out of Bikrampur? While strangling the life at Bikrampur, they have choked to death all the people of East Bengal.

As they came to fill their pitchers with water at the riverbank, shy women would glance through their veils at the men coming back from the marketplace. In their countenance, I could see the faces of my own relatives, my cousins and sisters-in-law and my aunts. I don't know where these well-loved relations are now. Maybe they could not escape with their dignity intact. Young girls are being treated disrespectfully all around. When will my Motherland arise and claim vengeance? She is a woman too. How can she bear to see women shamed so? How long can India last, being chopped off like this and constricted? Earlier on, women were held in high esteem. They were placed on pedestals. A woman shamed would bring shame on the whole country. Where has this mentality gone now? Hindus and Muslims, Sikhs and Christians had always respected women. Yet what has happened to the same men today? Is the difference in caste and creed so important that the truth is denied and men of one community can, without concern, shame the women of another.

I would go into a trance after all these thoughts. The old boatman would stir me awake.

'Come, Sir. We have reached Tongibari.'

Then we are very close to my destination! I have come here so many times to do the shopping! After my work was done, I would stand on that small bridge and just do nothing. Many a day, I would help carry home the purchases of Moti kaka, no relative but a neighbour from my own village. He used to always treat me afterwards to batasha and water. He used to ruffle my hair, smile, and say, 'Ginger does not lose its sharpness when it dries. When I was your age, I used to bring home 40 to 50 kgs of goods.' In those moments I could feel that Moti kaka and his wife were very close to me. Muri, batasha, narkoler naru, sweets made of grated coconut and molasses, used to tempt us to his home. I do not know where they are now. Wherever they are, let them be happy, let them be in peace. If they are alive, I will certainly meet them some day. I find it difficult to understand the logic behind certain things. Those who had distributed the above sweets freely to all, are perhaps today without food and are staring hungrily at these things from afar. This is the irony of Fate. I can understand this very well from my own life. When I see the selfishness of others to share some lentils and rice with the hungry, I am puzzled indeed.

After Tongibari, I remember Munshibari. During the days of the nawabs, this village had been smothered in luxury. The villagers lived in style and without care. Money flowed like water. Numerous temples and mosques dotted the village. In the burning ghat, the temple of Kali and Shiva exist since the days of the nawab. People came from distant villages to the shrine of Kali to pray for good fortune and miracles. Muslim brothers too would fold their hands in prayer before Her. When they were healed or their prayers fulfilled, they used to come with double offerings of goats to be sacrificed before the shrine. I have never seen such unity between these people of different religious beliefs anywhere else. Yet, why did Ma Kali too turn her face away from us? Why was I made to leave my ancestral home, leave all my wealth and security behind and step into the unknown? This temple was a haunt of our childhood days. During the scorching summer we would gorge ourselves on mangoes and jackfruit there. We used to steal date juice at night and fill the clay pots left to collect the nectar with water so that the farmers would not notice!

On the day of the immersion of Durga, on the last day of the festivities, we used to go wild with joy in the fields before this temple. While the drums were beaten we watched fascinated the dance before the Deity being performed by the priests with burning lamps held in their hands. If I could not go home for the Pujas one year, I used to become mad with frustration. The Pujas come regularly each year now but I cannot go home. How can I describe this pain? My eyes are filled with tears whenever I remember the past. The temple is still there and maybe it is still a landmark to the local people. Maybe they even bow in reverence before her image. But that easy and happy atmosphere is missing today. People have sacrificed unity and brotherhood and lost these qualities for ever.

I cannot forget the shrine at all today. Many memories crowd my mind. This shrine was the central point from which inspiration had been drawn for the struggle for independence. This was the first 'office' as it were of those rebellious youngsters who wanted to free their country from the hands of the British. The rebels faced the tyranny of the police bravely and tales of their heroism abound even to this day. Young boys were tortured inhumanly by their own countrymen who were the slaves of the British. Young boys were frightened to stay in the village after that. The work of freeing the motherland however went on silently. Ma Kali is the sole witness. Her swords flashed in defence of her sons those days and she gave her blessings to them unstintingly. Yet she remained aloof when they fought amongst themselves. Why did she become indifferent when they needed her the most?

I remember the illustrious people of the village. Some were college professors, some joined the civil services, some went abroad as representatives of a free nation. A girl from this village first had the honour of winning the prestigious Premchand Raichand scholarship. Yet they have no roots there. They had left the village long ago. They are huge trees and you can rest awhile in their shade but if you want to really have a good chat you will have to go where the fishermen live or to the shop of the local grocer or to the potters' wheel of Bishwambhar Pal. Individual joys and sorrows were shared by all. Their liveliness, their sincerity still thrills my lonely life. I remember that once I had made the comment that because winter had come late that year, the monsoons would be late too. Kali Bhuimali had concurred with my views. 'If a month sees 5 Sundays,' he said, 'then there will be floods or drought.' I was embarrassed that day to realize that these people were really knowledgeable about such things and their knowledge was based on ancient science. Their knowledge was the knowledge of the entire past and was a part of their daily lives. I had tried to teach them about the weather! The traditions of Bengal were living among these people, no matter in how thin a trickle.

Our village would have a celebration every month. Now I hear that it is difficult to find people there at all. The houses still stand but are in ruins and covered with wild shrubs. Is that tamarind tree still there? We used to sit in its shade and talk and talk. My heart twists in pain and tears flow freely. Will I never be able to regain those carefree days of my youth? Could we not all unite in praying to the Lord Varuna once more? In the month of Chaitra, we would pray for rain before Lord Varuna. We tried to please the clouds so that they would bring rain fast to us. Those prayers brought instant and miraculous results. With the strength of a mad elephant, a stiff gale would blow, dark clouds formed over the horizon and the blessed rain would fall on us in torrents. Life was filled with peace and uninterrupted by danger.

Can we not cool the heated souls of men today with the same prayer-song? Cannot the same stream of peace and prosperity fall on us once again? Have those days of happiness left us for good? When the monsoons arrive I feel no urge to go fishing anymore. Yet in my youth, I would get up at midnight and carry my fishing tackle to the river. I would cross the river Padma in a dinghy and go to the canal on the other bank where the fish came to spawn. The force of the water brought the canals to life as it were during the rains and a life force filled the fields all around. I am still fascinated by the memory of it. Let the force of peace and prosperity flood the barren burning ghat with life and hope. Let the droplets of peace and happiness anoint each head. Lead us, O Lord, away from fear and towards security. From an inert existence lead us into a new life, O Lord. I cannot bear this existence where I live only because I

must. The humility tears into me. Day and night, in this small
cubicle of a room, like a faint oil lamp, the black smoke fills my
life with darkness. Life is falling apart, divided into moments.
Like Rabindranath I pray:

> Like a swift and unerring eagle, lift me up, O Lord,
> From this morass of dark slush.
> Place me face to face with glorious Death
> In the light of flashing thunder . . .

('Barshasesh' from *Kalpana*)

Translated by Kumkum Chakravarti

16

Widows of Brindaban: Memories of Partition

INTRODUCTION

At present, 2910 Bengali women, mostly widows, are struggling to survive in Brindaban. A few of them have crossed 100 years and some are in their teens. These women live in abject poverty, with many of them depending totally on charity for their survival. A number of them came to Brindaban during Partition. They came directly, without a halt or they spent some years after crossing the border in West Bengal, Tripura and Assam before 'delivering' themselves to 'Radheshyam'. Even now, more than three decades after the creation of Bangladesh, Brindaban exerts a pull on the hapless and the helpless spending uneasy days and nights in Khulna or Chittagong. They still come, though in far-reduced numbers. Subhoranjan Dasgupta interviewed some of these women and chronicled their agonizing memories of violence and displacement. Here are the tales of widows of Brindaban who came from the east and are now living in 'Amar Bari' (My House), a shelter for the old and the helpless. Some of them submerged in despair, are waiting to die, but there are a few who have been able to rise above their sufferings. Let the women speak for themselves.

IIA BANDYOPADHYA

Aged 88 years, she came to Brindaban straight from Brandipara in Jessore district in 1947.

'I came to live in Brandipara after my marriage. My in-laws were well-placed and influential. My husband was an MBBS doctor. I had three sons—the oldest was in Class X, the next in Class V and the youngest in Class IV. They went to the market and did not return, not one. No trace of them could be found. After that our house was attacked and our dispensary was burnt down. At that point my husband decided, 'We are going to leave today.'

'At the dead of the night we left and entered Bongaon. There he said, "We have had enough of sansar [the world], let us go to Brindaban straight. We shall die there." Since then, we have been living in Brindaban. My husband who died ten years ago used to pray at Paglababa's ashram and I used to chant Hari's name in a dharmasala. We have had no ties with the outside world. No one has come to visit us, we know nothing. From 1947 to 2000, I have only chanted the name of God. Well, a little peace I have won here. Till I die I shall chant Hari's name, I do not want to go anywhere. I cling to my Gopal.'

Anusuya Roy, the caring matron of 'Amar Bari' told me, 'She weeps softly at night.'

GOPIKA SAHA

Aged 70 years, she left East Bengal in early 1960s and came to Brindaban in 1995.

'When riots broke out in 1960 we crossed over to Belonia in Tripura—my husband and my two sons, a few Gossains and I. It was no longer possible to survive in East Pakistan. From Agartala, we came to Calcutta. My age then was 30-31, my two sons were 7 and 8 years old and my husband used to work in the village grocery shop. We tried to settle in Jadavpur. I worked as a cook in middle class homes and

my husband found a job at the local ration shop. We tried
to bring up our children in the best possible manner, the
older is now married and works in a shop at Howrah and
the younger is a bit unbalanced. My husband died ten to
twelve years ago and since then, I did not find peace in
Calcutta. My son was not well-placed and I did not want to
be a burden on him and his wife. I decided to leave. First, I
went to Nabadwip and then for the last five years, I am
here at Brindaban. My life here began at a dharmasala
where I used to sing Radheshyam. From there, I have come
to "Amar Bari" and I shall stay here till I die. My life is
dedicated to Gobinda and Radharani. I have encountered
and suffered a lot—loot, plunder arson on the other side
and a desperate struggle for survival on this side. Now I
want to live in peace in the way I would like to. I left my
son's family in sorrow, I did not inform him. I do not want
to hurt anyone nor would I allow anyone to hurt me. I do
not want to recall Noakhali and my life there. Now that I
have lost everything, my only refuge is Radharani and
Gobinda. I chant the whole day. My son and daughter-in-
law do not know that I am in Brindaban.'

SUSHILA DE

Aged 82 years, crossed over in 1947 and came to Brindaban in
1960.

'I was given to marriage when I was 12 years old. I lost my
husband when I was 16 years old. I had a daughter. I used
to live with my parents after I became a widow in Ubata
village in Habiganj subdivision. My in-laws left some land
for me, which my parents took away. I could not protest
because I could not speak. When riots broke out in 1947, my
parents left me with my aunt and crossed over to Assam.
Then my aunt's brother put me and my daughter in a
packed train–everyone was fleeing. We went to our parents
in Badarpur, from there we were sent to a relief camp in
Silchar. There were many like me in that camp. Everyone
shouted and screamed when food was distributed. We had

to fight for our food and during one such fight, I also tried to make sounds desperately. Suddenly, at that point, my tongue got loose and I began to talk. We were taught to weave in the camp. Fourteen years I spent there. When the camp closed down, I went back to my parents who promptly sent me to Brindaban. In the meanwhile I had got my daughter married, my daughter died during childbirth.

'My first shelter in Brindaban was Gotkunja. I used to sing Radheshyam and earn money. For a single room, I paid a rent of Rs.5 per month. In 1999, I came to "Amar Bari". I have no one in this world. Where shall I go? No one looked for me in the last forty years. I shall continue to live and die in Brindaban, Radharani will care for me.'

CHAPALASUNDARI DHAR

Aged 92, she crossed over when riots broke out in the 1960s. She came from Noakhali district, village Dakshinbaria.

'I was married at the age of 11, I became a widow when I was 14. My husband was killed by his own relatives who eyed his property. When riots broke out in 1960, we came to this side—my one brother and four sisters. My brother and three sisters live in Tripura, they are well placed. Another sister lives in Delhi, she is also well placed and has repeatedly asked me to live with her there. They communicate with me, from time to time. But I shall not leave Brindaban. You see, my brothers and sisters are good people but their lifestyle is different. They eat onions and garlic, I do not touch them. Here I live in peace, I pray to Radheshyam, chant bhajans, take part in household chores.

'Yes, why did we leave? Riots had just broken out and my brother said, "No, we cannot live here any longer. Women will be dishonoured." We left everything behind—house, land and crossed over empty-handed. We paid for our escape so we did not face any problem on the road. Luckily, my father had already bought some land in Tripura and my brother began to work on it.

'I came to Brindaban willingly. Even before settling here, I had come here twice. You see, I am a child-widow, I have never had my own home, so I do not even know what it is like. Hence, I have no craving, no feeling of loss. I am devoted to my Radharani and I spend my days in peace.'

While answering questions, Chapalasundari (she was strikingly beautiful in the past) laughed. She has one wish—to get the young matron Anusuya married to a worthy 'boy'. However, with one condition attached—Anusuya and her husband should continue to live in 'Amar Bari' because Anusuya is irreplaceable!

PART III

Creative and Literary Texts

17

Poems on Concord and Rupture

INTRODUCTION

Jibanananda Das came from Barisal in East Bengal and experienced Partition. Arguably the greatest Bengali poet after Tagore, his two poems recreate the beauty, harmony and peace of undivided Bengal replete with the blessings of nature, and myths and legends. The two poems of Taslima Nasreen, 'Broken Bengal' and 'Denial', which follow, recreate the agony and unreason of Partition in a diction that is harsh yet nostalgic. The two poems of Jibanananda Das are a part of his incomparable cycle of lyrics entitled *Rupashi Bangla*. During the Liberation War of Bangladesh, Bengali freedom fighters kept *Rupashi Bangla* in their camps and read the poems as a source of inspiration. These four poems, in fact, capture the complete psyche of the Bengali people: from idyllic harmony to cruel separation and then from divided nationhood to a thirst for reunion. Translations are by Subhoranjan Dasgupta.

RUPASHI BANGLA by Jibanananda Das

GO WHERE YOU WILL

Go where you will—I shall remain on Bengal's shore,
Shall see jackfruit leaves dropping in the dawn's breeze,
Shall see the brown wings of shalik chill in the evening,
Its yellow leg under the white down goes on dancing
In the grass, darkness—once, twice—and then suddenly

The forest's hijal beckons it to its heart's side,
Shall see sad feminine hands—white conch-bangles
Crying like conch shells in the ash-grey wind:
She stands on the pond's side in the evening,

As if she will take the parched rice-hued duck
To some land of legends—
As if the fragrance of the fables clings to her body,
As if she is born out of kolmi clusters in the pond's nest—
Washes her feet silently—then goes faraway, traceless
In the fog—yet I know I shall not lose her
In the crowd of the earth—
She is there on my Bengal's shore.

I HAVE SEEN BENGAL'S FACE

I have seen Bengal's face, hence I do not go seeking
The beauty of the earth anymore: I wake up in the dark
And see the doel of dawn perched under the parasol-like
Huge leaf of the fig tree—on all sides I see heaped up leaves
Of jam, bot, kanthal, hijal, aswath lying still,
Their shadows fall on the clumps of cactus and spurge.
Who knows when Chand from his madhukar boat
Saw such hijal, bot, blue shadows of tamal near Champa
Incomparable beauty of Bengal.

Behula too floating on raft on Gangur's water one day,
When the full moon of the twelfth night died
    on the river's shoal,
Saw countless aswath and bot beside the golden grain,
Alas, heard the tender songs of Shama—
and on reaching Amara
When she danced like a torn khanjana in Indra's court,
Rivers, fields, bowerblooms of Bengal
Wept at her feet like ankle bells.

TWO POEMS by Taslima Nasreen

BROKEN BENGAL

There was a land watered and fruitful,
People of that land used to swing on festive days
Just as the golden paddy swung in the breeze,
There was a land which held happy fairs,
Merging the smell of soil in soil
When autumn clouds held fairs in the sky.
There was a land of mangoes, jackfruits
Where one could get soaked to the skin,
Returning home in rain then faintly tremble,
Or bask in the sun after the fog cleared.
There was a land—yours, mine, our forefathers'?
Some suddenly halved this land of love into two.
They who did it wrenched the stem of the dream
Which danced like the upper end of the gourd,
Dream of the people.
They shook violently the roots of the land
And people were flung about who knows where,
None kept account of who perished who survived.
Residents of Bikrampur landed on Gariahata crossing
Some came to Phultali from Burdwan,
Some fled to Howrah from Jessore,
From Netrokona to Ranaghat,
From Murshidabad to Mymensingh.
The outcome was inevitable,
As when you release a wild bull in a flower garden.
Two parts of the land stretch out their thirsty hands
Towards each other. And in between the hands
Stands the manmade filth of religion, barbed wire.

— From the selection *Behula eka bhasiyechilo bhela*

DENIAL

India was no discarded paper that you had
   to tear to bits.
I want to erase the word 47
I want to wash away the inkstain of 47
With water and soap.
'47—the word pricks like a thorn in my throat,
I do not want to swallow it.
I want to vomit it out,
I want to regain the undivided soil of my forefathers.
I want Brahmaputra as much as I want Subarnarekha.
I want Sitakunda Hills as much as Kanchenjungha.
Srimangal as much as Jalpaiguri.
I want the sal forests of Bihar,
As well as Ajanta and Ellora.
If Curzon Hall is mine, Fort William belongs to me too.
That man who fought in '71 and won.
That man who thrashed away the two-nation theory.
He can never accept defeat at the hands of '47.

From the selection *Ay Kosto Jhenpe, Jiban Debo Mepe*,
Gyankosh Prakashini, Dhaka, 1994. Published by kind
permission of the author. © 1994 Taslima Nasreen

18

Not Possible
Santosh Kumar Ghose

DON'T STAND straight. If you do, the flower in your hair will remain hidden. Tilt your shoulders a little, not much, just a
little. Now the flower can be seen. Not all of it. If all of it could
be seen, it wouldn't look good. Just a few petals are enough. But
how long could she remain in this posture? After a while, the
top of her shoulders would start aching.

Arati had managed to get a huge gardenia from the garden
next door. She was examining herself with mirror in hand,
standing in the inner verandah, and muttering to herself.

At one point she said, terrible, it hasn't worked at all.
One's looks can't really bloom with a white flower. It would
have been much nicer if she could have got a red flower. Then
she would have bloomed. He is so fastidious—cannot stand
bright colours. He gets mad at the sight of anything scarlet. I
haven't been able to touch my brown printed sari because I was
afraid he wouldn't like it. It's remained in a corner of the box
ever since it was bought. Isn't it a pain that, as the saying goes,
you can eat according to your own taste, but when it comes to
what you wear, you must go by the taste of others, particularly
in the case of women. Only one worry—what will HE think of
it. He, he, he.

Arati spoke in a mimicking voice, but only inside herself.
Not a red or a white sari. Instead she would have to wear this
ash-coloured one. A sari, was it, or simply ashes? It had been
worn so much that it had grown threadbare. A couple more

launderings, and then I'll say good-bye to it. I'll buy some utensils, some cups and saucers in exchange for it. And I'll serve
Saroj tea in that cup.

Arati put a tiny bindi in the centre of her forehead. Had
she managed to get it exactly in the middle? Who knows. She
had the mirror, itself blurred, in one hand, held high—how
much could one primp oneself in that awkward posture? It
would have been so nice if she had a large mirror. It would
have hung on the wall just as high as her throat or the border
of her blouse. It would have been even better if the mirror had
been fitted with a low table.

Now Arati sighed a little. Such luxuries were not possible
in this home of theirs, this room with a tin roof and a fence.
Maybe somewhere else. Perhaps in this self-same city, somewhere north of the level-crossing, in a cleaner area. What was
the name of that area of which Saroj was talking the other day,
where he was thinking of getting a two-room flat?

Arati took the container for the kohl in hand, and moistened her lips to wipe out the greed. Until then—until then she
would continue to hold up her mirror and put on her bindi and
kohl and do her hair. One of these days, the applicator for the
kohl would pierce her eyes. And she would moan in pain like
that bird called chokhgelo (eyes-gone). Saroj wouldn't even
spare me a glance. And if my eyes go, I won't even know
whether he looks at me. Her thoughts were all higgledy-
piggledy. Instead, I'll try on the grey sari and see what I can do
with it. There's no alternative, I'll have to wear it. Even if I
don't like it, even if it doesn't please anyone else, he will like
it. He'll give a little smile, and say, 'Fire hidden by ashes.' Who
knows whether that's jest or earnest. There was no trusting
him—his eyes always twinkled with mischief.

Arati rolled her eyes at the friend inside her, and said,
don't put on so much powder, he'll notice. And if you sweat in
the heat, it'll be a mess. Not that he minded people dressing
up, that after all is women's second nature. But he cannot stand
any excess. He says that cosmetics shouldn't enhance but rather
reveal beauty. Just as we underline the important lines in a text-
book. Making up is the work of underlining.

She didn't have much of a singing voice, not one she would
care to make others listen to, but to her own ears it didn't sound

bad. She began singing and stopped immediately. Let it rest, what would her mother think? Her mother had been sitting by the chulha since the afternoon, frying savoury snacks for Saroj. Her face was heated. But she wouldn't let me near the place to help. Apparently the heat of the chulha would spoil my looks. But I could have at least helped her with things. I like Ma's enthusiasm, but it also makes me laugh. Already she has asked three times, 'Has Saroj come? I wonder why he hasn't come yet? Will he definitely come? When did he tell you?'

Oh, he'll come, he'll come, he'll come—why was Ma so worried? If he were not going to come, then why was the afternoon sky so beautiful today with these light clouds? Why was the green water in the pond rippling gently in the breeze? Of course he'll come.

At this peak office hour, one had to let three or four buses go before managing to get onto the bottom step of the next one. It's only half past five or six now—I'm sure he'll come by half past six. Those who had gone from this neighbourhood to his still hadn't returned.

Arati brought a cloth embroidered with flowers and spread it on the low stool. Great, it looked nice now. I had embroidered those flowers with aching eyes, now that ache has been worth it. Suppose we had many other cloths and curtains? In that case, I would have covered up all the places where our want and poverty show up with sharp, jagged edges. I'd cover up that faded trunk and that unclean bed made with planks.

Anyway, where's the need for such cover-ups? There was nothing to hide from Saroj. He knows the innermost pulses of our lives. Right from the time when we landed up at Sealdah Station. He took us to the refugee camp, after a long search. Who was it who got my brother into the book-binding trade? Who was it who made such an effort and put up this hut in this colony? Through whose efforts did I get my job in the primary school?

All through Saroj. Ma says that there isn't another man like him anywhere. Arati laughed a little to herself. I know what sort of man he is. A large heart, a broad chest—all of that is true. He leaps into the breach to help other people. But Ma has only seen that side of him. She hasn't experienced his anger and sulks. He was so mad because he had to wait half an hour

for me in that tea-shop in Dharamtolla. I was saying this and
that to him, and he simply wouldn't answer. In the end I
pinched him gently with my hand under the table. Then he
ended up laughing. We had been supposed to see a film. He
said that if I had been late by five more minutes, he would
have torn up the tickets.
    How could I not be late? Do I have a car? One has to de-
pend on buses. You are men with so much physical strength; if
someone touches you, you can cope—yet even you let bus after
bus go. How can we women get on a bus that quickly? One has
to consider these things.
    Hearing someone's steps outside, Arati went to the veran-
dah. It was someone else. And, today you yourself are late, do
you think I'm not entitled to get angry? Suppose I sulk, and
don't say a word?
    No, I won't waste time today by sulking. There are many
important things to speak about. Now we have a home, and
even my younger brother is managing to eke out a living. Today
we must come to some sort of decision about us two. The moment he comes I'll take him somewhere private. Where shall we
go, màybe beside the pond? But there's no privacy there. Shall
we talk while strolling down the street? No, the neighbours
would stare. This verandah was far better. Ma wasn't going to
leave the kitchen.
    Ma had not slept, but was only pretending to be asleep.
Arati realized that standing on the threshold of the room. I've
been sleeping beside my mother since I was tiny, so I understand when she's asleep. When she sleeps, her looks are transformed. And maybe Ma doesn't know that she cannot sleep flat
on her back like that. There were a few other telltale signs as
well.
    Arati took off the grey sari and folded it with care. She took
up the sari she usually wore. The mirror was on the trunk, but
she didn't feel like looking at her face. She felt disgustingly hot.
Shall I go to the kitchen and see whether there is any food kept
ready and covered there? Would Ma not be asleep even by then?
    Arati splashed her face and eyes with water and thought, I
really don't care whether you do or don't sleep. Asleep or not,
you won't get a word out of my mouth. For two reasons.

Firstly, I am tired. Secondly, I don't want to disappoint you. The whole length of this afternoon you have sat by the heat of the chulha and prepared teatime snacks. When Saroj took me out, you probably sat there, your heart bursting with joy, looking at auspicious times in the almanac.

Ma, you are older than me only in years. You can't understand anything from looking at people's faces. You don't understand the wiles and strategies of everyday life.

Arati returned from the water-tap and sat down on a stool on the verandah, but she did not say a word. What was the point of entering the room in which she would be subjected to a cross-examination? Ma has not realized by looking at my face that I have come back after ending it all today. Does Ma have any inkling that I am very tired, that I want to weep?

She does not. She shall not. I won't say anything. At least not today. Arati said all this inside herself; it was as if she made a vow on a yellow star in the southern sky.

It was impossible to sit on the stool for very long, since the mosquitoes were bugging her. Better to sit on the floor with feet folded underneath her. Ma had not realized that anything was wrong by looking at his face—but I had. At first he was trying to speak with ease, and was breaking the nimkis into pieces and eating them; but when he half-finished his cup of tea and forgot the rest, I had to remind him. When he finished the rest at one gulp, then I felt a niggle of unease. He also seemed to answer a couple of questions haphazardly. It was as if he had not heard them. Right then I called him away and said, come, let's go out. I said to Ma, 'Ma, we are going out for a while.' Ma said, 'Go, but don't be too late.' I knew, though, that Ma would not mind even if I was late.

Arati mentally gathered together the threads of what happened at their meeting. They had walked side by side for a long distance, saying only a few inconsequential things. Then they had found that garden and that seat built round a banyan tree. It was quiet and private.

Arati had said, 'Now tell me.'

Saroj had turned his face away. 'What should I say?'

'Don't lie to me. I know that something has happened to you.'

Saroj had yawned. His attitude was indifferent, detached, and somewhat hard.

'Nothing has happened. I shall go away from here, I've decided.'

'Where will you go?'

'Certainly, outside Bengal. I don't like it here anymore.'

'What's happened?' Arati had taken his hand and said, 'Please tell me.'

'I keep telling you, nothing has happened.'

'You are hiding something.'

Until then Saroj had been quite controlled, but suddenly he stood up and turned around.

'It's not I who have hidden anything—you have.'

'I!'

'Yes, you! I hadn't wanted to say anything. It's because you insist that I'm telling you. I find it distasteful.'

'Let's drop the pretence. You have to tell me what you've learnt, what I've hidden from you.'

In a measured, grave voice Saroj said, 'You have hidden your past.'

'I've hidden that? Didn't you know how poor we were? Didn't you know that we lived in the railway station for three months after we left the village?'

Saroj had said, 'I had known all that. What I did not know was that you—you are not what I thought you were.'

'I am not?'

'No. "They" had captured you and taken you away two months before you left East Bengal. You were in their hands for two months. Finally, you somehow managed to get free and fled to your mother, and then you came here.'

'And?'

'And?' Saroj had looked at her with a blank gaze. 'No, there's nothing else.' While he was saying this, he sat down on the seat again, as if he was exhausted, and said to her in a pained voice, 'Why didn't you all come away a few months earlier, Arati, as so many people did. Then this disaster wouldn't have happened.'

'No.' Arati said very slowly, 'No, it would not have happened. Saroj, then you would have got a chaste virgin.'

Saroj seemed disconcerted. 'You are making a joke of it.

You know that I myself have no prejudices. But my sister—'
'No, it wouldn't be right to deceive her.'
'You keep misunderstanding me. My sister met a man from your village the other day.'
'He volunteered this piece of news?'
'No, it wasn't quite like that. It suddenly came up while talking of other things. He is an honourable man, and he doesn't even know about you and me. You don't know what anguish I've been in since then, Arati. Just tell me once that what I have heard is untrue.'

Arati had said tightly, 'No, it's not untrue. It's true to the letter. Forgive me.'

There had been nothing more to say. Arati had walked home quickly.

Saroj had begun to follow her, but Arati had turned around, looked at him, and said, 'What's the point of your coming any further? I'll manage to get home by myself. And—' Arati had forced a little smile, 'and even if something happens, what's the harm? Now you know my history. What new harm can come to me?'

Ma was restless in her room, Arati knew. She was curious, and afraid. Why wasn't Arati entering the room? What was she doing on the verandah? Ma was prone to such fears, fears for any and no reason at all. She had received many blows in life, so she could never be secure, only afraid. The doctors had said that it was a kind of nervous disease.

No, Ma could not be told. Arati tiptoed to her room and lay down. What was that underneath her chignon? Of course, it was that gardenia. It still hadn't dropped off? Arati thought of throwing it outside her window. Then she thought better of it. It was only a flower, after all, with a tiny lifespan. In any case it would drop, dry, and become stale. Let it remain in her chignon. Let it remain. And this was the last time she would wear a flower in her hair: he would never come again.

And yet who would have guessed that Saroj would come again just two days later, early in the morning, on a day when the weather was terrible. It had rained late in the night; the open drains were flowing with water; the clouds had not cleared. The rain was pelting down. It was as if every so often a horde of horsemen would ride from one end of the horizon to the other. A ghostly wind would pursue them with banners waving.

Arati was lying down and watching all this. It was the kind of day when even the birds were afraid of the sky and did not fly. They were not flying today. Arati saw that the thin oleander tree was bent over, as if it was protecting its children, the flowers.

At that moment, Saroj came. Why had he come today? Why today? Why did he have to disturb my morning languor? She'd have to get up right away, straighten her sari, maybe change the sari—no, why should she do all that? It was all over, anyway. I'll go just the way I am.

'Oh, dear, you're soaked.'

It was not only that Saroj was wet. He was also looking dishevelled. He hadn't even buttoned his shirt properly. Arati said, 'I'll get a towel—wipe your head. You'll catch a cold. Shall I make tea?'

Arati was just turning round, perhaps to go and make the tea, when Saroj caught the end of her sari and detained her. He said with intensity, 'Arati, forgive me.'

'Let go. Ma is in the other room. She might suddenly come here.'

Saroj did not heed her. He grasped both her hands and said, 'I have behaved like a cad.' Arati thought, I am weakening. What can I do? He has realized his own mistake, he has come in this tempestuous weather—what should I do? Arati marshalled all her strength and said, 'Calm yourself and sit down. One can't talk like this.'

Saroj had sat down on the stool and put his head in his hands. In a dry, broken voice he had said, 'I haven't been able to sleep these last two days.'

Arati looked into the house with caution. Ma wasn't coming, was she? What if she did? Ma would be pleased. After all, she too had not slept these last two nights. Even so, Arati looked towards the interior of the house with caution and modest embarrassment, then ran her fingers through Saroj's hair and said, 'Don't speak like that. I haven't been able to sleep either. It's enough that you have come back. We make so many mistakes.'

Saroj raised his eyes and said, 'Wasn't it a terrible mistake to have made? You must have been deeply wounded that day, which is why you deliberately didn't tell me I had been mistaken. But I know now.'

Arati's voice trembled. 'What do you know?'

'I managed to find that gentleman after looking round for two days. I asked him in detail. He is a distinguished gentleman; as I said, he wouldn't lie. After we had spoken for a little while, he realized that he had made a terrible mistake. You are not the girl he had spoken of. He was embarrassed and begged my pardon many times. Arati, I've raced here this morning to ask your forgiveness. Tell me you've forgiven me?'

'I have.' Arati said this in a low voice, but unknown to herself, she slowly retreated some steps.

'Call Ma. I'd like to tell her and touch her feet.'

Arati said, 'Not today. Saroj, shall I bring your tea now?'

There was something in her voice which made Saroj start and look at her with a piercing gaze. In a stiff voice he said, 'What's wrong with you? Aren't you happy?'

Arati turned away her eyes towards the window. 'The clouds haven't cleared—Saroj, how will you return? The rain hasn't stopped yet.'

Saroj grew restive and said, 'You are avoiding the issue. You keep talking about my going back. Haven't you got over your hurt yet? I'm saying it, and I'll say it again, I made a mistake. There is no stigma attached to you.'

Saroj stood up. Perhaps he had moved forward a step to take Arati's hand again, but Arati moved further away, and stood at the threshold of the two rooms. Saroj pleaded with his eyes, 'Come.'

Slowly Arati said, 'It is not possible.' Saroj said with yearning, 'Why is it not possible, Arati? I no longer have any suspicions! I've raced to you knowing that it was all untrue.' Arati remained standing at a distance and said in a very low but distinct voice, 'That's why it is not possible. Saroj, you have come knowing that it was all untrue. You would not have come knowing that it is all true.'

Translated by Barnita Bagchi. 'Hoina' by Santosh Kumar Ghose, from *Galpa Samagra*, vol 2. Kolkata, Dey's Publishing, 1994. Reproduced by kind permission of Kakali Chakravarti. © 2003 Kakali Chakravarti.

19

Natun Yehudi (The New Jews)
Salil Sen

INTRODUCTION

The play *Natun Yehudi* (The New Jews) written by Salil Sen (first performance in 1951 and published in 1957) is one of the most renowned plays on the Bengal Partition. Though relegated to oblivion now, it was a great success in the fifties. It labels the uprooted people of East Bengal as the 'New Jews' and dramatizes their agony and struggle in a remarkably realistic manner. Here we offer a translated version of the second and third scenes which graphically portray the diurnal trials faced by two displaced families. Struggling for a niche in Sealdah Station, abject dependence on morsels of rice supplied by aid societies, intimidation by volunteers, fleecing by landlords, no privacy for women, abysmal poverty and hopelessness, souring of familial relations—all these bitter experiences are the stuff of these two scenes.

DRAMATIS PERSONAE

MANOMOHAN BHATTACHARJEE (Panditmashai)—head of the uprooted brahmin family who was school teacher in East Bengal.
DUIKHA—second son of Manomohan (Mejda)
MOHAN—youngest son of Manomohan (Chorda)
ANNAPURNA or MOTHER (MA)—wife of Manomohan
PARI—daughter of Manomohan

KESTODAS—a Namasudra peasant who was Manomohan's tenant-farmer.

ASHALATA: Kestodas's wife

BHIKHUA: A coolie working in Titagarh

SCENE II

(*Calcutta, part of the Sealdah Station. A piece of cloth has been hung, in order to create something like two rooms. The brahmin family has taken shelter in one, the namasudra family in the other. In the background, the noises of the station, the whistling of the trains, the cries of the vendors, etc., can be heard. In one room Annapurna and in the other Ashalata are busy with domestic duties. Duikha comes and approaches his mother.*)

DUIKHA: Ma! Mohaina, father—has none of them returned?

MOTHER: No, Why?

DUIKHA: It's really something. They themselves will go out right in the morning, wander about, see so many things—and they won't let me go out. Ma, shall I go with them—to see the Howrah Bridge—they are going—

MOTHER: Since they have forbidden it—just sit still for a few days. After we have found a home and settled down a bit you can go where you like. We don't know when we have to move from here. If something had been settled, I would have let you go.

DUIKHA: Eight days. We have been stuck here for all of eight days. And I haven't been anywhere. They go about themselves—only as far as I am concerned—

MOTHER: Go and see why Pari has not yet returned from bathing. Just go and see—

DUIKHA: She's not likely to be drowned. She's just gone to the tap to have a bath.

MOTHER: Better if she had been drowned. Can a girl take a bath before a whole crowd of people, before the eyes of so many men! Just go and see.

DUIKHA: I won't go anywhere—

MOTHER: That's a bit of good sense, at least (*Duikha is about to go*). Where are you off to now?

DUIKHA: I am going to get some milk from the volunteers—over there—

MOTHER: No, I forbid you. You don't have a baby that's crying, do you. Why should you beg milk? Pregnant women aren't getting milk—and his lordship is going to fetch milk. [*Enter* Pari. *She has not bathed.*] You haven't bathed all this time?

PARI: Is it possible to bathe in the middle of all this? All around there are people, simply staring at me. All the time, who are you, Miss, from where have you come—how many people are there in your family? And the fight for water; I won't bathe.

MOTHER: All right, all right, don't bathe. You won't die if you don't take a bath for two days. It's just your luck. We are camping in the street like gypsies—I never thought we would come to this. (A volunteer *enters*) What's this? What's this? Why are you coming in—

DUIKHA: Can't you see, cooking is being done here? Why have you come in, wearing shoes—

VOLUNTEER: Shut up. Who is Manomohan Bhattacharjee? How is he related to you?

DUIKHA: He's my father.

VOLUNTEER: Where has he gone?

DUIKHA: Do you think he has told us, that we can tell you?

VOLUNTEER: You have said that you won't go to the refugee camp?

DUIKHA: When have we said we won't go?

MOTHER: No, my son, we will stay here.

VOLUNTEER: You can't stay here. Either you have to go to the camp, or empty the station. Besides, you won't get rice.

DUIKHA: What fine rice! Half of it is nothing but stones. And you are threatening to stop it!

VOLUNTEER: You have become arrogant feeding on free rice. A strong young man like you, sitting idle. Can't you get some job? Do you suppose you will be able to live on relief all your life? God knows what will happen to you.

MOTHER: Don't mind him, my son. He's just a fool. We will go away as soon as we get a house. Just have pity on us for a few days.

VOLUNTEER: All right, all right. Who is this? Kesto Das Bhui—

MOTHER: Our tenant farmer—

VOLUNTEER: So you have brought your whole zamindari along with you!

DUIKHA: Of course we have! Do you think we are beggars like you folks! Don't you dare to glare like that! I'll put out your eyes. You don't know the sort of chap I am.

VOLUNTEER: You scoundrel, you are going too far—I'll give you such a slap.

DUIKHA: Just try it and see.

MOTHER: Stop it, Duikha, I feel like hanging myself. How your nature has changed—(Enter Mohan).

MOHAN: What's your business here? What do you want?

VOLUNTEER: Are you related to those people?

MOHAN: Yes, I am.

VOLUNTEER: Are you related to Manomohan Bhattacharjee?

MOHAN: He's my father.

VOLUNTEER: You two brothers here, one sister and mother, these make up your family, doesn't it?

MOHAN: Yes.

VOLUNTEER: One-two-three, two—five people?

MOHAN: Yes.

VOLUNTEER: You won't get rice any more, unless you go to the camp. Last week you brought rice for seven persons—then why didn't you give Kesto his share?

MOHAN and MOTHER: We didn't give it?

MOHAN: We did give, we gave half of that rice.

VOLUNTEER: They have complained against you and taken rice for two. Why?

MOHAN: I don't know.

VOLUNTEER: What do you mean, you don't know.

MOHAN: Perhaps they have learnt this in Calcutta.

VOLUNTEER: Never mind. Tell me your full names and age, all of you. I must write it down.

MOHAN: How many people must write down our names? You have decorated the station by hanging up a thousand banners. And a thousand aid societies have taken down our names in their notebooks. We have understood everything. Get out now.

DUIKHA: Always finding some excuse to write down our names! We have had enough. Get out. Don't make us more angry.

VOLUNTEER: O.K. I have come with a false excuse have I? No more ration unless you go to the camp—got it?

MOHAN: Yes, we've got it.

VOLUNTEER: You must leave the platform.

MOHAN: Very well (*Exit* volunteer). They are all going about asking our names. Whether we take milk or not—what's your name. Whether you take medicines or not—what's your name. Whether you are vaccinated or not—what's your name. A thousand chaps just writing down our names and Kesto has learnt his lesson well—complaining against us, to get rice. Hey Kesto—Kesto—

KESTO'S WIFE: He isn't here—

MOHAN: Do you know where he's gone?

KESTO'S WIFE: He will buy land. He has gone to see it.

MOHAN: He will buy land? Where? He hasn't said anything.

KESTO'S WIFE: Someone he knows will sell him two bighas of land for three hundred rupees—he has gone to see it.

MOHAN: Where? Within Calcutta?

KESTO'S WIFE: Who knows? I don't know exactly.

MOHAN: In Calcutta, a katha of land costs five or six thousands.

KESTO'S WIFE: Then may be somewhere outside. (*Exit* Kesto's wife)

MOHAN: Well, it's possible.

DUIKHA: Mohan, will you buy for us also? Tell Baba—

MOHAN: Somebody who knows Kesto may be doing him a favour. Why should the chap help us.(*Enter* Panditmashai)

PANDIT: Listen, I have fixed up a room. We must go at once, or someone else will get hold of it.

PARI: How many rooms, Baba?

PANDIT: How many! Only one costs 100 rupees as 'selami' and twenty rupees as rent.

PARI: How can we and Keshto's family all live in one room?

PANDIT: Kesto's family! Is Keshto still here?

MOTHER: You needn't worry about Kesto any more. He has learnt to get rice by lodging complaints. He's buying land.

PANDIT: Buying land? He never said anything about it—

MOHAN: Two bighas for three hundred rupees.

PANDIT: It seems cheap. A hundred rupees 'selami' for one room—compared to that it seems cheap. He never said anything—

MOTHER: In case, you should ask for it. You needn't worry about him. He has learnt to fend for himself.

PANDIT: Have you started cooking?

MOTHER: Just going to—

PANDIT: Then cook after going there. If we are late, we may not get that room either. The scoundrel didn't even give a receipt after taking the money. We're done for, if he denies everything. Come quickly. Give that to Duikha there. (*The whole family leaves. Then the wife of Kestodas enters and starts doing domestic chores. A little later Kestodas comes in panting and sinks down on the floor.*)

KESTO: I am ruined, I am ruined—What's the matter, why are you crying like this?

KESTO: Those scoundrels, robbers have tricked me of everything! They have sucked my heart's blood—tricked away my three hundred rupees!

KESTO'S WIFE: Please be quiet—don't go on like this.

KESTO: The thieving scoundrels tempted me and took away all I had. Oh, God, look, three hundred rupees . . .

KESTO'S WIFE: Oh, Ma, oh, Pari-di—come and see how he's crying on—(*She runs to the abandoned place of Panditmashai*)

KESTO: Be quiet—don't call anyone—be quiet, be quiet.

KESTO'S WIFE: (*returning*) The masters have gone off somewhere, leaving us here in the soup.

KESTO: Let them go. Everyone will leave me, I am a luckless fellow. Let them go. I am not expecting anything from anybody. Don't weep, you bitch, shut up.

KESTO'S WIFE: (*crying*) How can I be quiet? You have ruined everything and I must keep quiet? At that time, I told you many times not to sell our house. A home is like an altar of Lakshmi.

KESTO: Shut up!

KESTO'S WIFE: I am never allowed to talk. I can never explain what I suffer in this home. Why should you take my advice? I asked you not to sell the house—shut up. I asked you to consult master before buying the land—shut up.

You went in secret to buy land saying, I've got a friend.
You have got lots of friends—to trick you out of your
money, to ruin you. There's another scoundrel of a friend,
all set to give you big jobs. Awash with jobs, isn't he? A
bunch of thieves, that's what they are.

KESTO: Shut up. How dare you—calling Bhikhua a thief? I'll
break your teeth. Do you know how many times he has
advised me to take a job, to start some business with the
money I had, I have ruined myself by not listening to him!

KESTO'S WIFE: Go on, cry and keep on saying, 'What have I done,
what have I done', I know we won't ever have enough to
eat. But you have also spoilt our chances of getting a home.
Today they have given us notice, we must leave the station.
Now where can we go, where can we get a shelter. O Ma
Lakshmi! What have you done! Where have you fled, after
driving us from our homes and turning us into beggars?

KESTO: Shut up, shut up, will you! (Enter Bhikhua)

BHIKHUA: Hey Kesto! What's up? Why for are you crying like
this?

KESTO: They have tricked me of my three hundred rupees—I
can't buy land any more.

BHIKHUA: Very sad, very sad. But what's the good of crying?

KESTO: The masters have left us, gone off I don't know where.

BHIKHUA: Where have the masters run away to?

KESTO: They have told us nothing before going—left us in such
danger.

BHIKHUA: What to do? It's all because of money.

KESTO'S WIFE: Didn't you say, you would get him a job?

BHIKHUA: I? But that's over here—in the brick kiln.

KESTO'S WIFE: (To Kesto) What's the matter? Why don't you say
something?

BHIKHUA: But if he goes there, he will get a job for sure.

KESTO: I'll buy land—

BHIKHUA: Buy land later, now come to the brick kiln for a job.

KESTO: You're asking me to come—where shall we stay?

BHIKHUA: What's the problem? We two will stay in my room—

KESTO: My wife? Where will she stay?

BHIKHUA: Send her home.

KESTO'S WIFE: We're in such a mess because of selling our home and tricking the master. He's paying for his sin by losing his money.

KESTO: Shut up. We have no home in our native place, brother. If you could fix a room for us—

BHIKHUA: Oh. . . I see. I'll try . . .

KESTO'S WIFE: Will you get a job in the brick kiln?

KESTO: Didn't you hear him. He says I'll get a job. Let me go and see—

KESTO'S WIFE: Then let's go. It's better that way. (*Almost weeping loudly*) We won't stay here anymore—not anymore. (*End of the scene*)

THIRD SCENE

(*A Calcutta slum. A room in a slum, a little verandah in the front. In the midst of sorrow, the appearance of each one has changed a little. Mother and daughter can be seen on the stage.*)

MOTHER: (*in an excited voice*) We won't pay the rent. Do what you can.

PARI: Ma, come away. They can talk to my father or brothers.

MOTHER: Shut up. That bitch talks in a way not to be endured, Curse your luck—

PARI: Let them say what they like.

MOTHER: Why, what for should they talk like that? Just because we are a little late in paying our rent one month, they have the right to say what they like? They charged us a rent of twenty rupees for this month. We didn't say a word. Other tenants pay eight rupees—you don't dare to say anything to them. You took a selami of a hundred rupees, we didn't say anything. We endured everything in silence. Let them return home today, we must fix something. What a lot of low-minded people we have come to—what a shame. You can't be a gentleman just because you look like one. Accursed luck.

PARI: Be quiet, Ma. Chorda (*second brother*) and father will come and . . .

MOTHER: Be quiet, I know what they are worth. They have sold the house without telling me. I am an illiterate woman. I understand nothing. They told the landlady to come in the afternoon, then left the house. Why do I have to face the music?

PARI: They have left because there's news about getting a job, perhaps.

MOTHER: Yes, of course, jobs are going abegging.

PARI: (*after thinking a little*) Ma, shall I wash the clothes? It's three o'clock, almost time for the tap water.

MOTHER: Leave it now. Let them come and eat first. How many times I have told them not to go about in this heat. What if they fall ill? Does anyone listen to me? It's so late, yet none of them has come. It's not fated that any of us should have a bite of food in peace.

DUIKHA: (from outside the door) Ma, open the door—Ma!

MOTHER: Duikha's come. Open the door. (Pari *goes out, Enter* Duikha *and* Pari)

DUIKHA: Is the cooking done?

PARI: No, we've been waiting for you.

DUIKHA: Then give something to eat quickly, Ma.

MOTHER: What's the hurry? Let them return, you can all eat together.

DUIKHA: No, I'll eat.

PARI: Won't you have a bath?

DUIKHA: No, I won't have a bath. I'll eat and go somewhere at once. Give me food, Ma—

MOTHER: Sit down, (*to* Pari) Dear—fill a glass of water.

DUIKHA: Quickly—give the water, Pari.

PARI: What's the great hurry?

DUIKHA: Give it quickly. Today, there's free entry to the zoo. Give it quickly. If I am late, it will be closed and I'll have to wait another month.

MOTHER: You wretch, you are just interested in such things. Why don't you look for a job? The other two are simply exhausting themselves.

DUIKHA: Just chattering! Give me rice.

MOTHER: Rice! I feel like serving ashes on your plate.

DUIKHA: Then I won't eat.

MOTHER: Don't put on airs. Soon, you won't get even this food. (Mother *sets a plate of rice in front of Duikha. He starts eating.*

Panditmashai *comes in.* Pari *lifts the shawl from his shoulder.*)
PARI: Baba, have you got a job?
MOTHER: Let the man rest, fan him a little. Can't you see the
state he's in? (Panditmashai *sits down.*)
PANDIT: I don't think there's a job to be had, anywhere . . .
DUIKHA: (*suddenly*) Isn't there anything else?
MOTHER: Haven't I given everything? If you want more rice
DUIKHA: Nice thing to eat so much rice with just a handful of
fish. And you are asking, if I want more rice—
MOTHER: Can't you see, how someone is just worn out with
worries about providing this food. Finish what you have
and get up.
DUIKHA: I won't eat. Only rice with just a little fish . . .
MOTHER: If you won't eat, get up.
DUIKHA: If you won't eat, get up! I won't eat, never, to hell with
it. (*Throws away the rice.*)
PARI: Mejda, you have thrown away rice?
PANDIT: You scoundrel! You're thrown away rice! (*Trembling with
excitement, gives Duikha a slap.*) The whole country is crying
out for rice and you . . . and you . . . . (*He can't go on.*)
DUIKHA: You hit me. You hit me! I won't stay here. (*Duikha goes
out, weeping*)
PANDIT: Go where you like. (*After a while*) Pari, go and see if
he's really gone (*to* Mother). You have spoilt them—I have
never been allowed to hit any of them. Go—go and see.
(*Enter* Duikha *and* Mohan. Duikha *is still weeping.*)
MOHAN: What's the matter? Why was he weeping out in the
street?
PARI: Baba hit him because he threw away rice.
MOHAN: Hit him! My God! Mejda come and sit here. Mother,
take these ten annas. (*Gives a few coins to his mother.*) Tomorrow, Mejda—
MOTHER: How did you get money? Where from?
MOHAN: Don't worry, I haven't stolen or begged. I have earned
this money. Father, I have brought your form. As the family of a martyr, we can ask for help. It must be sent to a
government office. And send a letter to Maulavi kaka for
that gratuity money.
PANDIT: Asking money as the family of a martyr. (*Becomes em-*

barrassed, as he thinks of it.)
MOHAN: There's no guarantee that you'll get it even if you apply. Write, all the same. If something—it's better to try something than starve all together.
PANDIT: I'd rather wait for the gratuity money.
MOHAN: Write both letters. I'll post them today.
MOTHER: Will you be just sitting round today?
MOHAN: No, I'm just getting up.

(*End of scene*)

Translated by Sudeshna Chakrabarty.

The translation is based on the test of *Notun Yehudi* that was published in *Bohurupee* 54 (October 1980). Reproduced by kind permission of *Bohurupee*.

20

Meghe Dhaka Tara
Ritwik Ghatak

INTRODUCTION

If you are asked to choose a single film which captures the trauma and tragedy of the Bengal Partition with unmatched power and sensitivity, you choose, without a question, Ritwik Ghatak's *Meghe Dhaka Tara* (The Star Veiled by Clouds, 1960). This classic is built on a simple story line: how the eldest daughter of an uprooted family, in a stifling, desperate environment, turns into the breadwinner and ultimately sacrifices her life. In fact, Nita, the protagonist in the film, has become a deathless symbol of Partition itself and the uprooted woman's tragic struggle against it. Here we present a translation of the last part of the screenplay where Nita after fulfilling her mission succumbs to tuberculosis. Her piercing cry 'I wanted to live' sums up the essence of all displacements, exodus and partitions.

CHARACTERS/ACTORS AND ACTRESSES

BABA (father), TARAN MASTER: Bijan Bhattacharjee
MA (mother): Geeta Dey
SHANKAR: eldest son: Anil Chatterjee
NITA (Khuki), eldest daughter: Supriya Chaudhury
MONTU, younger son: Dwiju Bhawal

GITA, younger daughter: Geeta Ghatak
SANAT, Geeta's husband and Nita's former friend: Niranjan Roy
BANSI, a grocer in the refugee settlement: Gyanesh Mukherjee.

SCREEN PLAY

SCENE 88
Day time. Baba's room

Shankar and Ma enter Baba's room. Baba is reclining back in his chair.
MA: We'll never get over the problem of eviction. In the middle of all this, people take courage, think of building homes—forget their sorrow.

[*Shankar touches his father's feet.*]

Tell him, how long we have wanted a two-storey house. Why not break the house and build a two-storey one. Let the kitchen remain, as it is. It will be enough, if it's repaired.
BABA: Repair? [*Putting his head on his breast, leaning forward.*] Will you be able to repair my heart—will you? So that I can enjoy reading Wordsworth again? That Swan and Shadows float double!

[*The reflection of Shankar in the wall mirror. Ma waves her hand and says to Shankar*]

MA: He's quite mad.
SHANKAR: Eh! Where's Khuki?

[*Ma standing beside Baba.*]

MA: Khuki!

[*Khuki/Nita's room. She goes out to work, then stays put in that room. She eats there. She has no connection with anyone else. She hides everything. She has fever, she's ill and tells no one. She even washes her own utensils. Tabla is added to the background music. Baba leans forward a little. Ma is standing on one side, Shankar goes out with his bag.*]

SCENE   89
Day time. Nita's room.

[*The background music continues. Nita is sitting on the bed and coughing. Shankar comes in, puts down the bag and looks at Nita. Nita lies on her stomach and tries to hide something beneath the pillow. Shankar sees it.*]

SHANKAR: What's it Khuki? Getting love letters in your old age, eh? Let me see!

[*Pulls out the hidden object from underneath Nita's pillow*]

NITA: Let go, let go, Dada!

[*Nita tries to stop him. Shankar pulls out the hidden handkerchief. Then starts and drops it to the ground. Shankar stares in amazement at the handkerchief which has fallen on the ground. Stunned. The sound of the Bhairon raga in the background Shankar stares at the handkerchief, paralyzed with fear. The playing of the veena Nita's profile. Nita lying beside the window. Nita raises her head and sits up, coughs*]

NITA: I was just thinking about you all. How nice, that you are all earning and standing on your own feet now.

[*Shankar, nervous, looks at her in amazement; music in the background—sarod and tabla. Nita tries to smile*]

It's like childhood. I don't have any responsibility any more. [*Shankar stands for a while, then goes out. End of background music*]

SCENE 90
Day time. The 'dawa' (verandah) and courtyard outside Nita's room.

[*Shankar comes out of Nita's room, into the courtyard. Gita is in the front. Father and mother at one end of the dawa*]

GITA: What's the matter, Dada?

[*Shankar looks at the sky and walks about in a restless manner. (Thunderclap)*].

SHANKAR: Khuki has got TB. A very advanced stage.

[*Gita and Shankar. In the courtyard.*]

GITA: How sad. Poor Didi!

[*Baba, standing in the dawa raises his finger and points forward, saying—*]

BABA: I accuse.

[*Shankar and Gita. Shankar turns to father, saying—*]

SHANKAR: Whom?

[*Baba lowers his finger.*]

BABA: Nobody.

[*Montu standing on the dawa of the house, his back turned.*]

SHANKAR: I will make arrangements for her treatment and return, no matter how late in the night it is. I'll stay here today.

[*Shankar goes out, carrying an umbrella. Background music, sarod and tabla: raga, Mian ki Mallar. Montu lowers his head in a helpless manner*]

SCENE 91
Night, Baba's room.

[*The background music continues. Baba is sitting on a chair with a worried look on his face. Ma is standing. Lightning flashes outside the window.*]

SCENE 92
Night, Nita's room.

[*The background music continues.The iron bars of the window. Heavy rain. The camera pans to show Nita lying with her eyes closed. Baba silently strokes her head. The shadow of the tree, half dark, half light on Nita's face. Baba points with his finger*] *towards the back of the room and remarks—*]

BABA: I have packed your clothes!

[*Then he slowly moves towards the door. He turns round once and looks at Nita, who sits up. Baba speaks, waving his hand*]

Go away, go away. They are dreaming of a two-storey house. You are successful. You have got them all to stand on their feet.

[*Nita stands up.*]

NITA: Ba—ba!

BABA: [*his voice is heard but he is not seen*] Don't stay here any more. They pity you now.

[*Nita stands up, bending her body, the bundle close to her throat.*]

You were unable to bear a burden, my dear, yet you had to do it. Now you yourself have become a burden. Your breath is poisonous.

[*Nita lowers her eyes. Baba says, raising his head*]

A mother and a newborn baby are coming to this room.

[*The childhood photo on the table, Nita takes it up. Nita clutches the photo to her bosom. Baba says, waving his hand—*]

Go away, go away, go away.

[*End of the background music. Nita clutches the picture to her bosom. Exit Baba. Nita stands up, carrying the bundle and the picture. She advances towards the door and opens it. It is raining heavily outside.*]

[*Song in the background*]

Come , Uma, let me take you in my arms.
Putting on your neck a garland of
Juin flowers. I know, my daughter,
The sadness of your heart,
Go my girl, to your husband's home.

SCENE 93
Night. The 'dawa' and the courtyard.

> [*Rain. The face of Nita seen in half-light, half-darkness. She comes into the courtyard and covers her head with the edge of her sari. She is smiling. Flash of lighting. Sadness. Song in the background—'Go my daughter, to your husband's home' . . . Baba is weeping. Song in the background—'leaving my home empty . . .' Nita is smiling. Her head is covered. Seeing the rain, she turns and goes down into the courtyard. Song in the background—'How can I live, my unhappy daughter/having said farewell to you'.*]

SCENE 94
Night. *The outside room.*

> [*Heavy rain can be seen through the door of the room. Nita runs out.*]

SCENE 95
Night. In front of the house.

> [*From outside the house. Nita can be seen running out. Shankar lowers his umbrella. Shankar and Nita face each other in front of the gate. Shankar stops Nita. Theme music—sarod, flute.*]

SHANKAR: Where are you off to?

> [*As Nita tries to back away, the photo falls from her hand. She stoops, picks up the rain-washed picture and looks at it. Shankar holds up the umbrella. Nita is beside him. Heavy rain.*]

Idiot. I've just arranged your stay in a sanatorium in the Shillong mountains. Then, yes—mountains. After all this time you will finally see the mountains.

> [*Nita listens, looking at Shankar's face. Nita turns from Shankar's side and appears in front of the camera. The rain*

washes her face and eyes. End of theme music.]

SCENE 96
Day. The Shillong mountains

[*Different parts of the mountain and the street can be seen. The mountainous road below. (Background music: sarod, flute, pakhoaj, tabla. The steep mountain to the left. The mountain slopes towards the right. As the camera pans towards the left, extensive mountainous areas, veiled by the clouds, can be seen.*]

[*Mix to cloud-veiled mountains. Mountain stream.*

Mix to pine forests. The valley can be seen.

Mix to rows of trees, human settlements, the sky, etc., can be seen. End of background music]

[*Fade in, fade out*]

SCENE 97
Day. The local market.

[*Background music—folk tune of the mountain. Shankar is standing, holding a basket of fruits. By going around, it is possible to see the bazar area*]

SCENE 98
Day. In the middle of a field.

[*Mix to*]

[*The background music continues. Shankar comes with the basket of fruits from the left to the right. The mountain in the distance. The mountain people, human settlements, trees can be seen. Children are playing.*]

[*Mix to Shankar with the basket of fruits in his hand. Nearby the mountain. The camera pans towards the right showing the board, 'Read Chest Hospital', on the side of the road. The road beside it goes on straight. End of background music.*]

[*Mix to Shankar giving the basket of fruits to a sister in the hospital, who gives it to another employee. The latter takes it away. Background music.*]

SISTER: Come with me.
SHANKAR: Yes.

[*Sister speaks while moving away*—]

SISTER: She likes the hills?
SHANKAR: Oh, very much, very much . . . right from her childhood.

[*While speaking, they are going inside the sanatorium. Two sisters and an employee pass by them.*]

SHANKAR: Hello!
THE EMPLOYEES: Hello!

[*Mix to*]

[*They pass various parts of the hospital while talking*]

SISTER: We make her sit there. She is better now.

[*Mix to*]

SHANKAR: Oh, yes, I am happy, I am . . . happy sister.
SISTER: But remember, don't excite her. She may have a relapse . . . Her sickness might increase . . . which is dangerous. Keep her happy.
SHANKAR: Yes sister, yes.

[*Sister takes Shankar up to a house, towards the left of the hospital. Says*—]

SISTER: She is there.
SHANKAR: Thank you . . . sister . . . thank you.
SISTER: Need not mention.

[*End of background music*]

[*Nita sitting on a stone, far away. The sky in the background. The mountains, mountain songs in the background. Shankar sees Nita. The camera pans rightward from a pine tree. Showing the mountain, sky and Nita. Nita has a shawl wrapped around her and a letter in her hand. She looks up. Shankar looks at Nita from the back. Shankar enters the frame from the left. Nita sits with her back to him, absorbed in her own thoughts. As Shankar clears his throat, Nita turns and looks at her brother. Shankar comes and sits beside Nita. Shankar and Nita sit, with their backs turned. The mountain, trees in the distance. The sound of bells*]

NITA: That star veiled by clouds . . . yes . . . Sanat's letter.

[*Theme music*]

[*Nita drops the letter, Smooths her hair with her hand. Shankar and Nita. Nita straightens her hair. She rests her cheek on her hand, leans forward and says—*]

I don't know why I preserved it so long.

[*Shankar looks at Nita, then laughs suddenly and says*]

SHANKAR: Do you know, our house has two storeys now. And Gita's son—he has learnt to walk now.

[*Nita turns her face, looks at her brother and says—*]

NITA: He plays a lot doesn't he?
SHANKAR: [*smiling*]Yes.

[*Nita turns her face.*]

NITA: He romps and plays a lot, doesn't he?
SHANKAR: He has turned Baba's life into hell.

[*Shankar, while speaking, goes out of the frame. A hill boy is seen passing by. Shankar enters, talking.*]

SHANKAR: He is always climbing up the stairs, alone. [*smiling*] The child is so lively, always making a racket. How he enjoys going up the stairs!

[*End of theme music*]

[Nita *suddenly lifts her face, saying*—]

NITA: Dada, but I wanted to live!

[*The Bhairon raga is played. The mountain—forest—sky move away. Shankar is in the front, looking at Nita.*]

SHANKAR [*in the background*]: Khuku?

[*Nita, with her face raised, is looking at her brother. She lowers her face. Shankar nods twice, smiles and says*—]

SHANKAR: Yes! Idiot.

[*Nita sobs aloud.*]

NITA: Dada I—

[*Nita with her back turned. Shankar in the front. At the back, mountains— sky.*]

NITA: I really wanted to live.

[*Background music— sarod. Shankar appears helpless*]

NITA: Dada, I love living.
SHANKAR: Khuku—
NITA: Dada, I will live, Dada, I will live.
SHANKAR: What are you doing, Khuki.
NITA: Dada, tell me just once, I am going to live.

[*Nita lets go of her brother's hand and lowers her head. Shankar straightens up and calls loudly*—]

SHANKAR: Nurse!

[*End of background music*]

[*Nita suddenly raises her face and stands up, facing Shankar. She flings herself on her brother's chest, puts her head on his shoulder and utters a shattering scream*—]

NITA: Dada, I shall live—Dada, I shall live.

[*Nita's desperate cry is echoed in the sky and the mountains. The camera pans to the left, over the mountains and forest. Nita con-*

tinues to say, 'Dada, I am going to live.']

SHANKAR: Khuki—i

NITA: Dada, I am going to live.

[*Nita, resting her head on her brother's shoulder, continues to cry and weep.*]

Dada, I am going to live—

SHANKAR: Khuki, have you gone mad?

[*A mountain river. Nita from outside the frame keeps on saying, 'Dada, I am going to live.' Pine trees. Human settlements to the right.*]

NITA: [*in the background*] Dada, I am going to live . . . Dada, I—Dada—

SHANKAR: Why are you shouting like a mad woman. Khuki . . . Khuki . . .

NITA: I am going to live.

[*The camera leaves the mountain and pans over the sky, to the right. In the background, Nita breaks into wild weeping.*]

I will live ... I will live ... I will live.

SHANKAR: [*in a low voice*] Khuku.

NITA: I will live ... I will live ... I will live.

[*Mix to*]

[*The pine forests, human settlements, the mountainous road, the sky.*]

SCENE 99
Day. Bansi's grocery shop.

[*Bansi is weighing the goods. He looks up as he sees Shankar and says—*]

BASNI: Hello . . . Shankar, old pal, you've come back after visiting your sister? How is she?

[*Shankar comes and stands in front of the shop of Bansi.*]

SHANKAR: Eh!

BANSI: Why don't you speak? Say something.

[*Comes and stands in front of the shop. He is shattered. He listens . . .*]

BANSI: No one even remembers now that such a person existed. That she went out in the morning, with the slapping clip-clopping sound of her chappals and came back in the evening. Such a quiet young girl . . . she didn't deserve such suffering. What do you say, old pal?

[*Background music—flute, sitar.*]

[*Shankar does not answer, manages to control himself somehow. He stands with a bag on his shoulder, in front of Bansi's shop. A girl from the neighbourhood is seen coming with a bag on her shoulder. A shop on the left side of the road. Shankar notices the girl. She comes forward and suddenly bends down and looks at her feet. The girl's feet. Her slipper is torn. She bends and sees that the strap is indeed torn. Shankar is looking at the girl. She looks at Shankar in an embarrassed way and lowers her eyes. In the background, a song starts*]

Come Uma, let me take you in my arms . . .

[*End of background music*]

[*The girl looks at Shankar, smiles in an embarrassed way and looks at Shankar. The song continues in the background, the sound of crickets. The girl goes forward, wearing her chappals and dragging along her feet. The chirping of crickets in the background*]

You belong to a sorrowful woman . . .

[*Shankar stands looking at the sky.*]

Come Uma, let me take you in my arms . . .

[*From the back, the girl with the torn chappal can be seen dragging her feet along the road of the colony. The song can be heard in the background.*]

[*Background music—sarod, sitar*]

[*Shankar covers his face with his hands*—]

SHANKAR: Oh, God!

[*Fade out*]

Go, my girl, to your husband's home,
Leaving my home empty
How can I live, my unhappy daughter,
Having said farewell to you.

Translated by Sudeshna Chakrabarty. Reproduced by kind permission of Ritaban Ghatak, on behalf of Ritwik Memorial Trust.

PART IV

Documentary Evidence

21

East Is East, West Is West

Ashoka Gupta, Bina Das, Amar Kumari Varma,
Sudha Sen, Sheila Davar and Suniti Pakrashi

INTRODUCTION

There was A consensus among refugees, social workers, politicians and the Government of West Bengal that the Central Government did not treat the displaced persons of the East and the
West in equal measure. This accusation was repeated many times.
The thousands who were forced to migrate from East Bengal
were discriminated against and at times this discrimination was
blatant. The 'Report of a Tour of Inspection of Some of the Refugee Homes in North-Western India' presents an eyewitness account as well as a comparative analysis and shows how the
discrimination was practised.[1]

Through the kindness of the Central Ministry of Relief and
Rehabilitation a body of non-official women social workers of
West Bengal were able to visit several Homes and training centres for refugees, women and children, in the states of East
Punjab, Pepsu (hilly areas that were later included in Himachal
Pradesh) and Delhi, and make a detailed study of the steps
taken to rehabilitate them in those states under the guidance of
the Government of India. The experience was valuable as af-
fording a yardstick with which to measure the steps taken in
West Bengal to tackle similar problems in this side of India and
to suggest what further liberalization of the measures of relief
were necessary so that the displaced women and children of

West Bengal could at least march in step with their sisters from West Punjab and Sind. We cordially thank Shri Mehr Chand Khanna and his ministry for the opportunity thus given and the officials of all the organizations we visited for sparing no pains to make our visits as comfortable and instructive as possible. In the following paragraphs we propose to state briefly what we saw and learnt during our visit.

THE ITINERARY

The first batch of social workers including Sm. Bina Das, Sm. Sudha Sen and Sm. Sheila Davar accompanied by Sm. Suniti Pakrashi, Deputy Director of Women's Rehabilitation in West Bengal, left Calcutta on 19 March, 1955, and reached Dehra Doon on the 21st morning. The second batch consisting of Sm. Ashoka Gupta and Sm. Amar Kumari Varma left on the following day and joined them at Jullundur on the morning of the 22nd. The following chart will show the places visited, the name and nature of the institutions inspected and the date of the visit:

Date	Name of Institution	Description
21.3.55	Bapu Industrial Training Institute (Dehra Doon)	Non-residential training centre for women
22.3.55	Gandhi Banita Asram (Jullundur)	Home for unattached women and their dependants
22.3.55	Lady Kusum Trivedi Sevasadan (Jullundur)	Home for unattached young women and girls
23.3.55	Widow's Home (Hoshiarpur)	Home for widows and their dependants
24.3.55	Kasturba Sevasram (Rajpura)	Home for unattached women and their dependants
	Nai Taleem School for boys	Day school
	Nai Taleem School for girls	Day School
	Work Centre (Rajpura)	Training-cum-Production Centre for men and boys
	Sri Jainendra Gurukul (Panchkula)	Boys' Home and School

25.3.55	Kasturba Niketan (New Delhi)	Orphanage for boys and girls
	(Morning)	
	Kasturba Niketan (New Delhi)	Home for unattached women and children
	(Afternoon)	
	Kingsway Colony Work Centre (New Delhi)	Non-residential work-cum-training centre for boys and girls
	Bengali Market Work Centre	–Do– For women
	Connaught Circus Work Centre (New Delhi)	–Do– For women
26.3.55	Arab-ki-Sarai (New Delhi)	Training-cum-Work Centre for boys
	Lajpat Nagar Work Centre (New Delhi)	–Do– For boys and girls
	Malviya Nagar Work Centre	–Do– For boys and girls
	Kalkaji Work Centre	–Do– For boys and girls
27.3.55	Women's Home (Faridabad)	Home and Work Centre run by Kasturba Trust for unattached women and children.
28.3.55	Central Infirmary (Rewari)	Infirmary for old and invalid men and women and their families

HOW THE INSTITUTIONS WORK

1. Bapu Industial Traning Institute, Dehra Doon

This Institution works in two sections, one for about 200 refugee girls and women under the control of the Rehabilitation Department and the other for local women under the control of the Department of Labour. The trades taught are tailoring, embroidery, calico printing, fruit preservation, hosiery, weaving and stenography (English and Hindi). The Labour Department prescribes the syllabus, conducts examinations and awards certificates. The hostel attached to the Institute contained 44 boarders on the date of the visit. The point for special notice is the liberal expenditure allowed which amounts to Rs 80 per month per

capita, Rs 30 given as stipend and Rs 50 allowed for other
charges, such as establishment, training fees, etc. The school and
the hostel buildings are spacious.

2. Gandhi Banita Ashram, Jullundur

Originally started to accommodate abducted women and children from West Pakistan, this commodious building was later
converted into a Home for displaced destitute widows (with their
children) and unattached children from general Relief Camps as
well as from outside when the recovered abducted persons were
either restored to their families or otherwise re-settled. At present
there are 1235 destitute women and children and 134 unattached
children in the home.

The educational and training facilities of the inmates are
worth noting. Within the Home itself there is a middle school
where education is free and reading and writing materials are
also provided. There are also a junior teachers' training class for
45 students and an adult literacy class where grown-ups are
taught. For those children who have outgrown the teaching
provided within the Home, arrangements are made with outside institutions, such as local schools and colleges for higher
education where they are admitted to free studentships or the
Normal School at Jullundur, the Training Institute at Hurdwar
and Karnal and the Institute at Pilani for professional and technical training where the students are paid a stipend of Rs 30
per month. The handicapped children are sent either to Lady
Nye Deaf and Dumb School, New Delhi, or the Blind School or
the Khalsa Orphanage at Amritsar with a stipend of Rs 25 per
head per month. A large number have been transferred to
Panchkula for education up to the Matriculation Standard or
for vocational or technical training with a stipend of Rs 30 per
head per month.

To teach crafts to grown-ups to make them self-supporting
there is a training-cum-production centre within the Home
where tailoring, weaving, machine embroidery, plastic and
leather work, soap making, etc, are taught, under expert guidance, and the trainee receives wages in proportion to his
outturn. For the illiterate and the less skilled, work is provided

in hand-embroidery, achar making, domestic service, etc. A very large number of women have been sent to different institutions for being trained as midwives, nurses and dais. For children below school-going age, nurseries and creches have been set up to enable mothers to work in a training centre or outside.

Besides these facilities for education, training and work the inmates are entitled to maintenance which takes the form of a monthly cash allowance on the following scale:–

(a) For a family of one person	Rs 18 per month
(b) –do– two persons	Rs 16 per head per month
(c) –do– three persons	Rs 15 per head per month
(d) –do– four persons	Rs 14 per head per month
(e) –do– five persons	Rs 13 per head per month
(f) For every additional member beyond five	Rs 10 per month.

No distinction is made between children and adults and all are paid at the same scale. In addition to such cash allowances every person gets Rs 2 per month for clothing. Physical and moral training is organized and intellectual exercises, such as debating, are provided for and encouraged. There is a ten-bed hospital within the Home for the sick and invalid.

On completion of training the inmates are usually fixed up with the help of the Occupation Organiser Centre in some suitable job with a rehabilitation grant of Rs 250. Some have been allotted lands and a few have received interim compensation at varying rates. Some inmates run shops within the Home on a cooperative basis. A marriage grant of Rs 200 is paid to each girl on the eve of her marriage.

3. Lady Kusum Trivedi Sevasram

This is a hostel for grown-up girls with a present strength of 219 inmates. There is a well-run community kitchen and provision for many-sided cultural activities. A special feature is its cooperative store where articles with marked prices are purchased and the prices deposited in a box without the intervention of a salesman.

4. Widow's Home, Hoshiarpur

Situated at the foot of the Siwalik Hills on spacious and well laid down grounds and containing 28 palatial structures in rural setting but within a reasonable distance from the city boundary, this Ashram has many outstanding advantages of which it has made the fullest use. The entire land and property has been acquired at government cost for the benefit of the Ashram where it has its own school, its own post office, its own hospital and library, its own bazar and its own religious halls. The present number of inmates is 1162.

The chief pride of the Institute is its adult education work which was started with voluntary services but has now got sanctioned posts for three salaried teachers. The absorption of a number of women trained in these schools in gainful occupation, such as teachers and dais has led to a very great increase in the demand for such education in recent years, followed by a course of junior training or nurse and dai training. Those who passed the Matric, get trained for Anglo-Vernacular or Basic Schools or as full-fledged nurses and get easily absorbed. Besides academic education training is imparted in crafts, such as tailoring, spinning, weaving, hosiery, embroidery, etc, and some women run shops or keep livestock and poultry on a cooperative basis which yields an income ranging from Rs 5 to Rs 25 per head. There are provisions for sports and physical culture and students are keen on dramatic representation of Indian mythological tales. The efficiency of the teaching methods and the keenness for education, especially adult education, are proved by the fact that a course which would normally take three or four years is covered within a single year. The discipline maintained within the Home is admirable. The government grant per capita is Rs 25. Out of this cash dole is in the scale as mentioned above.

5. Kasturba Sevasram, Rajpura, Pepsu

This is a home for unattached women and their dependants managed by the Kasturba Trust which draws a grant at Rs 25 per capita for running the institutes. It has a pre-basic school for very young children, while slightly grown up children attend one or other of the three basic schools run by the Nye Talim Sangha within the township. After eighteen, a selection is made for technical or vocational training in centres run by the Rehabilitation Ministry. The total number of inmates now is 800. Nearly all the able-bodied women are gainfully employed and earn a monthly wage in addition to doles. Land, building, capital grant for equipment, furniture, etc. are not included in the above figures.

6. Work-cum Production Centre, Rajpura

Originally started in 1949, it was later expanded to train 300 persons (mostly refugees with 5 to 10 per cent non-refugees) in different crafts of which carpentry, brick-laying, furniture polishing, cane and bamboo work, tailoring, compositors' work and sign-board and commercial painting are found most suitable for rehabilitation. The other crafts taught are blacksmiths and sheet metal work, motor-mechanism, foundry, weaving, hosiery and leather work.

Each refugee trainee gets a stipend of Rs 30 per month. The initial capital cost of land, building and equipment (totalling Rs 18.38 lakhs) was paid by the Government of India who also paid in 1954-55 a further capital grant of Rs 2.13 lakhs and a special grant of Rs 7,000 for setting up a motor mechanic section. For recurring cost the Government of India pay Rs 25 per trainee per month plus Rs 50 per trainee per annum for capital. The training period is one year and quarterly assessment tests are held. On completion of training a few are absorbed in the Production Wing, but the majority seek jobs outside. The total number of persons trained up-to-date is 1144 and the number absorbed in the Production Section averages from 120 to 180. The earning of persons so absorbed varies from Rs 1/8- to Rs 2/8 per day according to their skill and efficiency. The Production Wing is expected to be self-supporting and is largely patronised by the Pepsu Government for supplying hospital furniture of all kinds, hosiery goods, bed sheets, dusters, uniforms, etc.

In this connection something must be said about Rajpura Township itself, which was constructed in record time to house the refugees of Bahawalpur and provide them with some modern amenities. There are 2572 single-room tenements, 525 shops, a hospital (called Ajit Jain Hospital complete with X-ray apparatus and costing Rs 4.5 lakhs in construction alone), three basic schools and an infirmary for 500 old and destitute people—all constructed at the cost of the Government of India, though the management of most of them has now been transferred to the State Government. Large-scale and small-scale industries are being attracted to the place by leasing out lands and granting 50 per cent of the cost of the machinery. A Bone Mill, a Cycle Factory, an Iron Melting Factory, a Factory for manufacturing tyres and tubes are some of the industries that have been or are being set up to provide occupation to the refugee population.

7. Shri Jainendra Gurukul, Panchkula

This as its name implies, is a residential school run by the Jain community with 774 refugee-students on its roll. It has a big permanent building where students are taught up to the Matriculation standard together with instructions in crafts, such as spinning, weaving, tailoring, tin-smithy, carpentry and agriculture. The per capita expenditure sanctioned by the Rehabilitation Ministry is Rs 30 per month and is amply justified.

8. (1) Kasturba Niketan, New Delhi; (2) Women's Home (Orphanage); (3)Lajpat Nagar Work Centre, New Delhi.

All the three are run directly by the State Directorate of Social Welfare and Rehabilitation and are very well organized. The special features are: (a) an efficient Bal Mandir for little children; (b) neatness in the dormitories and the dining halls; (c) efficiency of the training-cum-work centre; (d) an adult education class; and (e) physical training and parade. School-going children attend primary and secondary schools outside the Home. There is a creche adjoining the work centre. Each family is housed in a large well-ventilated room and a small verandah which serves as kitchen.

9. Kingsway Colony Work Centre
10. Bengali Market Work Centre
11. Connaught Circus Work Centre
12. Arab-ki-Sarai

13. Malaviya Nagar Work Centre
14. Kalkaji Work Centre

These are a few of the 22 training-cum-work centres started in Delhi and its environs. The general pattern is the same and the only difference is in degree. Some are non-residential and some have hostel accommodation for a fraction of the trainees. Some are coeducational and some are exclusive to one sex. The period of training varies from one year to two years. Refugees receive a stipend at Rs 30 per month. There is generally one teacher for 16 or 20 trainees. The buildings are spacious and in most cases were provided and are maintained by the Central PWD. The usual crafts are taught, but no employment is guaranteed, though in the Production Wing large Government orders are received and executed in which the passed trainees have an opportunity to earn wages. Nearly all the trained students are said to have been provided with employment in the Production Wings or outside.

15. Women's Home, Faridabad

This Home with a sanctioned strength of 1500 inmates has at present 1326 inmates accommodated in five different blocks. The grouping is made on certain well-defined principle, the aged and infirm people (mostly single) being in one block, those capable of absorbing better education in another and the rest in the other three. A stipend of Rs 25 is paid per head from which each refugee gets a cash dole on the scale mentioned before and the rest is available to the Institution for payment of the staff and establishment, house rent and other incidental expenditure. There is one Superintendent (Rs 300), 7 supervisors, each Rs 90, 5 Instructors, each Rs 100), 1 Accountant (Rs 175), 1 Storekeeper (Rs 120), 1 Occupational Organiser (Rs 150), 1 clerk (Rs 115), 1 typist (Rs 110) and several peons, durwans and sweepers, each Rs 65). The crafts taught are spinning, weaving, tailoring, soap making, envelope making, etc.

16. Central Infirmary, Rewari

Established in June 1950 it has now 1837 inmates of which 1777 are in receipt of cash doles, while 60 are provided with cooked food. There are two primary schools and a training-cum-work centre for children and young wives of old men. Trainees get, in addition to their cash doles, a stipend of Rs 5 per head per month for the first three months after which they get wages for their work at piece rate.

COMPARATIVE ANALYSIS

REFUGEES FROM WEST PAKISTAN

1. Immediate recognition of the size, gravity of the problem and early construction of new townships like Faridabad, Rajpura and Tripuri led to the permanent rehabilitation in pucca houses of many refugees and provision for their employment either in work centres or in industries attracted to those townships provided with hospitals, schools, infirmaries, etc.— all at government cost.

2. The reception camps, homes, training-cum-work centres and infirmaries are of a superior kind.

(a) There are pucca permanent buildings with running water, separate kitchen, good sanitary arrangements and bathrooms and latrines laid up in spacious grounds (witness, for example, Gandhi Banita Asram at Jullundur and Widows' Home at Hoshiarpur).

(b) In most cases one and some-

REFUGEES FROM EAST PAKISTAN

1. Although there was a steady influx of refugees from 1948 onwards which reached a peak after the riots in 1950, no planned large township worth the name was ever built (except Fulia) which could go towards permanent rehabilitation of even a fraction of the 60 lakhs of refugees already in West Bengal.

2. (a) & (b) Reception camps in West Bengal were the decaying bamboo hutments with CI roofs left by the military authorities. This was bad economy for the recurring repair cost during the last seven years has gone up to lakhs. Even jute godowns and aluminium huts for storing grains have been pressed into service as reception camps where many families had to stay on for more than three or four years awaiting final rehabilitation or transfer to a better site.

times two or three small families are accommodated in one room, but allowance of space per head seldom goes below 30 sq ft, so that there is hardly any congestion. The rooms are well lighted and ventilated and each one has a kitchen attached to it so that no cooking is done inside the living room. There is ample courtyard space for camps and physical exercises even when there is no gymnasium.

(c) Cash allowance for food (and not cooked food) is paid in accordance with the scale mentioned in connection with Gandhi Banita Ashram at Jullundur. In addition, Rs 2 is paid to each person per month for clothing which the recipient is free to spend herself, though purchase of garment and materials prepared in the Home Production Centres is encouraged. In the Homes managed by Kasturba Trust the inmates of the Home concerned consume the khadi produced at the Home on cash payment. Each worker is allowed to receive and retain the wages earned by him or her in the work centre or elsewhere without reduction to their maintenance dole.

Lack of privacy and of kitchen space was notorious. Scanty water supply with hand pumps and congested rooms with leaking roofs have led to a number of strikes in P L Camps. All the camps that we have visited here in West Bengal for P L women and children, lack workrooms, creche rooms, playground, separate kitchen, common prayer room even after seven years.

(c) Cash dole for food is not paid at uniform rates for an adult and a child. The scale of doles here is Rs 12 for an adult and Rs 8 for a child below eight, and up to a maximum of Rs 60, whatever may be the number in the family. Whereas in East Punjab the scale is as follows:—

1 unit family   Rs 18
2 person family   Rs 16
3 person family   Rs 15
4 person family   Rs 14
5 person family   Rs 13
and plus Rs 10 for every additional member.

In P L Camps and Homes for the aged and the infirm no such regular work centre was ever sanctioned to enable them to learn and earn something. Even when some work centres or training centres were sanctioned, it was for a short period only and no wages were paid for the goods produced by them after the training was completed. The plea given for this is that they are fed and clothed at Government expense. Women are therefore reluctant to come and work at the work centres or training centres. There was a proposal to start khadi production for which they were to be paid wages. Our information is that the Government of India wanted to cut doles for these earnings. Consequently the proposal for giving occupation to persons willing to work failed. Allowance for clothes at Rs 2 per capita is never given to the camp inmates in cash. Sarees, dhuties and garments are supplied by the department twice during the year, but the result of such bulk purchase is that the garments seldom fit the person to whom it is given. For bedding the inmates are provided with one mat each, and a thin cotton blanket for a family of three supplied by the Ministry from Delhi. No charpoys or 'razias' are provided as is done for West Punjab refugees. In the damp Bengal climate the bedding provided is very inadequate.

(d) Some work centres are only training centres without provision for residence, but each Home is a complete unit providing not only residence but also education in different stages, professional or practical training and employment for at least a short length of time. One (e.g. at Hoshiarpur) is a small town in itself. Others (e.g. at Jullundur) have in addition to other facilities their own hospital. All have creches to enable mothers to leave their children and go out to work. The Kasturba Homes in Rajpura and New Delhi have their own pre-basic schools. Almost all have their Bal Mandirs or middle schools and when inmates outgrow the education provided within the Home, arrangement is made with outside institutions to continue the training till he or she is fit to take up a vocation (witness the steps taken by the Gandhi Banita Ashram at Jullundur Widows' Home at Hoshiarpur and the Kasturba Homes at Pepsu and New Delhi in this connection). The stipends are allowed to these trainees if they go out of Homes for further training. The dependants of the trainee remain and get maintained in the Homes even after they have secured jobs.

(d) No Home or a P L Women's Camp, however long it may have been established, has been provided with any facilities for education at nursery or pre-basic stage. No crèche is supplied. There are no middle school in any of the P L Camps. If there are schools nearby, they are allowed to attend; if not, they go without further education. When women are sent for training in vocational training centres, their children are looked after in the Homes, established for trainees' children, but the day they finish their training, their children are generally discharged and handed over to them, although they have not secured any jobs yet. No woman is allowed to go and work in the adjoining city or village even if she is willing. We have seen a number of women in the P L Camps engaged in Bidi or Paper-bag making but they do it secretly because they are afraid of their doles getting cut.

(e) The rate of grants are of a generous scale. It is seldom below Rs 30 per month and is sometimes at a higher rate according to the professional training chosen. Some privately managed Homes for children (Khalsa Orphanage at Amritsar, Lady Nye Deaf and Dumb School, New Delhi, Kasturba Sevasram) receive Rs 25 per refugee admitted to their Institutions. The Jainendra Gurukul at Panchkula receives Rs 30 per child. But each training institution for adult in addition to the maintenance grants receives capital grants for equipment, building, raw materials, establishments etc.

(e) The rate of grant is almost the same but several categories are excluded from this privilege. Women refugees taking a course of training in teaching or nursing in a recognized institution or hospital are not given any stipend but are only allowed to attend the vocational training centres specially set up for refugees.

(f) In addition to the stipends amounting to Rs 30 per head to the trainees government provides the houses, the establishment and equipment cost and a revolving cost of raw materials. In Rewari a revolving cost of Rs 5 lakhs has been recommended.

(f) Except in Titagar and Gariahat Work Centres (which are for men) the grants for women under these heads in West Bengal are very meagre. In non-residential training centres women are given stipends @ Rs 15 only.

(g) In Work Centres there is one teacher per 16 to 20 trainees. The Superintendent holds gazetted rank with drawing and disbursing powers and powers to sanction leave and take disciplinary action, is able to purchase at his discretion up

(g) In our Camps and Homes the Superintendent does not have gazetted rank and has no power to sanction leave to staff or take disciplinary action against inmates. The general assistants have no knowledge and experience and serve no

to Rs 300 in each transaction, and to secure orders and to sell. There is an Assaistant Superintendent where the number of inmates exceeds 500. The clerical staff is adequate—pay being

Accounts-cum-Cashier Rs 175/-
Clerk Rs 115/-
Typist Rs 100/-

useful purpose. The pay of the clerk is Rs 47 plus allowance and is too inadequate to attract good officers. We recommend gazetted status to the Superintendents engaged in West Bengal. They should be experienced, middle-aged social workers with high academic qualification. Pay scale should be the same as that of East Punjab. (Rs 300+Rs 50 for supervising Work Section)

(h) Some Homes (Kusum Trivedi Sevasram) claim to have successfully achieved moral rehabilitation. Others claim that almost all their trainees have been provided with jobs either within the workshop or outside. There is no doubt that the occupational organizer centre within some of the Homes is a great help in finding employment for the trainees.

(h) There is no social or cultural life, no Puja room or prayer hall and no arrangement for library, reading room and indoor games in any of the Camps in West Bengal. There is no occupational organizer within the Homes or attached to the Government who can help in finding employment for the trainee.

(i) The expenditure of the Homes for PL category is on an average per capita Rs 25 only which roughly covers all the expenses.

(i) The expenditure in the Camps (running since 1949) for PL category here in West Bengal are run on Rs 14 per capita only which covers all their expenses.

(j) Admissions—Hard cases are still admitted and the average number of such admissions of women and children is 100 per month. These cases relate to persons who migrated in 1947.

(j) New arrivals in Sealdah are admitted in the Camps only after a thorough enquiry and scrutiny. But in case of old arrivals, hard cases are admitted after a long process of investigation which takes months.

RECOMMENDATIONS

1. All the Permanent Liability Camps and Infirmaries should be raised to the status of 'Homes' and 'Work Centres'.
2. The present huts should be replaced by pucca structures and each family unit must have a room and a kitchen. Running water and an adequate number of bathrooms and pucca latrines should also be provided in every woman's Home. Besides these minimum requirements each family should have a small allotment to be used as a kitchen garden. There should be in each Home school rooms or nurseries for the very young and classes for the adult, prayer halls, workrooms and godowns. Schools should be provided where there are no such schools in the vicinity, but this need may be obviated by siting the Homes near a district, a sub-divisional or an industrial town where grown up children may have their education and training in the schools meant for the general public and probably find occupation on the completion of training. Within the Home boys above ten should have separate dormitories. There should be playgrounds and courtyards and each big building block within a Home should be linked with other similar blocks by metalled pathways. Pucca boundary walls are necessary in Women's and Children's Homes but not in Infirmaries. Overcrowded Camps should be thinned out by transfer of the latest arrivals to other Homes. There should be a Training-cum-work Centre in each Home.
3. The Superintendent of the Homes should have gazetted ranks with drawing and disbursing powers and powers to sanction leave and make purchases etc similar to what is enjoyed by her opposite member in the Punjab.
4. The scale of doles should be exactly the same as in the case of West Punjab Refugees. The cloth allowance should be paid in cash with a directive that they should purchase the 'Home' product preferably Khadi and make their own garments rather than buy from the bazar. Charpoys or taktaposh should be included in bedding, especially in Children's Homes and Infirmaries and jute and cotton blankets should be replaced by 'razias' of reasonable size.

Spinning should be made compulsory for these who can do light work not only to keep them busy but for production of khadi cloth.

5. Inmates of Homes should not be prevented but should be encouraged to take temporary jobs outside for which leave should be granted. For the period their doles may be cut but their names should not be struck off the register until it is proved that they have been permanently rehabilitated.

6. Immediate steps should be taken in respect of the refugees (women and children) in permanent liability category who have been kept in camps since 1948 on a meagre cash dole of Rs 12 and Rs 8 respectively. Because a few cases have not been properly screened or are doubtful, there is no reason why the genuine cases which constitute the large majority should not be placed on the same footing as their sisters in East Punjab. Doubtful cases may be kept as they are in the dole camps in the old scale till the enquiry is completed. A periodical screening of the doubtful cases may be carried on in the homes and P L Camps even at a later period.

7. New arrivals should be admitted after enquiry at the Railway Station but for old hard cases there should be a nonofficial Committee to scrutinize their genuineness and admissions should be made on their recommendation.

8. It must not be forgotten that the refugee problem in West Bengal is likely to be a recurring phenomenon for many years to come and is not a closed case like that in West Punjab or Sind. It would therefore be extremely unwise to fix a dateline and to state that future arrivals after that date would be denied any special consideration. That would not only be untrue historically but would aggravate the situation by accelerating migration at about the prescribed dateline. Facts should be faced and the door should be kept for treating as refugees any Hindu who permanently come away from East Pakistan on account of political tension whenever such tension may arise.

9. We have gone through the recent Circular issued by the Ministry of Rehabilitation, Government of India—G. O. No 15(7)(1)/54 dated 15 March 1955—meant for the refugees

from West Punjab and Sind. We are in general agreement
with the suggestions made in the Circular and insist on
their being made applicable also to the refugees from East
Bengal.

Signed

Ashoka Gupta
Bina Das
Amar Kumari Varma
Sudha Sen
Sheila Davar
Suniti Pakrashi

NOTE

1. We are grateful to Ashoka Gupta for kindly making the report
    prepared by Ashoka Gupta, head of the delegation that included
    Bina Das, Amar Kumari Varma, Sudha Sen, Sheila Davar and
    Suniti Pakrashi available; and for permission to reproduce it.

22

Statements

Gobindalall Banerjee

On Continued Exodus

If exodus be the criterion of judging the failure and success of the Indo-Pakistan agreement, as has been said by its authors, there is nothing but disappointment for them and as a matter of fact the whole of East Bengal has turned into a veritable station-platform so far as the minorities of the province are concerned. Everybody from the lowly to the high up speaks in the language of the people gathered in a station-waiting room. The agreement is looked upon as a tolerable charter for migration, although the authors conceived it otherwise.

This is due to the failure of the Government to restore confidence in the minds of the minorities, particularly the upper strata of the society by taking prompt and exemplary action against the wrong-doers and undoing the wrong done to them. Unlike West Bengal, hundreds of houses belonging to the minorities of the East Bengal living in the District Towns have been taken over either by requisition, just or unjust, legal or illegal, or by forcible occupation or by compelling the owners to part with their houses under duress. No action could be taken against the trespassers and generally no compensation due to these houses could be realized either from the Government or from the civilian occupants. In this regard the Government and the trespassers stand on the same platform. No catalogue of the innumerable and varied wrongs done to the minorities and not undone need be given here because it has now become common knowledge and the cumulative effect can be found in the volume of exodus.

There is a great misconception about the purpose of the agreement in the administration and also amongst the leaders. The absence of mob violence of February-March days is looked upon as the result of the implementation of the agreement and it is for this reason perhaps that Janab Liaquat Ali Khan depending upon the reports of the administration did not hesitate to say to the people that the agreement was working splendidly. Pandit Nehru also said that on the whole the result of the agreement was generally good. We do not know for whom these statements are made. Nothing can be more unfortunate than this. The mob-violence of February-March days has stopped no doubt but it has taken different shape and form. There is not the slightest attempt to make good the damage done to the minorities by the social-quake caused by the communal violence. If the absence of mob violence be the proof of restoration of normal conditions in which the minorities may come back and stay on, there will never arise the necessity of erecting or repairing the embankment which has been washed away or damaged by flood after it has receded or stopped, for the growth and preservation of the crops, but the failure of the crop will surely remove the illusion, and wisdom will be made to prevail. Let the two Prime Ministers come and visit Sealdah Station and other refugee camps and make these statements in the face of reality.

The two Minority Ministers and many leaders of public opinion are moving about the countryside and telling the people to implement the agreement, although there is nothing in the agreement which can be implemented by them. It is for the Government to take actions and maintain law and order. It is very often said and it has also been given place in the agreement that the rights of the minorities are to be protected. But is there any bundle of rights which can be called minority rights? The relation between men and men, men and the state are guided by codified laws of the land,

viz., the Penal Code, the Tenancy Laws, the Laws of Inherit-
ance and so on so forth. There is nothing particular for the
minorities. Therefore protection is to be given to law and
order- of the State and it is the primary function of the
State's to maintain it. The wave of lawlessness was set forth
by thoughtless policy of the Government and indiscreet action of its officers. Therefore these Ministers and Leaders of
goodwill missions should settle matters with the Government first and the people will readily follow.

Our society is an integrated whole. If the lawyers,
doctors, teachers and professors, men of property and busi-
nessmen who form the upper strata of the society be on
move, it is impossible for the rest of the community to
stay on. Many of the famous idols of Gods and Goddesses
of the society, which were honoured by successive Moghul
Emperors, have been removed from East Bengal. Women
and children have been removed. Hindus are living there
without their Gods and Goddesses, without their women
and children and under constant apprehension of losing
their property and residential houses and every day they
are feeling the artificiality of their social life and seeking
opportunity to leave the place.

Depopulation itself has become a cause of exodus
which has now gained its own momentum. Damage to
Hindu social life has been so deep and extensive that even
if it be granted that henceforward there will be no communal violence in any form, exodus will not be stopped and
there is nothing on the horizon at the present moment
which can prevent the tragedy being enacted to the full. If
the minorities of East Bengal are an integral part of the
Province, the Government will surely take a grave view of
the ever-increasing exodus. And if Pandit Nehru does not
pose the problem as a case of 15 million minorities of East
Bengal against 300 millions of India he will also have to
take similar views of the matter, because every refugee, in
the circumstances in which they are placed today is bound
to turn enemy of both the States. The Korean aggression
and the possibility of third world war may be their grave
concern but the home front, particularly the situation in the
two Bengals and Assam is no less serious than International

front. Should it so happen that the Korean War will burst into a world conflagration the people of Eastern part of the Indo-Pakistan sub-continent will surely lend their support to the forces represented by Soviet Russia, because in that event they will free themselves from communal oppression once and for all.

It is very often said that if anything happens in one of the two Bengals it will have its repercussion in the other and on many legislative and administrative matters reference is freely made by the one to the other. It makes the life of the minorities of both the Bengals precarious and subject them to victimisation for no fault of theirs. This is an impossible position as a citizen of a sovereign state. If there be so much of reciprocity between the two Bengals on so many matters including law and order, there must be some sort of administrative alliance between the two for the good of both the Provinces.

It is hoped that the two leaders of India and Pakistan are alive to the situation and therefore the two Prime Ministers together should immediately meet the representatives of the minorities in conference and try to find out a formula for the speedy solution of the problem. The minorities of East Bengal met in a convention in Mymensingh in June this year and have passed a resolution on the situation after due deliberation. The text of the resolution may be made the subject matter of the discussion in the proposed conference. If some such move be not taken without a moment's delay, arguments and mathematical figures will not be able to save the situation, which is bound to jeopardise the well-being of the two States and the two Heads of the States will have to answer the charge of ruination of the minorities.

Khulna,   (Gobindalall Banerjee, MLA)
East Bengal   Chief Whip, East Bengal Congress
25.7.1950   Assembly Party

From Ganendra Chandra Bhattacharya, M.L.A. (Dacca)

To H.E. The Governor, East Bengal
Dacca

Dear Sir,

I beg to tender my resignation from membership of the East Bengal Legislative Assembly.

I believe I owe an explanation to the Government, to the people and specially the Electors for this action of mine.

I can assure you that I have been forced to take this decision out of desperation after a strenuous struggle for giving some service to the suffering people. I have not acted hurriedly but after great deliberation and hesitation.

The present administration in Pakistan has chosen a policy definitely anti-progressive and detrimental to the interest of the common people in the State. The Pakistan administrative policy is not only anti-democratic, it is also undoubtedly anti-Hindu. This naked truth cannot be hidden from even a casual observer by piling heaps of falsehood upon it.

The Muslim League organization nurtured by British imperialists had been all along obstructing Indian struggle for freedom, jeopardizing the best interests of the people, including those whose cause they profess to champion. The leaders of that organization for their self-aggrandizement played to the tune of the foreign rulers even at the time when the Imperialist Force after severe battering by the world war became prostrated and too weak to hold the imperial reign and gave them an opportunity to score a diplomatic gain which has made the country crippled and weak and possible ground for further exploitation.

However, this could have been partially remedied by joint endeavour of all citizens after mobilization of available forces, but unfortunately for all concerned the League leaders decided otherwise. Though the country was divided by agreement between the Congress and the Mus-

lim League with clear understanding that all citizens including both the Hindus and the Muslims will live at
their own places in both the parts, enjoying equal opportunities and full citizenship rights, Pakistan has negatived
that totally.

Various measures, including daily tortures of pinprick
nature, unprovoked humiliation, economic pressure, forcible eviction, insecurity of life and property, crime against
women, onslaught on culture and religion, physical oppression culminating in mass killing in 1950, have been
adopted to drive the Hindus out of Pakistan.

Now a fresh sinister move is afoot to cut at the root of
political existence of Hindus in Pakistan by forcing separate electorate.

Some Hindus have migrated to take shelter in India,
leaving behind their ancestral home and vast property,
and others are helplessly staying on with great suspense,
so the stream of moving Hindus from Pakistan has been
unceasingly flowing with ebbs and tides, varying with the
amount of pressure put on them. This cursed policy pursued has made the State poorer by driving the Hindus out
who would have been good assets to the State and has
made the Hindus miserable. That has also heavily damaged the moral foundation of a large section of Muslims
who were utilized for such anti-social activities or were
allowed to do all this with a sense of impunity.

So one, who has got eyes to see, looks at the State with
great dismay. Your Excellency is well aware of the fact
that for about fifty years prior to Independence the whole
of East Bengal had been pulsating with lively political and
social activities mainly led by Hindu workers, but today
the whole atmosphere is dull and dreary: progressive and
humane activities have almost come to a dead stop. Sometimes a small section of Muslim young men in their
youthful exuberance tries to do something, but unfortunately they fumble and fail for obvious reasons.

Schools in East Bengal now languish and vanish in an
uncongenial atmosphere where people one day could take
pride in their love for education.

The foreign policy is equally ruinous. Apart from apprehended serious consequences of the present foreign policy in the event of another world war, continuous hostility with India is sure to obstruct the path of progress, though this may earn a few pats and even some gain of transitory nature from countries abroad whose interest is to see these two States in perpetual feud. The Pakistan State being composed of two small slices of India, her economy naturally depends greatly on that of the bigger partner.

As a servant of the people I consider it my duty to raise a voice against the wrong line of action of the Government, but I cannot make any effective protest as the whole atmosphere is so much surcharged that fanatical uproars overpower all counsels of reasoning.

On this background, it is impossible for me to discharge satisfactorily my duties as a Legislator. One who watches the proceedings of the East Bengal Legislative Assembly may witness the exhibition of hideous fangs of communalism displayed by a section of Muslim League members, particularly when the grievances of the Hindus as such are discussed there. Even in the matter of ordinary legislation, despotic ways of the Government often deny the opportunity of fruitful debate. The proceedings of the House are neither correctly reported nor regularly published, and unscrupulous press and politicians take advantage of that for their sordid game.

Besides ineffectual efforts in the Legislature, the only work that could remain for me was of arranging some help to the people in distress, but attempts in that direction have also met with failures. Representations to the authorities, made jointly with my other colleagues and sometimes made separately by me met the same fate of being kept in cold storage. Though much pained, I have not been surprised at the failure of my last effort to arrange help for rehabilitation of the unfortunate Hindus, some of whom lost their relatives and all their belongings, including houses. When repeated prayers for help yielded no result, I thought it prudent to acquaint Dr. A. M. Malek, the Hon'able Minister then in charge of Minority Affairs, with the real position, and submitted to him a list of riot-affected villages showing the scandalously meagre amount of help given to the suffering families. Dr. Malek was very kind to visit two or three of those villages near the Dacca City with the District Magistrate to make immediate arrangements for rehabilitation of the unfortunate people there. But his request has also had the fate of our prayers. Credulous people who readily believed that the Pakistan Government would sincerely implement the terms of the Delhi Pact [Liaquat-Nehru Pact] have now been disillusioned. It is now clear even to the man-in-the street that the Pakistan Government entered into the Pact only in their eagerness to screen off their atrocious crimes, simultaneously warding off the danger of immigration of Muslims from India, and to take more time for consolidating their position to squeeze out the Hindus.

Evidently, as every effort of mine has been made ineffective in every sphere of my activities, no useful purpose, I consider, may be served by my continuing as a member of the Legislative Assembly.

I withdraw with a heavy heart, yet with the hope that the young generation in Pakistan will realise the perils of the situation before it is too late to save the country from an impending disaster.

Yours faithfully,

Signed G.C. Bhattacharya
21.11.51

NOTE

The editors are grateful to Ashoka Gupta for permitting the reproduction of these two documents.

A Select Bibliography and Films on Partition

LITERATURE: NOVELS (West Bengal)

Bandyopadhyay, Atin, *Nilkantha Pakhir Khoje*. Kolkata: Karuna Prakashani, 1986.

Basu, Manoj, *Setubandha*. Kolkata: Bengal Publishers, 1967.

Bhattacharjee, Bijan, *Ranipalanka*. Kolkata: Bengal Publishers, 1960.

Das, Jibanananda, *Jalpaihati*. *Jibanananda Samagra*, vol 1, edited by Debesh Roy. Kolkata: Pratikshan, 1985.

Devi, Jyotirmoyee, *Epar Ganga Opar Ganga*, vol 1. *Rachana Sankalan*, edited by Subir Roychoudhuri. Kolkata: Dey's Publishing and School of Women's Studies, Jadavpur University 1991.

Gangopadhyay, Narayan, *Lal Mati*. Kolkata: Anjali Prakashani, 1998.

——, *Bidisha*. *Narayan Gangopadhyay Rachanavali*, vol 9. Kolkata: Mitra and Ghosh, 1985.

Gangopadhyay, Sunil, *Arjun*. Kolkata: Ananda, 1971.

——, *Atmaprokash*. Kolkata: Ananda, 1972.

——, *Purva Paschim*. Kolkata: Ananda, 1988.

——, *Jochana Kumari*. Kolkata: Ananda, 1990.

Ghosh, Amarendra, *Bhangche Sudhu Bhangche*. Kolkata: 1951.

Ghosh, Gourkishore (epic trilogy on Hindu-Muslim relations in Bengal and on Partition), *Jol Pore Pata Nore*. Kolkata: Ananda, 1978.

——, *Prem Nei*. Kolkata: Ananda, 1981.

——, *Protibeshi*. Kolkata: Ananda, 1995.

Ghosh, Sankha, *Supuriboner Sari*. Kolkata: Aruna Prakashani, 1990.

Majumdar, Amiyabhusan, *Gar Srikhanda*. Kolkata: Aruna Prakashani, 1957.

Roy, Prafulla, *Keyapatar Nauko*. Kolkata: Karuna Prakashani, 1996.

Roy, Prafulla, *Nonajal Mithemati*. Kolkata: Dey's Publishing, 1959.

Roy, Sabitri, *Meghna Padma*, vols 1, 2. Kolkata: Mitralay, 1964-65.

——, *Swaralipi*. Kolkata: Ratna Prakashan, 1992.

——, *Badwip*. Kolkata: Nabapatra, 1972.

Sanyal, Narayan, *Bakultala P L Camp*. Kolkata: Bengal Publishers, 1955.

Sanyal, Prabodhkumar, *Hasu Banu*. Kolkata: Bengal Publishers, 1952.

NOVELS (East Pakistan, Bangladesh)

Ahmed, Kayes, *Nirbasito Ekjan. Kayes Ahmed Samagra*. Dhaka: Mowla Brothers, 1993.

Elias, Akhtaruzzaman, *Khowabnama*. Kolkata: Naya Udyog, 1996.

Fazl, Abul, *Ranga Prabhat, Abul Fazl Rachanabali*, edited by: Alauddin al Azad. Dhaka: Bangla Academy, 1994.

Hossain, Selina, *Kantatare Projapati*. Dhaka: Jatiyo Sahitya Prakashani, 1989.

——, *Japito Jiban*. Dhaka: Bidyaprakash, 1996.

——, *Gayatri Sandhya*. Dhaka: Bidyaprakash, 1995.

Ishak, Abu, *Surya Dighal Bari*. Dhaka: Nowroj Sahitya Sambhar, 1995.

Jainuddin, Sardar, *Anek Suryer Asha*.

Kaiser, Shahidullah, *Sangsaptak*. Dhaka: Pallab, 1993.

Karim, Rashid, *Uttam Purush*.

Nasreen, Taslima, *Phera*. Kolkata: Ananda, 1993.

Rushd, Abu, *Nongor*. Dhaka: Bud Publications, 1970.

SHORT STORIES: ANTHOLOGIES (West Bengal)

Bandyopadhyay, Manabendra, ed, *Bhed Bibhed*, 2 vols. Kolkata: Dey's Publishing, 1992.

Bhalla, Alok, *Stories about the Partition of India*, 3 vols. Delhi: Indus/ Harper Collins, 1993.

Imdad-ul-Haq, Milan, *Deshbhager Par*. Kolkata: Ananda, 1998.

Roy, Debesh, *Raktamanir Hare*. Delhi: Sahitya Akademi, 1999.

Sen, Kamalesh, *Dangabirodhi Galpa*. Kolkata: Ratna Prakashan, 1991.

SHORT STORIES/ANTHOLOGIES (East Pakistan, Bangladesh)

Azad, Salam, *Deshbhager Galpa*. Kolkata: Mitra and Ghosh, 1998.

Hussain, Akhtar, *Sampradayikata Birodhi Galpa*. Dhaka: Jatiya Sahitya Prakashani, 1991.

Haq, Hasan Azizul, *Rarbanger Galpa*. Dhaka: University Press Limited, 1991.

TWENTY UNFORGETTABLE SHORT STORIES ON PARTITION,
DISPLACEMENT, MEMORY AND HINDU-MUSLIM RELATIONS

Ahmed, Kayes, 'Paran'
al-Azad, Alauddin, 'Chhuri'
Bandyopadhyay, Dipendranath, 'Jatayu'
Bandyopadhyay, Manik, 'Chhelemanusi'
Bhaduri, Satinath, 'Gananayak'
Bose, Samaresh, 'Adab'
Chanda, Somen, 'Danga'
Devi, Jyotirmoyee, 'Sei Chheleta'
Elias, Akhtaruzzaman, 'Khoari'
Ghatak, Ritwik, 'Sfatikpatra'
Ghosh, Santosh Kumar, 'Hoina'
Haq, Hasan Azizul, 'Parabasi'
Hossain, Selina, 'Dwanda'
Imdad-ul-Haq, Milan, 'Deshbhager Par'
Khan, Rahat, 'Amader Bisbriksha'
Mitra, Narendranath, 'Jaibo'
Osman, Soukat, 'Akheri Sangkranto'
Rahman, Hasan Hafizur, 'Aro Duti Mrityu'
Sen, Rameshchandra Sen, 'Sada Ghora'
Waliullah, Syed, 'Ekti Tulsigacher Kahini'

NB Many more unforgettable stories have been written on this theme.

PLAYS

Bandyopadhyay, Digindrachandra, Tarang. Kolkata: Pustakalay, 1947.
——, Naya Shibir. In Trisrota, Kolkata, Nabapatra, 1982.
——.Bastubhita. Kolkata: Bengal Publishers, 1948.
——, Masal. Kolkata: Pustakalaya, 1954.
Bhattacharjee, Bijan, Gotrantar. Kolkata: Jatiya Sahitya Parishad, 1959.
Ghatak, Ritwik, Dalil. Kolkata: Jatiya Sahitya Parishad, 1952.
——, Sanko. In Natya Akademy Patrika, Kolkata, 1999.
Lahiri, Tulsi, Chhera Tar. Kolkata: Jatiya Sahitya Parishad, 1994.
Mitra, Sambhu, Ghurni. In Prarombhik. Kolkata: M C Sarkar, 1996.
Samaddar, Sekhar, Tirtha Jatra. SAF Journal 10, Kolkata, 1993.
Sen, Salil, Natun Yehudi. Kolkata: Indiana, 1957.

POEMS (West Bengal)

Chattopadhyay, Birendra, 'Visa Officer Samne'. In Sreshtha Kabita, 1970.

Das Jibanananda, *Rupashi Bangla* . In *Kabya Sangraha*, 1993.
——, '1946-47'. In *Sreshtha Kabita*, 1954.
Dasgupta, Alokeranjan, 'Seemante'. In *Jhorche Katha Atas Kanche*, 1985.
De, Bishnu, 'Hasnabadei'. In *Sandwiper Char*, 1947.
De, Bishnu, 'Jal Dao'. In *Anvista*, 1950.
Gangopadhyay, Sunil, 'Keu Katha Rakheni'. In *Bandi Jege Acho*, 1974.
Ghosh, Sankha, *Gandharva Kabitaguccha*, 1994.
Islam, Kazi Nazrul, 'Kandari Husiyar'. In *Sanchita*, 1952.
——, 'Pact'. In *Sanchita*, 1952.
Mitra, Arun, 'Prati Bidaye' In *Sreshtha Kabita*, 1972.
Mukhopadhyay, Subhas 'Parapar'. In *Sreshtha Kabita*, 1970.
Sen, Samar, 'Janmadine'. In *Samar Sen-er Kabita*, 1987.
Sengupta, Achintyakumar, *Pub Paschim*, 1983.

POEMS (East Pakistan, Bangladesh)

Ahsan, Syed Ali, "Amar Purba Bangla.'
Al Azad, Alauddin, 'Exodus.'
Jafar, Sikander Abu, 'Bangla Chharo.'
Haider, Zia, 'Rabindranath.'
Huda, Mohammed Nurul, 'Amra Tamate Jati.'
Mahmud, Al, 'Sonali Kabin.'
——, 'Bharatvarsha.'
Rahman, Hasan Hafizur, 'Ekhan Juddho Amar.'
Rahman, Shamsur, 'He Amar Balya Bandhugan.'
——, 'Barnamala, Amar Dukhinee Barnamala.'
Nasreen, Taslima, 'Asvikar.'
——, 'Bhanga Banga Desh.'
Siddiqui, Zillur Rahman, 'Amar Gaurab.'

The poems selected here are to be found in two anthologies: Daud Haider, *Bangladesher Kabita*, Kolkata: M.C. Sarkar, 1985; and Sakti Chattopadhyay, ed, *Purba Banglar Sreshtha Kabita*, Kolkata: ·Aruna Prakashani, 1970.

Shamsur Rahman's poem, 'He Amar Balya Bandhugan' is in his *Sreshtha Kabita*. Dhaka: Jatiya Sahitya Prakashani, 1976. Taslima Nasreen's poem 'Asvikar' is included in *Ay Kasto Jhenpe Jiban Debo Mepe'*. Dhaka: Gyankosh Prakashani, 1994; and 'Bhanga Banga Desh' in *Behula eka Bhasiyechilo Bhela*, Dhaka: 1993.

Poems from West Bengal and Bangladesh evoke many emotions and moods—some recollect the beauty of old, undivided Bengal with the help of legends and myths, some glorify the Language movement and War of Liberation, some lament the division of Bengal, some pay and War of Liberation, some lament the division of Bengal, some pay homage to Tagore and the Bengali language as the unbreakable bridge, some stress the intrinsic oneness of the Bengali people professing allegiance to two nations.

MEMOIRS (West Bengal)

Bagchi, Jasodhara, and Abhijit Sen, eds, *Shatabarshe Ashalata*. Kolkata: Stree, 1996:
Bandyopadhyay, Hiranmoy, *Ja Dekhechi*. Kolkata: Nabapatra, 1997.
Basu, Dakshinaranjan, ed, *Chhere Asa Gram*. Kolkata: Jingasa, 1975.
Bose, Nirmal Kumar, *My Days with Gandhi*. Kolkata: Nishana, 1953.
Chattopadhyay, Ranu, *Bangladesher Smriti*. Kolkata: Paschimbanga Ganatantrik Mahila Samiti, 1984.
Das, Bina, *Srinkhal Jhankar*. Kolkata: Jayashree Prakashan, 1992.
Das, Hena, *Smsritimay Dingulo*. Kolkata: Script, 2002.
Dasgupta, Kamala, *Rakter Akshare*. Kolkata: Sishu Sahitya Sangsad, 1995.
Ghosh, Dastidar, Sankar, *Sesh Anurodh*. Kolkata: Forward Publishers, 1998.
——, *Smritituku Thak*. Kolkata: Naba Chalantika, 1990.
——, *Mane Pare*. Kolkata: Kranti Prakashani, 1993. •
Gangopadhyay, Shyamal, *Jiban· Rahasya*.Kolkata: Mitra and Ghosh, 1992.
Ganguly, Indubaran, *Colony Smriti*. Kolkata: published privately, 1997.
Ghosh, Santisudha, *Jibaner Rangamanche*. Kolkata: Jayashree Prakashan, 1989.
Gupta, Ashoka, *Noakhali Durjoger Smriti*. Kolkata: Naya Udyog, 1999.
Gupta, Priyabala, *Smritimanjusha*. Kolkata: Dey's Publishing and School of Women's Studies, Jadavpur University, 1999.
Gupta, Saibal, *Kichu Smriti, Kichu Katha*.Kolkata: M C Sarkar, 1994.
Lahiri, Abani, *Tirish Challiser Bangla,* edited by Ranajit Dasgupta. Kolkata: Sariban, 1999.
Majumdar, Romesh Chandra, *Jibaner Smritideepe*. Kolkata: General Printers and Publishers, 1978.
Mukherjee, Shyamaprasad, *Leaves from a Diary*. Kolkata: Oxford University Press, 1993.
Nag, Nepal, *Smriticharona*. Kolkata: National Book Agency, 1996.
Pal Chaudhuri, Aparna, *Nari Andolan : Smritikatha*. Kolkata: Paschim Banga Ganatantrik Mahila Samiti, 1990.
Roy, Annadashankar, *Muktabangar Smriti*. Kolkata: Mitra and Ghosh, 1999.
Roychaudhuri, Tapan, *Romanthan Athaba Bhimrati Praptir Parcharitcharcha*. Kolkata: Ananda, 1993.

Sen, Ashalata, *Sekaler Katha*. Kolkata: Firma K.L.M, 1990.
Sen, Manikuntala, *Sediner Katha*. Kolkata: Nabapatra, 1982. Eng transl,
    In Search of Freedom: An Unfinished Journey, Kolkata: Str̀ee: 2001
Sen, Shanta, *Pitamohi*, Kolkata: Pratikshan, 1994.
Singha, Ava, *Darpane Barisal*. Kolkata: Anil Singha, 1998.

MEMOIRS (East Pakistan, Bangladesh)

Ahmed, Abu Mansur, *Amar Dekha Rajnitir Panchas Bachar*. Dhaka:
    Khosroj Kitab Mahal, 1995.
Azad, Salam, *Ethnic Cleansing*. Kolkata: Ratna Prakashan, 2002.
Das, Hena, *Ujjal Smriti*. Dhaka: Manab Prakashan, 1995.
Das, Suhasini, *Suhasini Das Sambardhana Grantha*. Sylhet: Sampadana
    Parishad, 1999.
Dasgupta, Ranesh, *Kakhono Champa, Kakhono Atasi*. Dhaka: Sahitya
    Prakash 1998.
Hashim, Abul, *Amar Jiban o Bibhagpurva Banglar Rajniti*. Kolkata:
    Chirayat Prakashani, 1988 (Dhaka ed,1978).
Huq, Hasan Azizul, *Chalchitrer Khutinati*. Dhaka: Jatiya Grantha
    Prakashan, 1998.
Karim, Rashid, *Jiban Maran*. Dhaka: Sahitya Prakash, 1999.
Sengupta, Kiranshankar, *Challiser Dasake Dhaka*. Dhaka: Sahitya
    Prakash, 1994.
Singha, Mani, *Jiban Sangram*. Dhaka: Jatiya Sahitya Prakashani, 1983.
Shamsuddin, Abul Kalam, *Ateet Diner Smriti*. Dhaka: Nawroj
    Kitabistan, 1968.
Waliullah, Mohammed, *Jugbichitra*. Dhaka: Mowla Brothers, 1997.

ANALYSIS AND CRITIQUE In English

Ahmed, Rafiuddin, *The Bengal Muslims 1871-1906:A Quest for Identity*.
    Delhi: Oxford University Press, 1981.
Bose, Pradip, ed, *Refugees in West Bengal*. Kolkata: Calcutta Research
    Group, 2000.
Bose, Sugata, *Agrarian Bengal: Economy, Social Structure and Politics
    1919-1947*. Cambridge: Cambridge University Press, 1986.
Chakrabarti, Prafulla K., *The Marginal Men*. Kalyani: Lumiere Books,
    1990.
Chatterjee, Jaya, *Bengal Divided: Hindu Communalism and Partition 1932-
    1947*. Cambridge: Cambridge University Press, 1995.
Das, Suranjan, *Communal Riots in Bengal,1905-1947*. Delhi: Oxford Uni-
    versity Press, 1991.
Datta, Pradip, *Carving Blocs: Communal Ideology in Early Twentieth-Cen-

tury Bengal. Delhi: Oxford University Press, 1999

Eaton, Richard. M. *The Rise of Islam and the Bengal Frontier 1204-1760.* Delhi: Oxford University Press, 1997.

Gupta, Saibal, *Dandakaranya: A Survey of Rehabilitation.* Kolkata: Bibhasa, 1997.

Geeti Sen, ed, Crossing Boundaries, Culture and Identity. *India International Centre Quarterly* (Monsoon 1997).

Kabir, Humayun, *Muslim Politics 1909-1942.* Kolkata: Gupta, Rahman, Gupta, 1943.

Murshid, Tazeen M., *The Sacred and the Secular: Bengal Muslim Discourses 1871-1977.* Delhi: Oxford University Press, 1995.

Pakrasi, Kanti, *The Uprooted: A Sociological Study of the Refugees of West Bengal.* Kolkata: India Editions India, 1971.

Roy, Tathagata, *My People Uprooted: A Saga of the Hindus of Eastern Bengal.* Kolkata: Ratna Prakashan, 2001.

Samaddar, Ranabir, ed, *Reflections on Partition in the East.*Delhi: Vikas, 1997.

Sarkar, Kamala, *Bengal Politics 1937-1947.*Kolkata: A Mukherjee, 1990.

Sen, Shila, *Muslim Politics in Bengal 1937-1947.* Delhi: Impex India, 1976.

In French

Ivekovic, Rada, and Ghislaine Glasson Deschaumes, eds. *Pays divisés, villes separées* (Divided Countries, Separated Cities). Paris: Transeuropeennes, 2001.

In Bengali

Bandyopadhyay, Hiranmay, *Udbastu.* Kolkata: Shishu Sahitya Sansad, 1970.

Bandyopadhyay, Sandip, *Deshbhag- Deshtyag.* Kolkata: Anustup, 1994.

——, *Deshbhag: Smriti ar Sattwa.* Kolkata: Progressive Publishers, 1999.

——, *Itihaser Dike Phire, Chhecholliser Danga.* Kolkata: Utsa Manush, 1992.

Biswas, Kalipada, *Jukta Banglar Sesh Adhyay.* Kolkata: Orient Book Company, 1966.

Chaudhury, Sirajul Islam, *Dwijatitattver Satyamithya.* Dhaka: Bidyaprakash. 1993.

——, *Bangalir Jatiyatabad.* Dhaka: University Press Ltd.

De, Amalendu, *Swadhin Bangabhumi Gathaner Parikalpana: Proyas o Parinati.* Kolkata: Ratna Prakashan 1975.

——, *Bangladesher Janabinyas o Sankhyalogu Samasya.* Kolkata: Ratna Prakashan, 1992.

De, Amalendu, *Prasanga: Anuprabesh*. Kolkata: Barnaparichay, 1993.

——, *Dwijatitattva o Muslim League*. Kolkata: Ratna Prakashan, 2000.

Ghosh, Shankar, *Hastantar*. Kolkata: Ananda, 1999.

Ghosh, Suniti Kumar, *Bangla Bibhajaner Arthaniti-Rajniti*. Kolkata: New Horizon Book Trust, 2001

Ghosh Dastidar, Sabyasachi, *Ei Bangla Oi Bangla*. Kolkata: Tulot, 1991.

Islam, Mustafa Nurul, *Bangladesh : Bangali, Atmaparichayer Sandhane*. Dhaka: Sagar Publishers, 1991.

Lahiri, Provaschandra. *Pak-Bharater Ruprekha*. Kolkata: Shyama Prakashan, 1968.

Mandal, Jagadishchandra, *Banga-bhanga*. Kolkata: Mahapran Publishing Society, 1977.

——, *Marichjhampi-Naisabder Antarale*. Kolkata: Sujon Publications, 2002.

Roychoudhury, Ladli Mohan, *Khsamata Hastantar o Deshbibhag*. Kolkata: Dey's Publishing, 1999.

Sammilito Samajik Andolon. *Nirjatoner Dalil 2001*.

Sengupta, Amalendu, *Uttal Challis, Asamapto Biplab*. Kolkata: Pearl Publishers, 1989.

Singha, Anil, *Paschimbange Udbastu Upanibesh*. Kolkata: Book Club, 1995.

Singha, Tushar *Maranjoyee Sangrame Bastuhara*. Kolkata: Dasgupta and Co., 1999.

Umar, Badruddin, *Bangabhanga o Sampradayik Rajniti*. Kolkata: Chirayata, 1987; Dhaka, 2001.

FILMS ON THE BENGAL PARTITION

Nemai Ghosh, *Chhinnomul*, 1951
Ritwik Ghatak, *Meghe Dhaka Tara*, 1960
           Komal Gandhar, 1961
           Subarnarekha, 1962
           Jukti, Takko ar Gappo, 1974
           Titas Ekti Nadir Nam, 1973
Shantipriya Mukherjee, *Refugee*, 1959.
Agradut, *Bipasha*, 1962
Bimal Basu, *Nabarag*, 1971
Masiuddin Shaker and Sheikh Niamat Ali, *Surya Dighal Bari*, 1979
Tanvir Mokammel *Chitra Nadir Pare*, 1999.

Index